Collective Goods and Higher Education Research

With this volume, the author demonstrates how a collective-goods approach to higher education research can alleviate problems of rising costs, declining resources, and growing concerns about undergraduate learning. In taking this approach, the author presents new tools of analysis—borrowed from cognitive science, economics, data analytics, education technology, and measurement science—to investigate higher education's place in society as a public or private good. By showing how these tools can be utilized to re-orient current research, this volume offers scholars and policymakers an argument for the large-scale use of scientific and economic approaches to higher education's most pressing issues.

Roger Benjamin has been president of CAE, an education assessment testing organization, since 2005.

Routledge Research in Higher Education

Articulating Asia in Japanese Higher Education
Policy, Partnership and Mobility
Jeremy Breaden

Global Mobility and Higher Learning
Anatoly V. Oleksiyenko

Universities and the Occult Rituals of the Corporate World
Higher Education and Metaphorical Parallels with Myth and Magic
Felicity Wood

Developing Transformative Spaces in Higher Education
Learning to Transgress
Sue Jackson

Improving Opportunities to Engage in Learning
A Study of the Access to Higher Education Diploma
Nalita James and Hugh Busher

Graduate Careers in Context
Research, Policy and Practice
Fiona Christie and Ciaran Burke

Narratives of Marginalized Identities in Higher Education
Inside and Outside the Academy
Edited by Santosh Khadka, Joanna Davis-McElligatt and Keith Dorwick

Collective Goods and Higher Education Research
Pasteur's Quadrant in Higher Education
Roger Benjamin

For more information about this series, please visit: www.routledge.com/Routledge-Research-in-Higher-Education/book-series/RRHE

Collective Goods and Higher Education Research

Pasteur's Quadrant in Higher Education

Roger Benjamin

Routledge
Taylor & Francis Group
NEW YORK AND LONDON

First published 2019
by Routledge
711 Third Avenue, New York, NY 10017

and by Routledge
2 Park Square, Milton Park, Abingdon, Oxon, OX14 4RN

Routledge is an imprint of the Taylor & Francis Group, an informa business

Library of Congress Cataloguing-in-Publication Data
A catalog record for this book has been requested

ISBN: 978-1-138-32076-5 (hbk)
ISBN: 978-0-429-45306-9 (ebk)

Typeset in Sabon
by Apex CoVantage, LLC

To Eva, Thomas, Arthur, and Elodie

Contents

Figures

Tables and Graphs

Tables

Graphs

Contributors

Scott Elliott, President, SEG Measurement

Stephen Klein, Director of Research, CAE (Council for Aid to Education), 2001–14

Julie Patterson, Course Mentor, Western Governors University, Adjunct Instructor, Central Texas College

Jeffrey T. Steedle, Senior Research Scientist, ACT

Doris Zahner, Vice President and Principal Measurement Scientist, CAE (Council for Aid to Education)

Preface

The Thesis

Higher education continues to attract illuminating publications by higher education leaders and thoughtful observers. These works aim to persuade current and future higher education leaders to change course either by increasing access, reducing costs or providing more public support, improving academic quality, or altering the mission of universities.

If we adopted the applied interdisciplinary empirical research approach for higher education that was adopted in agriculture, health, and national security at critical historical junctures in each policy area, we could envisage the development of a continuous system of improvement on the issues higher education institutions face. This study makes the case for evidence-based decision-making.

The subtitle *Pasteur's Quadrant in Higher Education* evokes the narrative of the study. Pasteur's professional life was motivated by the need to solve the problem of tainted milk by Typhus. To solve the problem, Pasteur invented the building blocks of microbiology. The issues facing higher education also present practical problems that warrant a similar use-inspired interdisciplinary approach. Applications of the approach on issues such as the role of the faculty in governance, inequality of economic opportunity of high-ability students from underrepresented groups, and the role of critical-thinking skills for the improvement of economic productivity are presented in support of the thesis.

The Puzzle: Why Don't We Connect the Dots? The Anatomy of a Critique

A well-regarded education policy expert (Zemsky, 2013), dismisses educational assessments like CLA+. He calls attention to the CLA's "wobbly methodology" (2013, p. 201) and summarizes his view of the CLA as follows:

> A more refined CLA is not what the academy needs. We don't need a single test that is expected to be equally relevant to all institutions;

> we don't need a test of dubious statistical value; and we don't need a test that principally rewards motivation, and whose results too often reflect a student's score on the SAT.
>
> (p. 201)

Zemsky is contradicted by measurement scientists that show that:

1. Student motivation is not a significant predictor of CLA performance (Steedle, 2010);
2. Although the CLA is correlated with entering academic ability, it does not test the same constructs as college entrance exams like the SAT or ACT (Klein et al., 2007; Zahner et al., 2012);
3. The samples drawn are representative—freshmen and seniors do not differ much from each other except for their CLA scores (Klein et al., 2008);
4. The CLA program rejects one-size-fits-all measures. Appropriate standardized tests that permit inter-institutional comparisons are necessary but not sufficient. Institutional comparisons are needed to frame within-institution formative assessments; and
5. The CLA is "not of dubious" statistical value. Measurement scientists representing ACT, ETS, and CAE found that the critical-thinking assessments, two of which are multiple choice and one of which is performance-assessment based, were all statistically reliable (Klein et al., 2009).

Zemsky's critique of standardized assessments like CLA+ and his proposed course of action, a "National Process of Continuous Improvement of the National System of Higher Education" (p. 219), would have been improved significantly if he had the benefit of the vigorous debates by researchers working in the educational assessment field exhibited in the publications noted here.

Bowen and McPherson, in *Lesson Plan* (2016, p. 134), end their book with a call for "enabling stronger leadership." However, they also indicate they do not have any recommendations to achieve this goal. Why do we not have stronger leadership in higher education that reflects the quality of former presidents like Robert Hutchins, president of the University of Chicago, or Clark Kerr, chancellor of the University of California? Would it not be preferable to provide stronger, more objective tools of analysis that higher education leaders could use to make better decisions?

Major Public Policy Comparisons

There are examples in public policy domains where widespread agreement among influential leaders crystalized in investments called use-inspired research (UIR) from which stronger science-based tools of analysis have been developed. At critical historical junctures, national leaders made the decision to invest heavily in scientific, evidence-based tools of analysis in agriculture, health, and national security, policy domains recognized as central to the wellbeing of the nation-state. Congress voted to establish land-grant universities in each state in 1862 during the Civil War, which were dedicated to transforming agriculture into a scientific-based enterprise. The results of this decision have changed agriculture throughout the world. Stimulated by the results of a survey of the health profession in the United States and Canada (Flexner, 1910), medicine has been transformed from a clinical to a science-based enterprise with dramatic success.

In agriculture, once the decision was made to shift the focus from the practice of agriculture by farmers only to a science-based development of agriculture with practitioners—the farmers—in the lead, biological technology and mechanization led to enormous progress (Ruttan and Hayami, 1987, pp. 2–3). Ultimately, agricultural economists succeeded in creating measures of the growth of agricultural productivity.

Based on the Flexner Report, a similar shift in medicine was seen; medicine changed from a clinical to a science-based enterprise with the doctor remaining in the lead, and improvement in healthcare diagnosis and medical procedures in the treatment of patients became the norm.

When the United States was faced with the Soviet threat after World War II, Congress founded the RAND Corporation in 1948, which tasked researchers from a variety of disciplines to develop objective tools of analysis for national security policymakers to use. Cost-benefit analysis, systems theory, game theory, and the prototype for the Internet were developed at RAND during its first decade of existence.

The leadership efforts required to make these paradigm shifts in these major policy fields were extraordinary, as is the case in any attempt to change the status quo state of affairs.

Is There a Model to Describe These Important Examples of Applied Interdisciplinary Policy Research?

The answer is UIR based on the analysis of Donald Stokes, who argued that the need to solve important practical problems has often driven the development of compelling, interdisciplinary, science-based research programs—starting with Pasteur's professional life experience. Passionate about solving the problem of tainted milk that created typhus, he created the initial building blocks of microbiology in the 19th century (Stokes, 1997).

There are many examples of scientific-based research relevant to higher education. However, there is no appetite for large-scale interdisciplinary investments in fields of research that share a commitment to transparency, peer review, the imperative to replicate results, or the core values of science. In fact, the few applications of economic approaches to higher education are ignored. Cognitive science findings are not being applied to the improvement of teaching and learning. Progress in educational technology, including artificial intelligence research, is more feared than embraced. Standardized educational assessment, a well-developed branch of statistics, is too often dismissed out of hand as antithetical to teaching and learning or is flawed methodologically.

Why do higher education thought leaders and education policy specialists ignore the findings of the measurement science community? What are the consequences, and what might be done about it? These are questions I attempt to answer in this book.

A Thought Experiment

The three distinguished higher education leaders noted above are among the most astute analysts of higher education. As a thought experience, imagine that the UIR approach discussed above has been adopted and there are numerous interdisciplinary research teams comprised researchers from economics, cognitive science, education technology, educational assessment, and data analytics throughout RI research universities. These teams are working on various parts of the system of higher education institutions. The main output (the nature of access, retention, graduation rates, and the quality of student learning), the throughputs (instructor/class-size ratio, online competency programs compared to traditional brick-and-mortar-based instruction), and the inputs (per student endowment) are among the major subjects studied. Over time, it would be reasonable to expect improved understanding of what factors contribute the most to improved skills of graduating seniors.

Would not experts such as Bowen, McPherson, and Zemsky note and applaud the record of continuous improvement corroborated by research findings that are peer reviewed and transparent, with the research results and data used for the research made public? If the UIR program achieved progress, I believe it possible to imagine the kind of progress we have seen in agriculture, healthcare, and national security policy coming to higher education.

We Have Made Progress in American Higher Education[1]

In addition to creating a science-based agriculture, the land-grant universities quickly rose to become serious contributors to fundamental academic research and scholarship. They also became the principal incubators for growing the private and public leaders in their states. Following World War II, the GI Bill gave millions of veterans the opportunity to go to college. The participation rate for college attendance rose for the middle class in the 1960s.

However, while the research productivity of the higher education sector has remained high as measured by external funded research dollars, patents, innovations in many fields, the heady years of Clark Kerr's multiuniversity seem in the distant past. Today the sector is clearly divided into a small set of approximately 143 selective colleges and universities (see Barron's selectivity index, *Barron's Annual Review* (2015) and approximately 3,000 colleges and universities in the less-selective group. The top 20 fundraising institutions alone, all in the selective category and equaling less than 1% of the nation's colleges, raised 27.1% of all 2016 gifts (CAE, 2017), which totaled $41 billion.

Meanwhile, the cost of higher education, as measured by the higher education price index (HEPI), is no longer held in check by the Consumer Price Index, as is the case with companies in the private sector. For its part, the administrative response to the increasing costs in less-selective colleges is to raise student tuition, just as many of the selective colleges do, but also transform their faculty from a full-time staff to a majority of part-time adjunct staff. Less than 25% of faculty holds tenure-track or tenured full-time positions. Since the department-based governance model has been the basis of decision-making for what subjects are taught, who should be hired to teach them, and how and when students should be assessed, this sea change that has hollowed out department-based governance should be undergoing scrutiny to understand its effects on teaching and learning. As of now, this is not happening.

The innovation ideas generated in education technology for improvement in teaching and learning and for cost reductions in higher education are burgeoning but do not appear to be gaining traction in the higher education sector. Overall, the higher education leadership seems to be in a defensive posture. The most esteemed recent public and private college presidents challenged the prevailing social and economic norms and were a source of inspiration and innovation themselves. James Conant, Robert Hutchins, Derek Bok, and Richard Atkinson come to mind. It may well be the case that today's higher education leaders struggle just to keep their institutions afloat. A recent special issue of *The Economist* concluded that it was no longer clear whether the U.S. higher education system would be able to surmount its current challenges to implement reforms sufficiently to continue to lead the world in higher education progress.

This study aims to persuade the reader that this negative scenario does not need to frame the prospects of the higher education sector. What is called use-inspired research has been employed historically to improve the outcomes in several institutions that are the delivery mechanisms of critical societal functions such as agriculture, healthcare, and national security. We should build on the expertise of researchers in academic disciplines that produce scientific-based research that bears on the subject of improvement of teaching and learning. We should align these disciplines with the experienced classroom teachers via new education technology tools and, through an interdisciplinary approach, commit to the development of a continuous system of improvements in teaching and learning that is similar in scale and effect to the dramatic successes achieved in agriculture, healthcare, and national security over time.

Note

1. The words postsecondary and higher education are used interchangeably throughout this study to describe what the French and the OECD (Organization of Economic Cooperation and Development) defines as the tertiary sector of the education system.

References

Barron's Profiles of American Colleges. 2015. New York: Barron's.

Bowen, William G., and Michael S. McPherson. 2016. *Lesson Plan An Agenda for Change in American Higher Education*. Princeton, NJ: Princeton University Press.

CAE, 2017. Colleges and Universities Raise $41 Billion in 2016. New York, NY: CAE News Release, February 7.

Flexner, Abraham. 1910. *Medical Education in the United States and Canada: A Report to the Carnegie Foundation for the Advancement of Teaching*, Bulletin No. 4. New York: The Carnegie Foundation for the Advancement of Teaching, pp. 346.

Klein, Steve, Lydia O. Liu, James Sconing, Roger Bolus, Brent Bridgeman, Heather Kugelmass. 2009. *Test Validity Study (TVS) Report*. Supported by the Fund for the Improvement of Postsecondary Education, U.S. Department of Education. Retrieved from http://www.voluntarysystem.org/docs/reports/TVSReport_Final pdf.

Klein, Steve, David Freedman, Richard Shavelson, and Roger Bolus. 2008. "Assessing School Effectiveness." *Evaluation Review* 32 (6): 511–25.

Klein, Steve, Roger Benjamin, Richard Shavelson, and Roger Bolus. 2007. "The Collegiate Learning Assessment: Facts and Fantasies." *Evaluation Review* 31 (5): 415–39.

Ruttan, Vernon Wesley, and Yujiro Hayami. 1971 (1st ed.) 1987 (2nd ed.). *Agricultural Development: An International Perspective*. Baltimore, MD: Johns Hopkins University Press.

Steedle, Jeffrey T. 2010b. "Incentives, Motivation, and Performance on a Low-Stakes Test of College Learning." *Paper Presented at the Annual Meeting of the American Educational Research Association*, Denver, CO.

Stokes, Donald E. 1997. *Pasteur's Quadrant: Basic Science and Technological Change*. Washington, D.C.: Brookings.

Zahner, Doris, Lisa M. Ramsaran, and Jeffrey T. Steedle 2012. "Comparing Alternatives in the Prediction of College Success." *Paper Presented at the Annual Meeting of the American Educational Research Association*, Vancouver, Canada.

Zemsky, Robert. 2013. *Checklist for Change: Making American Education a Sustainable Enterprise*. New Brunswick, NJ: Rutgers University Press.

Acknowledgments

I gratefully acknowledge the support, advice, and criticism without which this book would not have been written, starting with RAND—where I learned much about the field of public policy, especially from Steve Klein (retired senior scientist at RAND and the director of research at CAE from 2001 to 2014) and Steve Carroll (senior scientist emeritus, RAND). I thank my colleagues at the University of Minnesota, Raymond Duvall and Robert Kuderle, and Doris Zahner at CAE. I would like to thank Joseph C. Burke, Dan Fallon, Ted Marmor, Margaret Miller, Elinor Ostrom, and Bert Rockman. I also thank Richard Atkinson, Richard Foster, Ron Gidwitz, Katharine Lyall, Michael Rich, and Harvey Weingarten, members of the Board of Trustees at CAE who have been excellent sources of advice for this research. I appreciate the advice and support of Andreas Schleicher and Dirk Van Damme from the OECD (Organization of Economic Cooperation and Development). I also thank my colleagues Conor Sullivan, Tim Coussa, and Mi Sun Kwon for their editorial assistance on this study.

In addition, I have worked out some of my ideas in public. I am grateful for permission to repeat arguments here to the publishers of Anker Publishing and Change in Chapters 5, 8, and 10. Chapter 7 is reprinted from Assessing Quality in Postsecondary Education: International Perspectives, edited by Harvey P. Weingarten, Martin Hicks, and Amy Kaufman, Montreal and Kingston: McGill-Queens University Press, Queen's Policy Studies Series.

Part I

The Framework

1 Introduction

Introduction

Pasteur's Quadrant in Higher Education employs the logic and strategy of inquiry (Benjamin, 1980, 1982, and Benjamin and Duvall, 1985). In those studies, the last with Raymond Duvall, I described the structural changes that transformed the economic, social, and political systems of industrial societies into today's knowledge economy. The economic changes include a shift in focus from the principal production and consumption of physical goods to today's principal focus on the production and consumption of services, in particular "knowledge-intensive activities" (Pawell and Snellman, 2004, p. 199).[1]

Social values appear to be following a similar structural transformation from an emphasis on deferred gratification and subordination of the individual to the group in the industrial era to a greater focus now on "the individual over the group" and a transformation from an emphasis on deferred to immediate gratification (Benjamin, 1980, p. 50; see also Inglehart and Welzel, 2005).

The political institutions in the industrial era were based on the premise that "in size rests efficiency." However, from the collective goods literature we should expect that, in the post-industrial phase, demands for change increasingly challenge the authority of existing institutions and the focus shifts from a focus on growth to a focus on the quality of goods and services produced. Because of the growth of interdependence in the social-economic system, I argued the limits of politics itself would be redefined as citizens sought to reduce the increasing number of negative externalities that affected their wellbeing, including negative externalities from the local, state, and federal governments. Most importantly, I argued that the largely centralized institutions developed for the industrial era to deliver physical goods no longer achieved greater efficiency and effectiveness through economies of scale because of the inherent distortion effects on informative sensitive goods, which have come to dominate our post-industrial era. Flatter institutional arrangements more suited to respond to the need to improve the quality, not quantity of the services provided, are preferred.

Background

I became a participant observer of higher education in the wake of the research noted above. After serving as a dean and provost, I studied the empirical conditions associated with governance of postsecondary education in several settings around the United States and, with colleagues, recommended restructuring plans that involved substantial changes to institutional governance. Since 1999–2000, I have focused on the development and implementation of standardized assessments into postsecondary education while continuing to engage in strategic planning for individual universities and systems of universities. I also have observed the challenges higher education leaders, faculty, students, and policymakers face. Like many who have worked as faculty and administrators in universities, I have marveled at the disconnect between the success of faculty research and scholarship over the past several decades and the paucity of research and scholarship on higher education itself, especially the absence of progress in research that translates into improvements in teaching and learning, greater access, improved retention, and graduation rates of students from underrepresented groups. The trend of rising costs coupled with declining public resources is drawing comparisons with similar issues facing the healthcare sector. It appears that the higher education sector is at a tipping point.

What explains the disconnect between the apparent seriousness and urgency of the issues facing the sector and the lack of attention to it? What might be done about it? My goal is to answer these questions in this study.[2]

Chapter 2 presents a proposal for a new approach to research on postsecondary education. Figure 2.1 describes the growing cost problem in higher education. The most serious issues associated with growth in costs is captured in the higher education price index (HEPI), including student loan debt, the growth of teaching by adjuncts versus permanent faculty, the attainment deficit for students from underrepresented groups in access, retention and graduation rates, and employment in appropriate jobs after graduation.

The new approach is based on an intriguing idea of D. Stokes (1997). He points out that concern about major real-world problems drives the development of basic research initiatives as often as basic research leads to practical applied research. Stokes presents cogent examples of what he terms use-inspired basic research (shortened to use-inspired research, UIR here). Can this approach be used for research on higher education issues? Barriers to the application of the same scientific premises of research faculty use, to enormous effect for extending the frontiers of knowledge, appear to thwart use of these scientific premises on higher education itself.

An analysis of why outside, third-party research is resisted by departments is presented followed by a discussion of the most serious barrier that appears to be hindering innovations that might improve quality while cutting costs: the debate over whether higher education is a public or private good. The debate appears to be coalescing into what might be characterized as a permanent, common pool problem that may become a tragedy of the commons.

This situation makes the case for a new approach to research on higher education urgent. Higher education leaders and policymakers need new objective tools of analysis they can use to more effectively set academic and nonacademic priorities and, importantly, cut costs while improving the quality of undergraduate education.

A New Approach to Research on Postsecondary Education

Historical examples of UIR in agriculture, health, and national security are presented. The case for a UIR interdisciplinary approach for postsecondary education research comprised initially of several fields of inquiry that share the value system of science, including measurement science, is followed by a list of possible problems to solve. These academic disciplines initially include cognitive science, economics, data analytics, education technology, and measurement science. These disciplines should be joined with and guided by the practitioners who are engaged in teaching and learning. The contributions of measurement scientists and standardized assessments provide metrics of student outcomes that are essential to UIR because such metrics benchmark the proposed improvements in the quality of teaching and learning and other productivity.

Part II provides illustrations of how the UIR approach can **empower** stakeholders to make better policy decisions about critical policy issues. The intent of Part II is to provide motivation to support the focus of Pasteur's Quadrant in Higher Education on the use of an interdisciplinary approach, including educational assessment, for evidence-based decision-making,

- Should we fear that assessment in higher education will repeat the questionable high-stakes test purposes the way standardized assessments have been used in K–12 since No Child Left Behind (NCLB) was launched (Chapter 3)?
- Is it possible to use assessment as part of the education reform movement to transform teaching and learning from the current lecture format for instruction to a student-centered approach (Chapter 4)?
- Because the public research university has become highly factionalized, it is no longer accurate to claim the institution as a whole is

greater than the sum of its parts. Can assessments like CLA+ be used as a tool to assist faculty in gaining a stronger role in university-wide governance of the general education curriculum (Chapter 5)?
- Does the growing national problem of social-economic inequality manifest itself in the postsecondary sector? If so, what policy solutions might assist in reducing the problem? Can we use CLA+ data to estimate whether there is a market failure between college and career to provide empirical estimates of barriers that high-ability students from less-selective colleges face in securing jobs for which they are qualified (Chapter 6)?
- Can a generic-skills assessment of student-learning outcomes be used as a measure of the service sector of the economy to improve our understanding of productivity growth slowdown (Chapter 7)?

Part III presents evidence for the role of standardized assessments in higher education through the lens my colleagues and I used in developing the Collegiate Learning Assessment (CLA). Department-based governance privileges the role of department members in deciding what subjects to teach, who to recommend to teach the subjects, and how to assess students in their classes. This means that faculty tend to be wary of research findings from outsiders about their teaching practices and learning results. While faculty typically recognize other disciplines as legitimate in the Academy, they are more apt to question whether measurement science is itself legitimate. Many faculty members see standardized assessments as a threat to the relative autonomy granted to department governance. Such tests are not under the control of faculty members. Moreover, many faculty question whether standardized tests are reliable or valid. In part, this view may be a function of history.

Many faculty are ambivalent about multiple-choice tests. They prefer open-ended essay tests. Also, the recent history of the No Child Left Behind (NCLB) high-stakes testing regime implemented by the Bush Administration in 2002 has reinforced faculty skepticism about the potential role of standardized tests in higher education (see Chapter 9 for further discussion).

The case presented here rests on seeing appropriate standardized assessments as the important missing link needed to complete an interdisciplinary array of disciplines that could be brought together in an integrated way to generate much more successful, sustainable improvements in teaching and learning. Part III attempts to justify an important role for standardized assessments in higher education. The goal is to demonstrate that measurement science is a worthy candidate to be the anchor discipline that enables innovative interdisciplinary approaches to research on higher education to be developed. Part III also documents the path my colleagues and I have traveled to reach Pasteur's Quadrant in the higher education research space.

The three chapters that make up Part III, assisted by the comments and criticisms of critics, are devoted to the following issues,

- The case for comparisons between institutions: why are they important, and why are standardized tests important to use (Chapter 8)?
- What are the costs and benefits of performance-based assessments compared to multiple-choice assessments (Chapter 9)?
- Are critical thinking assessments, independent from academic disciplines, measurable and teachable? Do tests like CLA+ produce results that matter (Chapter 10)?

Among the many issues higher education faces, the market failure between higher education and career stands out. By one estimate (Chapter 11), over 1,500,000 graduating college seniors from less-selective American colleges and universities warrant the same designation as high-ability students as their counterparts in what Barron's called selective colleges in 2012 (Baron's College Selectivity Index, Barrons, 2015). The same year, 2012, the 143 colleges labeled selective by Baron's (2015) enrolled 940,000 students, of which 240,000 warrant being listed as high-ability students. If the criteria used to define high ability is credible, it means the less-selective colleges in the United States that enrolled 10,769,764 in 2012 graduated over five times as many high-ability students as their selective college counterparts. America's less-selective colleges educate the great majority of all students from underrepresented groups—African-Americans, Hispanics, and non-Hispanic white students—with Pell Grants.

This disparity in numbers of high-ability students in less-selective versus selective colleges runs counter to received wisdom, which privileges selective colleges as the principal choice of high-ability students. It suggests there is a market failure in the college to career space equal or even greater in magnitude than the similar problem identified by Hoxby and Avery (2012) for African-Americans entering college. Hoxby and Avery find that at least 10 times as many African-American college freshmen attain SAT or ACT scores that warrant admission to the selective colleges than previously understood. Even if the selective colleges were able to enroll all the eligible students from underrepresented groups, the problem of equal opportunity would not be solved. There would still be many high-ability students who would not have a place at the selective colleges. Of course, this is even more dramatic when one ponders the probability of selective colleges not enrolling their current cohort of students.

Employers report that millions of technology careers and jobs that require significant skills go begging. And what are the job and lifelong earning prospects for students who graduate from Ivy League colleges versus little-known public or private colleges throughout the United

States? If high-ability students from isolated small towns in rural settings are not recognized as worthy candidates for high-value jobs, what does this do to their morale, the morale of their family, and the attitudes of their K–12 teachers and local residents? In short, if today's social and economic inequality level is unacceptable and education increasingly recognized as the key for national human capital development and upward mobility for the next generation, why is today's division into selective and less-selective colleges allowed to be such a formidable barrier for either issue?

Notes

1. In 1980, it seemed appropriate to describe the structural changes in the society and economy in terms of the transition from the industrial to post-industrial phase of development. Because of the growth in technology-based services, the label knowledge economy is preferable to the more general post-industrial term used three decades ago (See Bell, 1973; Inglehart, 1971).
2. I use the Collegiate Learning Assessment (CLA), a standardized test of critical thinking skills, as my principal example of a standardized assessment because I am most familiar with its development. ETS, with its HEIghten Outcomes Assessment, and ACT, with CAAP (College Assessment of Academic Progress), also field standardized assessments that focus on critical-thinking skills.

References

Barron's Profiles of American Colleges. 2015. New York: Barron's.

Becker, Gary. 1993. *Human Capital: A Theoretical and Empirical Analysis with Special Reference to Education* (2nd edition). Chicago, IL: University of Chicago Press.

Bell, Daniel. 1973. *The Coming of Post-industrial Society*. New York: Basic Books.

Benjamin, Roger. 1980. *The Limits of Politics*. Chicago, IL: University of Chicago Press.

Benjamin, Roger. 1982. "The Historical Nature of Social Scientific Knowledge: The Case of Comparative Political Inquiry." In *Strategies of Political Inquiry*, edited by Elinor Ostrom, 69–82. Beverly Hills, CA: SAGE Publications.

Benjamin, Roger, and Raymond Duvall. 1985. "The Capitalist State in Context." In *The Democratic State*, edited by Roger Benjamin and Stephen Elkin, 19–58. Lawrence, KS: University Press of Kansas.

Bowen, William. 2012, October 10. *The Cost Disease in Higher Education*. Palo Alto, CA: Stanford University, The Tanner Lectures.

Hoxby, Caroline, and Christopher Avery. 2012. "The Missing "one-offs": The Hidden Supply of High-achieving, Low-income Students." *NBER Working Paper No. 18586*. Cambridge, MA: National Bureau of Economic Research.

Inglehart, Ronald. 1971, December. "The Silent Revolution in Europe: Intergenerational Change in Post-industrial Societies." *American Political Science Review* 65: 991–1017.

Inglehart, Ronald, and Christian Welzel. 2005. *Modernization, Cultural Change and Democracy: The Human Development Sequence*. New York: Cambridge University Press.

Pawell, Walter W., and Kaisa Snellman. 2004. "The Knowledge Economy." *Annual Review of Sociology* 30: 199–220.

Stokes, Donald E. 1997. *Pasteur's Quadrant: Basic Science and Technological Change*. Washington, DC: Brookings.

2 The Framework

Pasteur's Quadrant in Higher Education

Introduction

Human capital is increasingly recognized as the principal resource of the nation. The K–16 education system is the formal venue for preserving and enhancing it. Just as the historic decisions were made to introduce interdisciplinary, scientific-based research programs to agriculture and healthcare, a national-level decision can be taken to introduce a similar approach to postsecondary education. It is time to introduce the use-inspired research (UIR) approach to higher education.

The key problems facing higher education that comprise a compelling case to attack and solve are summarized. The principal obstacles inhibiting serious policy reform are reviewed, and a rationale for solving the problems presented is followed by a description of a proposal for use-inspired research by D. Stokes (1997). Historical examples of UIR then frame a proposal for how higher education can be the next candidate to benefit from UIR. The chapter concludes with suggested research topics to engage. An initiative called CLA+ Analytics that my colleagues and I are implementing to support the UIR approach in higher education is presented in the coda to this chapter, CLA+ Analytics, pp. 211–25.

The Case for Objective Tools of Analysis

Unless I can make a compelling case that decision makers in postsecondary education need these new tools to respond positively to the disruptive nature of a changed environment that features rising costs and declining resources—coupled with problems with the quality of undergraduate education—Pasteur's Quadrant is an academic exercise. Over time, critics and supporters of postsecondary education have reduced the argument to a binary choice: supporters argue postsecondary education is a public good that should be funded by the public sector, and critics argue that position is no longer viable or preferred. Postsecondary education produces private goods for students. Therefore, the public sector should not support the enterprise.

Noting the historic moves of agriculture and health policymakers to embrace use-inspired interdisciplinary empirical research, I apply a collective-goods approach to show why decision makers in postsecondary education require new tools of analysis developed by collaborating teams of researchers who share a commitment to the value system of science that privileges transparency, peer review, and the requirement to replicate results. This is the only way to build tools of analysis that are powerful enough to assist decision makers in breaking out of the dilemma they are in now, frozen over whether postsecondary education is a public or private good. In fact, the collective-goods approach leads us to understand the binary choice is the wrong way to view the problem. In fact, the question is which goods should be seen as public and which goods should be viewed as producing private-good returns to individuals who should pay for these goods. Empirical-based research is needed to determine whether to assign the goods produced as private or public.

Principles From the Collective-Goods Approach

Because I will employ principles from the collective-goods literature, I describe the rationale for this approach here.[1] The premise of the collective-goods approach is the methodological assumption of individual rational choice (Harsanyi, 1969). This deductive method emphasizes point predictions rather than the inductive, statistical-based method of explanation, which is more prevalent in the social sciences. When presented with evidence of social or economic change, the premise of methodological individualism directs the observer to look for changes in the environment that provide incentives or sanctions that drive individuals to change their behavior. Explanations based on "theories" about social systems or cultures are regarded as descriptions accounted for by mixes of incentives and sanctions, not explanations in and of themselves.

Recent public-goods theorists argue that the important distinction between public and private goods (Samuelson, 1967) requires revision due to the recognition of increased interdependencies in all aspects of the environment. In fact, today goods are rarely, if ever, purely public or purely private. Public goods, which, in theory, are supposed to be delivered to all members of a catchment, physical or otherwise, produce externalities that provide differential benefits to some and greater negative costs to others. The same distortion effects are found in the production and consumption of private goods. Therefore, one reads about quasi-public or quasi-private goods that form a continuum often called collective goods.

Previously, I, among others (Frolich et al., 1971; Furniss, 1978; Ostrom, 1990), have applied the collective-goods approach to the issue of how major social and economic institutions in society should be redesigned to meet the challenges of the Knowledge Economy. Large, centralized public and private institutions appear to have made sense in the industrial phase of U.S. development when manufacturing was the central driver of the economy. The production and consumption of physical goods are relatively free from distortion effects, also called negative externalities. However, the efficiency and effectiveness of large centralized institutions are challenged today because they are largely tasked with producing information-sensitive service goods, which are now the principal driver of the economy. Information-sensitive goods are more likely to exhibit distortion effects. Therefore, collective-good theorists posit centralization as likely to fall prey to diseconomies rather than economies of scale. This is because the collective-good approach is built on the methodological assumption of individual rational choice.

In theory, advancements in the organization come to those who perform assigned tasks most successfully; however, rewards are most likely to go to those who perform functions in a manner most congruent with the organization's latent goals. These include selection of such solutions that will preclude risking failure and, most important, the transfer of information that subordinates feel their superiors want to hear rather than what they may need to hear. Information about bureaucratic failure or a problem that must be solved is unwelcome because it may require action that may have uncertain consequences for the superior. All of this results in information bias; the more levels through which information passes, the greater the possibility that information will be biased.

The Research University Case

Research universities are examples of large centralized institutions, in their case divided into colleges separated one from the other. Higher education institutions produce service goods that are information-sensitive goods. Each college is made up of separate and relatively autonomous academic departments and programs that recommend what subjects should be taught in their fields, who should be hired to teach them, and whether and how students in their courses are to be assessed. As such, these institutions exhibit distortion effects about information in ways similar to all other centralized institutions.

Information that suggests the size of the department or supporting organization may be reduced in size or budget is typically unwelcome because that change would reduce the base of power and control of the leaders of the bureau or department (see Johnson, 1975). That same information bias occurs between departments within a college or colleges as departments compete for funds, power, and advantage within the larger organization.

"When we look at the relationship between size and efficiency from the collective-goods approach, we should therefore be prepared to find diseconomies as well as economies of scale."[2] Moreover, the focus should be on the need to differentiate among collective goods by asking: Is the size of the organization, public or private, delivering the good appropriate for the type of good being delivered?[3] Instead of governing the behavior of faculty and students in the institution through regulatory mechanisms themselves developed and applied by central bureaucracies, adherents to the collective-goods approach would suggest that outcomes-based metrics be developed to guide the behavior of individuals.

Existing economic metrics such as the concept gross national product (GNP) were developed in the industrial phase of social and economic development and privilege physical over service goods. Higher education institutions produce service goods that are information-sensitive goods. This is likely to produce several institutional redesign issues for postsecondary institutions that, like other institutions, were designed to be larger, centralized administrative structures in the industrial phase of development. Clark Kerr's celebration of the multi-university is a prime example of this preference (Kerr, 1995). I have attempted to apply several policy recommendations based on the collective-goods approach throughout this chapter. These recommendations include flattening hierarchies, which creates more effective ways to send and receive information horizontally between isolated organizations, and the creation of more horizontal pathways for stakeholders to communicate with each other.

Evidence That Higher Education Faces Significant Change

As measured by the higher education price index (HEPI), one sees that the costs of higher education have increased from 20% to 40% above the Consumer Price Index (CPI) on an annual basis from 1961 to 2015. This trend of higher education cost increases is dramatically higher than the increases in the CPI (see Figure 2.1).

Four Key Problems: A Possible Tipping Point

1. Rising Costs and Declining Public Support

The cumulative impact of the rising costs in postsecondary education, coupled with declines in public support for higher education, particularly since the financial crisis of 2008–09, are shown in the following examples:

1. The national student debt level is now over $1.3 trillion (Consumer Financial Protection Bureau, 2016).
2. One quarter of colleges and universities are on Moody's Financial Watch List (Woodhouse, 2015).

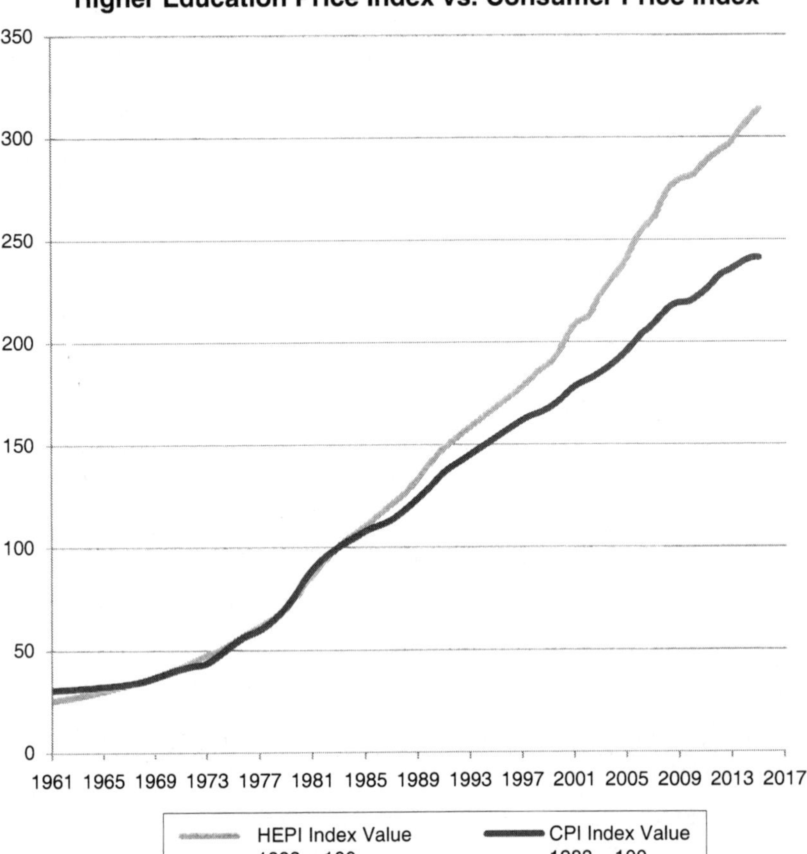

Figure 2.1 Higher Education Price Index Versus Consumer Price Index[4]

3. Permanent faculty lines (tenure-track or tenured) declined from over 85% in 1970 to less than 25% today (Schuster and Finkelstein, 2008; Finkelstein et al., 2016).

The first two examples on this list are functions of the colleges' and universities' need to raise tuition because of shortfalls in funding. The fact that many colleges are in financial stress continues to result in increasing revenues through raising tuition.[5]

The third example is also the result of funding shortfalls, but the implications of the large increase in adjunct faculty is not widely understood. The modern institution of higher education, developed in the late 19th century in the United States, delegates relative autonomy to departments to recommend what subjects to teach, who should teach these subjects, and how the students are to be assessed. As a result of the decline of permanent faculty to approximately 25% of all instruction in the higher education sector, most departments may no longer have the critical mass to manage the department's curriculum, to decide what subjects to teach and who should teach them, and to determine how and when students should be assessed.

The absence of a critical mass to sustain the department-based teaching and learning model is a major change for colleges and universities.[6] This hollowing out of the permanent faculty likely contributes to lower learning gains and lower absolute learning outcomes for undergraduate students. At this time, however, I know of no institutions that have conducted the assessments of student-learning outcomes that are needed to evaluate whether this is, in fact, the case.

2. *Decline in Major Indicators of College Success*

Only 40% of entering freshmen have reached college-level requirements in reading, writing, and math in recent years (ACT, 2014). In addition, despite the doubling of spending on K–12 education since the 1970s, the scores of nationally normed tests—such as the National Assessment of Educational Progress (NAEP), the SAT, and the ACT—have been flat or declining over the past 25 years.[7] Finally, employer surveys and research reports show an increasing dissatisfaction with the critical-thinking skills of college graduates applying for jobs (Hart Research Associates, 2014; Casner-Lotto et al., 2006; Liu and Grusky, 2013; National Research Council, 2012).

3. *The Impact of Disruptive Force, the Move From Place-Based to Internet-Based Education, Including the Change to Competency-Based Education (CBE)*

Instead of relying on the number of credit hours as the basis to certify student readiness to graduate with a bachelor's degree, many colleges and universities are introducing the idea to define readiness to graduate as a function of the demonstrated ability to pass the end-of-program assessments, which will demonstrate competency. As of 2015, at least nine nonprofit and for-profit colleges and universities offer solely competency-based degrees for 140,000 students. And between 60 and 100 colleges and universities offer parts of their academic programs as competency-based degrees (Kelchen, 2015). Many more colleges and universities appear to be planning to join this trend, a trend that may result in significant cost savings to colleges, including a move to a three-year bachelor's degree.

Internet-based education, often blended with place-based education and linked with CBE degrees, is also on the rise throughout the higher education sector. Internet-based courses offer cost savings in maintenance, instruction, and tuition for students.

These disruptive forces potentially offer new ways to reduce the cost problem for colleges and universities. However, there is a striking lack of credible research on the impact of the move to the Internet and competency-based education on the quality of undergraduate education.

4. The Market Failure Between College and Career

African-American and Hispanic students are often advised not to apply to selective schools, and they generally attend high schools that are not visited by college recruiters from elite institutions. Hoxby and Avery (2012) demonstrate that there are 10–15 times more African-American and Hispanic students than previously thought who have SAT or ACT scores that meet the admissions requirements of the most prestigious U.S. colleges. The SAT and ACT provide important additional information to complement students' high school GPAs (Kobrin et al., 2008), and these assessments help to overcome the market failure between high school and selective-college admissions. Lacking the SAT and ACT scores, admissions officers would only have students' high school GPAs to use for admissions decisions, and there likely would be even fewer students from underrepresented groups admitted to the most-selective colleges.

College-to-work readiness presents an even more severe market failure because there are no credentials or tests to accompany students' cumulative college GPAs that could control for the increasing grade inflation and variability of grades across colleges (Rojstaczer and Healy, 2012). Employers do not know how to evaluate the transcripts of students from less-selective colleges who may be as qualified as their counterparts from more-selective colleges. Employers have little choice but to consider students from the more-selective colleges as their primary job candidates because the branding of the colleges is seen as a proxy for quality.

In 2012 in the U.S., there were 10,764,489 students enrolled in four-year colleges. Less-selective colleges enrolled 9,823,718, which is approximately 10 times as many students as the selective colleges, which enrolled 940,771 students. If one were to focus on the top 10% of all graduating seniors, however, one would find that for every graduate from a selective college there would be eight graduates hailing from less-selective colleges, despite the lower percentage of high-ability students (defined by their CLA+ scores) in the top 10% (Barrons, 2014).[8] As a result, each year approximately 1,570,000 students from less-selective colleges do not get interviews for the higher-value jobs for which they are qualified (see Chapter 11).

Implications

Figure 2.1 implies that most of the new resources higher education institutions receive each year are eaten up by increases in costs. In turn, this means there are fewer resources to solve looming challenges, such as raising access, retention, and graduation rates. In addition, there are fewer resources to maintain or increase basic or applied research. The historical growth of the HEPI at a rate significantly higher than the CPI's rate of growth also means we can assume that little or no systematic efforts have been made to cut costs over the several decades covered by Figure 2.1 (p. 17). If this pattern remains unchanged, we can expect this assumption to continue to be accurate for the future as well.

The pattern of rising costs in higher education is reminiscent of the history of healthcare economics. It is reasonable to conclude that the higher education sector does not have the resources, and hence the decision-making tools, to make it the active shaper of social and economic change that thought leaders expect. This situation is unfortunate because the higher education sector is of the highest importance to the future of the nation. Here is why this is the case.

In today's Knowledge Economy, there is agreement that human capital—the skills, knowledge, and experience possessed by a nation's work force—is a nation's primary asset (Becker, 1993). Because technological innovation is central to high value-added economic growth (Kurth, 1979), human capital improvement is central to the nation's ability to preserve or enhance its comparative advantage in national security and other policy domains, such as healthcare, agriculture, energy, and transportation. The relationship between the human capital level of the workforce and economic growth is stronger today than at any other time, especially because the time between technological innovations is shorter than ever before (DeSilver, 2014; Miller, 2013). Higher education is critical to the K–16 education system because the requirements for graduation from college set the standards for teachers, students, and parents to achieve at the elementary- and secondary-education levels.

One implication of the importance of the human capital premise is the following hypothesis:

> The stronger a nation's human capital, the greater the probability its technological progress will remain at the peak of the economic product cycle where products of the highest economic value are created. Therefore, the principal obligation of the Nation State is to preserve and enhance the human capital of its workforce.
>
> (Benjamin, 2012a, pp. 20–1).[9]

Therefore, if the primary obligation of the State is to defend the security of the nation-state, human capital should be protected as its primary resource. This means it becomes critical to improve the quality of education because the ability of the State to provide national security, adequate healthcare, high-quality agricultural products, and energy and transportation enhancements all depend on the quality of a nation's human capital. Hence, human capital should be recognized as the necessary, but insufficient, condition for continued progress in these important policy domains. The improvement of the quality of undergraduate education should, therefore, become a principal focus of policymakers.

In sum, there is significant evidence that the postsecondary sector faces major challenges, perhaps a tipping point. Because higher education is so critical to the nation's future, why are higher education leaders, central administrators, and boards of trustees not attempting to deal with the challenges directly? One major reason is they do not have the tools to do so. If this is the case, why not? The answer, I will argue below, rests in overcoming obstacles to building and employing research-based tools useful for evidence-based decision-making embedded in the governance of the institution itself.

What Are the Obstacles to New Research Initiatives Like UIR on Postsecondary Education?

Many faculty do not grant the same respect to research on issues related to higher education institution matters that they grant to research from all fields on all other subjects. Although the standardized measurement of student-learning outcomes in undergraduate education is a branch of statistics, many faculty, administrators, and other stakeholders do not accept such research as reliable or valid. These same groups also do not welcome pertinent research on higher education by researchers in other science-based fields, such as neuroscience and cognitive science, data analytics, economics of education research, or technology-based innovations. These fields of inquiry, forming an interdisciplinary whole, could provide powerful new tools to assist in the quest to improve teaching and learning systematically.

Why this does not happen is a puzzle because of the shared assumption that many faculty hold called the parity of all fields of knowledge. The assumption that all fields are considered legitimate is in large part based on historical and practical considerations. The history of science teaches us that one cannot predict when fields of inquiry will suddenly take on urgent practical utility. For example, when the AIDS epidemic emerged, an obscure field of research on retroviruses in monkeys became a seminal building block for the response of medical science to this unknown malady. In a practical sense, faculty in university departments need to make it explicit to members of other departments that they grant the assumption that all other fields of inquiry are legitimate. There is no other way for all faculty to operate within the ecology of a college or university comprised colleagues from many academic fields of study. They do not have the time or expertise to make independent judgments about many academic fields outside of their own. Moreover, they want faculty members in other departments to grant their department and academic field similar recognition and legitimacy (Benjamin and Carroll, 1996).

Why are some research applications from several fields of inquiry, which are based on the logic of scientific inquiry, not granted the assumption that their research approaches are authentic and legitimate when they are focused on higher education itself? The answer to this question is twofold—first, department-based governance is a double-edged sword. Giving relative autonomy to the experts in academic disciplines to chart their course is the principal reason the U.S. research university became unrivaled on the world stage. However, the premise underlying department-based governance is a powerful hindrance to the introduction of the institution of higher education itself.

In the late 19th century, a consensus emerged that the best way to organize universities was through department-based governance. This meant encouraging qualified graduating college seniors to obtain PhDs in a field of inquiry of their choice. In turn, professionals in each field of inquiry organized themselves in departments around the structuring principle that only those qualified in a field of knowledge are equipped to govern themselves and, in turn, to decide which fields of inquiry within their discipline should be covered, what subjects should be taught, who should be hired and promoted, and how students should be taught and assessed. No matter how great their knowledge, skills, and/or accomplishments, outsiders were perceived to lack the shared understanding needed to contribute to these decisions in a meaningful way (Benjamin and Carroll, 1996).

Second, faculty are focused on academic fields of inquiry. Faculty are typically not interested in whether their instructional methods produce acceptable results based on independent, third-party assessments. Nor do they pursue different models of mission differentiation, which might create new opportunities for improvement in the quality of instruction and student learning.[10] Their interests do not extend to research findings that question the premise of department-based governance.

The result is the powerful commitment to the premise of department-based governance has led to a two-culture split within the Academy. Too many faculty resist science-based research on higher education. Thus, there is a paucity of evidence-based empirical research supported by the value system of science. Scholarship not based on the value system of science lacks transparency and clear peer-review standards and does not privilege the value of replication of research results. Without systematic, empirical-based evidence, it will not be possible to propose, develop, and implement effective remedies to the two-culture division.[11]

Another obstacle involves the split between stakeholders for and against the concept of postsecondary education as a public or private good. UIR is needed to assist in resolving these and other major higher education issues, just as it was, and still is, needed to assist in framing the health insurance policy debate, improving agriculture, and providing national security policymakers with the decision-making tools they need to ensure national security in today's Knowledge Economy. However, it is imperative to also register an important point about the relationship between UIR and formative-based assessment.

The formative-based assessment program in postsecondary education must not be cast aside. UIBR research alone will not fundamentally improve teaching and learning in undergraduate education. However, neither will the formative-based assessment program do the job. Both research programs should be linked as part of the UIR-proposed program for postsecondary education. This study makes the case that a number of fields of inquiry that share the same value system of science should be a major part of the integrated, focused research program to improve postsecondary education (see also footnote 25 below).

Why is the task of designing better objective tools for higher education leaders and education policy decision makers urgent? The debate about whether higher education is a public or private good is frozen in place. If this situation is not changed, there is potential for serious damage to the postsecondary education sector. Objective tools of analysis are needed to assist in solving this contentious debate. Here is the case for urgent attention to the public/private good debate.

Higher Education as Private or Public Goods: The Wrong Debate

Private goods are goods that are divisible when buyers and sellers can agree upon a mutually acceptable price and close the deal (i.e., the buyer agrees to pay price X for good Y). Since the price of private goods is set by the market, there are no spillover effects (i.e., "externalities") that benefit or harm third parties attached to the transaction. Private goods are neither overvalued nor undervalued because of the discipline of market-based competition.

Exponents for privatization of higher education point to the benefits of market-based efficiency in treating higher education as a private good. They agree that the treatment of higher education as an undifferentiated public good results in an inevitable upward spiral of costs to the major consumers of the good, to students, and to their parents. This is because there are no market incentives in place to limit increases in salaries of professors and the expansion of the administrators and staff that serve them. Public subsidies of any kind translate into further increases in tuition and other costs.

Adherents of privatization have seemingly unlimited numbers of examples of the misallocation of public resources that produce unintended consequences for all parties concerned. For example, privatization adherents agree with publications that argue for raising the amount of money for Federal Pell Grants simply results in increases to tuition for colleges and universities (Lucca et al., 2015; Giller, 2012).[12]

Citing the "invisible hand" argument (Bishop, 1995), the status quo is accepted as given. The "invisible hand" argument itself is based on the assumption that what is most important for individuals, individual families, and individual companies is to pursue their own self-interest. If they do that successfully, the public good will take care of itself.[13] In other words, it is assumed that the parts will add up to the greater whole. In sum, the "invisible hand" is well-aligned with the assumption that the status quo is the preferred approach to the problem. The status-quo argument involved in common problems is powerful and convenient for existing stakeholders. Moreover, often the status-quo situation has been in place for some time.

Adherents find it hard, or even impossible, to imagine a viable alternative to the status quo. It is based on the premise that the status quo is superior to all proposed reforms or improvements unless it is proven that the proposals are better than the status quo. It is always difficult to "prove" that proposed reforms are clearly better than the status quo. That is why they are called proposed reforms. However, holding to the status-quo position also assumes the status-quo position is itself not producing a variety of negative externalities, which may call for or require significant change, even in the absence of clear proof of the superiority of the proposed reform.

An example of the privatization position with respect to higher education is provided by a critique by Leef (2015) of a book by Lambeth (2014). Leef calls out Lambeth and the endorsers of the book's thesis, Pat Callen and James Duderstadt, by asserting that they commit the error of mistaking correlation for causation. Leef makes a reasonable case for this position by arguing that the decline of the government subsidy of higher education has not demonstrably "caused lost benefits in health, crime, welfare, human rights, political stability, or anything else" (Leef, 2015, p. 1). Since the adherents of the public-good case for supporting higher education do not "prove" their arguments, the privatization case against any public support is vindicated. This is so, Leef argues, because public support always stifles market competition, which, in turn, raises costs but not productivity.

At the same time, we are left to speculate what Leef's definition of the public good is. His critique of Lambert's work is based on the premise of the invisible hand in which it is assumed that if individuals pursue their own rational self-interest in improving their economic and social condition through education, benefits will accrue to the "greater" society. There is no need, however, to construct an argument for viewing postsecondary education as a public good because if that approach is implemented, rising costs will inevitably tip the postsecondary sector into ruin.

As Adam Smith noted, the "invisible hand" argument does not cover the needed social, economic, or political change (Harsanyi, 1969) that is championed by the academics who recognize that the ever-changing market dictates what types of goods can be designated as public goods. For example, the establishment of the principle that protection of the environment is important led to the establishment of the National Parks Service, the Environmental Protection Agency, and endangered species acts. Adherents to the invisible-hand position resist any argument for change because they note that the argument for change has not been proven to be a clear advance. However, adherents to the invisible-hand position do not calculate the opportunity costs of continuing to hold the status-quo position in the face of significant changes in the environment, as recognized in these examples by champions of establishing national parks.

To be fair, because the public good claims for higher education of Lambert and his supporters appear to be based on an oversimplified view of today's more nuanced understanding of the concept, Leef's critique of Lambert has merit. Yet Leef, too, does not present his definition of what the public-good concept entails. Neither Leef nor those he criticizes appear to accept the concept of negative externalities, which is an important concept that has provided the basis for fresh thinking about the distinction between public and private goods as a continuum of goods rather than the black-and-white distinction introduced by Samuelson.[14]

From Samuelson's (1954) definition, we learn that public goods are indivisible. If they are allocated to one member of a community, they cannot be denied to any other members of that community. National defense and K–12 education are often cited as examples. Upon study, most goods exhibit both positive and negative externalities.[15] For example, airlines may be "private companies," but a decision to discontinue flight service to a small city has significant negative externalities that affect all members of the city's population. The production of energy by power plants regulated by public authorities often produces unwanted carbon and other pollutants on the population at large. National defense benefits some localities where military bases are placed more than localities that do not have bases to benefit their economy. Therefore, it has become clear that goods form a continuum between the pure private and public good poles. That is why labels such as quasi-public, quasi-private, or collective are often used in describing a particular set of goods.

Postsecondary education comprises both private- and public-good benefits. Students and their families benefit from an undergraduate education. These are benefits that may be assigned to private individuals. However, the education and graduation of large numbers of undergraduates produce externalities that clearly also benefit the greater society and economy at large. Moreover, while it is possible to assign some of the costs of undergraduate education to the individual, private consumers of the good (the students), there are significant numbers of additional costs that cannot be designated as such. For example, many teaching professors received PhDs based on research funded by the federal government.

The publications of the professors on the basis of this federally funded research are in the public domain. Students and their families cannot be asked to pay for this funding. Research labs, research libraries, and physical plants are also benefits distributed widely and not easily reduced to a cost to be assigned to an individual student. This does not mean, however, that we cannot do a much better job of allocating benefits and costs to students and parents on the one hand and the public on the other.

Neither the privatization supporters nor the public-good exponents appear to acknowledge any truth in the positions of their opponents; the debate is frozen. Whereas privatization supporters see no merit in public subsidies for any part of higher education, supporters of the view that postsecondary education is a public good do not recognize the merit of the market having any role in higher education. There is little or no basis for a middle ground for compromise between the two positions. Unfortunately, there is no acceptance of any part of the other side's position. The end result is an underinvestment in the activities and components of higher education that are core public goods, necessary for higher education institutions to function. This is a serious problem, and it is urgent that the higher education sector responds to it.

Postsecondary Education as a Common Pool Problem (CPP)

We should view postsecondary education's problems as what economists call a common pool problem (CPP)[16] because there is not sufficient public or private investment for the postsecondary education good. CPPs develop whenever a group depends on a public good that is universally used but no one owns and where one person's use affects another person's demand for the good. The result is that either the population fails to provide the resources, overconsumes them, or fails to replenish them. Another important problem regards confusion about property rights. Examples include water, fishing or grazing rights, and climate change. If no solution to the CPP is reached, they can tip into a permanent crisis by which the problem can no longer realistically be solved. This is what Garrett Hardin calls a tragedy of the commons (Hardin, 1968).

To understand how Hardin's argument applies to postsecondary education, consider the following hypothetical example: the state budget retrenchment requires the governor to authorize a 10% cut in the higher education budget. What is the likely response of the sitting presidents in each of the state's higher education institutions? Will they volunteer to cut back 10%? No. There is no incentive for them to volunteer unless they are compelled to do so. Instead, they will attempt to resist any cuts to their budgets through a variety of imaginative strategies.

In Hardin's example of the tragedy of the commons, when the herd grazing on the commons grew too large and was in danger of starvation and decline, the rational behavior of each individual farmer was to increase the number of cows in his herd. This guarded against his herd sharing the same fate as the overall herd grazing on the commons. The problem, of course, is that what is rational for the individual farmer speeds the decline of the commons' herd overall. In this example, the farmers are the higher education leaders and the cows are the higher education institutions, which will suffer and decline if their leaders do not cooperate when the budget (the equivalent to the grass on the commons) collapses.

Many state universities face this same budget retrenchment issue today. There are few, if any, examples of cases where a state authority has had the discretion to compel behavior by individual colleges that was rational from the perspective of the state. For both access and fiscal reasons, in the future governors and state legislatures may well face the necessity of changing the rules of governance to come closer to creating a more realistic commons for higher education institutions in their states.

In the case of higher education, the most basic question is: Who is responsible for correcting the underinvestment in the higher education sector? Is it the students and their parents, the institution of higher education, or public authorities? Today, tuition revenues for public higher education outstrip local and state subsidies in over half of the states (Woodhouse, 2015). Most important, because there also is widespread confusion about what should be done about it, there is a need for serious empirical-based research to determine what alternative paths are available to solve the problem of underinvestment noted in Figure 2.1. In fact, there is very little recognition of the extent of the misunderstandings about what parts of higher education should be viewed as more "public" and which should be viewed as more "private."

CPPs, then, are collective goods that pit two sides against each other with no compromise envisaged by either side. No change, from the point of view of the privatization of higher education adherents, is imaginable. Those arguing to move away from privatization toward the public good need to make a much stronger case than they have to change the attitudes of their opponents. They must demonstrate how the institution of higher education can be redesigned (not restricted) to deal with the problems noted above. If proponents for change were able to do so, they would be better positioned to reframe the debate and draw supporters from the status-quo privatization camp. This situation must change if progress is to occur.

Once a CPP is locked in, it becomes more and more difficult to solve it. Meanwhile, we have witnessed the higher education sector become an unwitting party to the mal-distribution of human capital at the national level because of the absence of a level playing field for high-ability students in less-selective colleges. Higher education has become a positional good that determines the economic life chances of all citizens because the competitively branded colleges maintain a monopoly, controlling access to the jobs of higher economic value (Hirsch, 1976). The higher education sector appears to be losing the battle to improve student access, retention, and graduation rates. There are questions about the quality of undergraduate education as well. It does appear the higher education sector is at a tipping point.

Better understanding regarding the inevitable tradeoffs between all approaches to the production and consumption of goods is the first practical step toward decisions that benefit all parties who participate in the production and consumption of the principal higher education goods, research, and undergraduate education. Tools of analysis that can assist policymakers, higher education leaders, parents and students, and other stakeholders in understanding the tradeoffs between public versus private good positions regarding many issues in higher education are needed.

The Intriguing Idea From D. Stokes: Pasteur's Quadrant

The familiar assumption most researchers adhere to is that basic disinterested research drives applied, practical applications. Through a portrait of the motives that drove Louis Pasteur to find a solution that would prevent tainted milk from killing millions of children, Stokes (1997) describes how Pasteur ended up inventing the building blocks of microbiology as an unintended side benefit of his search for a practical solution to a major health problem. Pasteur's passionate and practical medical goal led to a breakthrough in basic research. Stokes labels this kind of research use-inspired basic research (UIR). He posits that in today's democratic societies, major public policy issues must be attacked by UIR programs because the nature of funding choices made by governments and foundations are driven by public opinion.

The question is whether use-inspired research makes sense for higher education.

Research in physics, such as the experiments run at Cern's Large Hadron Collider in Switzerland, is an example of empirical research used to corroborate pure basic research at one pole. Edison, on the other hand, did not focus on the research basis of the innovations he discovered. He represents the other pole.

Table 2.1 Quadrant Model of Scientific Research[17]

Research is inspired by:		*Considerations of Use?*	
		Yes	No
Quest for fundamental understanding?	Yes	Pure Basic Research (Bohr, Cern)	Use-Inspired Basic Research (Pasteur)
	No		Pure Applied Research (Edison, Marconi)

The Premise and Role of UIR

Many of the most important empirical research programs are based on the value system of science. Such research programs are the clearest strategy we have to develop continuous systems of improvement.[18] These research programs are based on the transparency of results, the commitment to make the results replicable, and the utilization of peer review to design and evaluate the progress of the research program itself. Popper (1959) breaks down the scientific research steps into the logic of inquiry, starting with the assumptions that underpin the research approach to the problem under study. The theory or theoretical framework postulated flows from the assumptions. From there, Popper shows why the concepts that measure the key dimensions of the theoretical framework are critical—e.g., whether the concepts are interval (precise gradations between the points in the intervals predicted), ordinal (categorized in more or less terms), or nominal (simple classification) in nature. He ends with descriptions of the hypotheses that flow from the conceptual framework, the data employed, the data analysis carried out, and the criteria needed for falsification of the hypotheses tested.

Discussions about the logic of inquiry inevitably turn into discussions about the strategy—the way the steps in the logic of inquiry are employed. That is what makes the research process so interesting (Kuhn, 1970; Lakatos, 1970). For example, with respect to assessment in higher education, the fundamental argument is not whether a particular standardized assessment is reliable or valid; rather, the argument lies between those who believe that the logic of scientific inquiry has no place in higher education assessment and those who believe it does have a role.[19] In other words, the debate is over first principles; should measurement science have a role in assessment in higher education? If this point is acknowledged, the discussion focuses on values of those who are for or against standardized assessment in higher education. Most college graduates do not have a problem viewing the physical and natural sciences as "real" subjects. However, the social sciences remain contested. I have argued elsewhere that social science is replete with scientific-based fields, but that the content these fields generate are historical-based (temporal) subjects (Benjamin, 1982). It may be enough to agree that the strategy of inquiry involves the way that steps in the logic of inquiry are put together to construct innovative research designs. The development of each scientific-based field consists of a constant search for grids that provide better coordinates with which to map and remap the part of the "real" world of interest (Maxwell, 1974).

Breakthroughs in scholarship and scientific research occur when a researcher or group of researchers decide to look at the relationship between different but related fields; for example, the relationship between medieval literature and medieval art (Pickering, 1970), comparative literature and linguistics (Godzich, 1994), engineering and chemistry (Aris, 1999), and physics and biology (Goldfarb, 2010). At the societal level, use-inspired based research, as shown by Pasteur's quadrant, turns into a larger focus on institutions at critical junctures of social, economic, and political change.

Looking back at the transformative change that occurred from the agricultural to the industrial era, we hold individual figures such as Max Weber, Karl Manheim, and John Maynard Keynes in esteem because their names are linked with the creation of new institutions designed to respond to and shape key components of industrialization. Weber is rightly credited with inventing the rational-legal bureaucracy to fill the need for a governance system in firms and governmental institutions rising in the industrial era. Manheim developed the concept of social welfare, including the institutions necessary to deliver welfare to the citizens needing it. Keynes formulated the concept of steering economic growth itself through pump/prime policies from the government.

Each of these innovations was based on a strategic assessment of the direction of social change and the institutional policies and institutional delivery systems that could shape the human response to the social-change process. The central premise of these institutional innovations at the onset of the industrial era of development is that centralized institutions bring with them economies of scale and, therefore, are more effective and efficient in delivering their services.[20]

In today's Knowledge Economy, where information-sensitive goods are the majority of goods produced and consumed, centralization may bring significant diseconomies of scale. Many private-sector organizations have recognized this, thus flattening their hierarchies and adopting outcomes-based accountability systems in response (Besley and Ghatak, 2003; Coram, 1996). The higher-education sector has not yet done so, but the time for redesign of the institution of higher education may be here. First, however, what examples of UIR can we point to besides supporting Stokes's conclusions that clarify the need for UIR in democratic societies (where public opinion matters)?

Examples of Use-Inspired Research

Of course, the distinctive histories of agriculture, health, and national security policy domains feature significant and contentious debates. However, one may point to critical inflection points when the thought leaders in each of these policy areas agreed to introduce scientific-based empirical research into their subject areas. One may also point to specific historical junctures when agriculture, health, and national security were each regarded as the central policy problem to solve. It is during these junctures that we find Congressional national policy actions that endorse a shift toward URI empirical research. Here is a description of each case.

1. **Making Agriculture a Science-Based Enterprise: The Morrill Act (1862)**

   The rationale of the Morrill Act (Geiger and Sorber, 2013) was that an integrated focus on the development of agriculture based on scientific research was critical to the future of the country. Biology, chemistry, economics, and ecology were applied in numerous integrated ways. Moreover, an innovative new institution, the agriculture county extension agent system, was created to transmit new agricultural innovations from the land-grant universities to the farmers. The result over the next century was an extraordinary increase in agricultural productivity that created the worldwide green revolution in wheat and rice production and improved many other areas of agriculture.

2. **From a Clinical to a Science-Based Medicine**

   The Flexner Report (1910), sponsored by the Carnegie Corporation, created momentum to transform medicine from a clinical profession to a profession based on the value system of science. It has been on this path ever since, although tension remains between the clinical and scientific groups attempting to make progress in medicine from their different premises. The recent progress in molecular biology may have been the tipping point in the transition of medicine into a science-based enterprise.

   In the 1960s, Congress passed Medicare and Medicaid, which meant that the federal government needed to determine the best-practice models for co-payment of health insurance. Analysts, tasked to find the best possible answers, conducted decades-long random trial experiments to determine best-practice models for the health insurance payment system.[21]

   A central goal of empirical-based research is to stimulate further research, leading to improved solutions to the problems being addressed. Dr. Theodore Marmor (private communication) suggests attention be devoted to comparing cost trends in postsecondary education with trends in healthcare costs. For example, he points out that single-payer healthcare systems like Canada and Western European countries have produced significantly lower cost increases in healthcare than the United States has. The reason for this, he suggests, is that single-payer systems are more likely to restrain cost increases than multiple-payer systems and that multiple-payer systems do not have as much authority as single-payer systems over healthcare providers. He wonders, therefore, whether the year-over-year cost increases in public colleges and universities is lower than year-over-year cost increases in private colleges and universities. The Common Fund, the host of the higher education price index (HEPI), has broken out HEPI year-over-year increases from 2001 to 2015 that show the total HEPI increase for public colleges and universities is 6.99% over the 15-year period, while the increase in costs measured by the HEPI are 7.97% for private colleges and universities over the same period. While the results are not statistically significant, this may be due to the small sample size. Research that compares cost increases in private versus public universities are needed.

3. **Objective Decision-Making Tools for National Security Policy Makers: The RAND Corporation**

   In 1946–47, the president and Congress became alarmed about the emerging threat from the Soviet Union to U.S. national security. In response, in 1948, Congress provided funding to support the establishment of the RAND Corporation and tasked researchers to create objective tools of research to assist national security policy advisors with making better decisions (Smith, 1965; Light, 2003, 2005). In the first 15 years of RAND's existence, game theory, cost/benefit analysis, systems theory, and the prototype of the Internet were invented (Dresher, 2007; Enthoven and Smith, 1970; Barran, 1964).

These examples may be amplified with other more specific examples, such as the invention of the transistor and laser at Bell Labs (Gertner, 2012), the program to place a person on the moon in the 1960s, and the mapping of the Human Genome Project in the 1990s. These three projects also greatly accelerated basic research in applied scientific fields that ultimately improved the quality of life for many individuals.

Finally, in STEM fields of inquiry and medicine, the case for more investment in interdisciplinary and multidisciplinary research appears to be growing. "Integration of the biological sciences with physical and computational sciences, mathematics, and engineering promises to build a wider biological enterprise with the scope and expertise to address a broad range of scientific and societal problems" (National Research Council, 2009). In addition, the American Association of Colleges and Universities (AAC&U) launched its STIRS (Scientific Thinking and Integrative Reasoning Skills) project, bringing an integrative approach to problem solving with the application of scientific principles across the arts and sciences to reform general education (see Peer Review, 2016).

In each of these cases, it is notable that policy issues and practical problems were selected to be the focus of researchers and practitioners from several fields of inquiry. These researchers shared a goal to create significant improvement in the performance of institutions or organizations, or within many groups and individuals. In each of these examples, an important objective was tied to an institution or a system of institutions (the delivery system), warranting an integrated research approach that combined scientific fields, each based on the value system of science. The movement toward broad-based integrative research that impacts policy and practice is widespread. What is distinctive about the commitment to UIR for agriculture, health, and national security policy domains is their scale and importance in the larger economy, society, and polity. Higher education is the logical next target for UIR that matches the other three national policy domains in scale and importance.

The Use-Inspired Research Model for Higher Education Is the Best Way Forward

Science-based research is essential to address any policy problem in education that has stakes attached to it. Researchers in cognitive science, macroeconomics and microeconomics, educational assessment, educational technology, and data analytics—to name a few—toil in independent silos, isolated from each other. However, they share a commitment to the logic and strategy of scientific inquiry. The premises of the value system of science, peer review, transparency, and the ability to replicate results are familiar to faculty and administrators. When paired with a coherent and compelling use-inspired basic research strategy, it is possible to imagine a more integrated, interdisciplinary approach to the challenges that higher education faces.

The Focus of Research on the Institution of Higher Education

I use the human capital premise to motivate how improvement and efficiency are defined in the analyses of higher education institutions. The use of this concept—from the level of the nation-state to individual returns to education—is powerful because of its importance to society and the economy and because it can be measured at different units and levels of analysis. Here are suggestions for a research program focused on the higher education institution, with the goal of improving teaching and learning while rebalancing the post secondary common pool cost/benefit equation for individuals and public authorities, which draws on the academic fields of inquiry discussed above in this chapter:

> Cognitive Science, itself an interdisciplinary field anchored in psychology, biology, neuroscience,[22] linguistics, computer science, and philosophy of the mind, among others, is comprised of a number of subfields such as the brain, learning, cognitive development, motivation, and memory. Research on the transfer of skills from one

academic subject to others is directly relevant to the measurement of critical thinking skills.[23]

Economics—see, in particular, the economic returns to education, the institutional design, and the behavioral economics literatures.[24]

Education Technology[25]

Data Analytics[26]

Measurement science—education assessment[27]

The challenge is to integrate these distinctive fields of inquiry, which are focused on different units and levels of analysis, so that their analyses add up to a whole that is greater than the sum of its parts when used together for research on higher education institutions.

The Principles of Use-Inspired Research (UIR)

- The research is based on the logic and strategy of scientific inquiry.
- The research results, including the methodology used in the study and the data results, are made public—peer review, transparency, and the ability to replicate the results built into the study are essential.
- A significant amount of the research is done by interdisciplinary teams to leverage the strengths of the different approaches to:
    - Bring together a significant number of researchers in the fields of inquiry noted to undertake a sustained research program on the institution of higher education and
    - Create links between institutions, centers, and researchers that enable them to work together collectively on higher education research topics. Practitioners, senior faculty, and former deans and provosts who possess the class knowledge of the institution of higher education are also critical to this use-inspired basic research program. They must be delegated the principal role in deciding how to use the results of use-inspired research and suggesting new topics.

Potential Projects

Here are possible projects focused on the institution of higher education that illustrate the potential of UIR.

Apprenticeships

Should the apprenticeship model be made available to exiting high school students, whether or not they have obtained a high school degree, to provide skills training to the many students who do not have the minimum skills needed for work in the Knowledge Economy?[28] In order to decide whether or how to provide pathways for members of this large class of individuals, the question that must be answered is whether there is a consensus that such pathways should be provided as a public good to this population. The answer to that question involves the use of the collective-goods approach combined with analysis of the costs of providing the pathways compared to economic returns to the individuals to whom the benefits are provided. The economic approaches developed by Heckman and Krueger (2003) are relevant. This question and the answers to it fall under the Common Pool Problem (CPP) heading.

Mission Differentiation

The Multi-University, celebrated by Kerr (1995), accepts the premise that research and teaching functions can and should coexist across the four years of college. Would significant cost savings be achieved by encouraging research universities to scale back their lower-division commitment to focus on upper-division and graduate education and research? Data mining is needed to analyze the benefits over costs of this potential new model. Assessments of student-learning outcomes are also needed to project the benefits over costs of this new type of differentiation of the higher education institution over the current type.

Institutional Redesign

The Need for Horizontal as well as Virtual Linkages: Faculty are organized into departments and programs. Authority is delegated to these units to recommend what subjects in their fields should be taught, who should teach them, and how students should be assessed. The academic departments and programs are typically organized into the life (or natural) sciences, the physical sciences, the social sciences, and the humanities. Each unit within these groups reports to an associate dean who, in turn, reports to a dean. The dean of the college of arts and sciences reports to a provost or vice president for academic affairs. In large public research universities, there are 10–15 colleges, which are each organized into vertical columns reporting to a provost. In comparison, there are few horizontal linkages between the colleges. In addition, there are vice presidents of administration, of finance, of agriculture (sometimes), and of student affairs, with many supporting administrative units reporting to each. CLA+ Analytics (see the coda, pp. 242–55) is designed to assist in the development of stronger horizontal linkages between offices across the university.

Universities, then, are unique in the sense that they are highly centralized but their major academic functions are delegated to department-based governance. While most public and private institutions have attempted to decentralize and moved toward an outcomes-based accountability system, the accountability system of higher education institutions remains largely built on a rules-based system developed by faculty and administrative committees, which is implemented by administrators. Research productivity is governed by measures of the quality and quantity of outputs aided by peer review, transparency of results, and a requirement that empirical research can be replicated. However, undergraduate and graduate level teaching and learning are not governed by similar outcome-based measures.

The universities' unique combination of centralization with regulation by rules is an outlier among institutions. Over time, the ratio of resources devoted to instruction compared to the resources devoted to administration has declined. It remains difficult to change the system toward a decentralized and accountability-based model without the creation of new models of institutional design that give promise of being more effective and efficient in delivering stronger student-learning results. In turn, this requires research that informs prospective institutional redesign ideas.

The Cost Reduction Problem

How might costs be reduced? Administrative functions should be audited with an eye to generating efficiencies and savings by two strategies. First, education technology has delivered a number of promising solutions to greatly reduce the costs associated with admissions, laboratory equipment, books, security, the library, and a host of other nonacademic functions. In addition, several functions are candidates for outsourcing, such as student housing, energy, policing, and renovating the physical plant. Second, because academic personnel costs comprise over 80% of university budgets, academic priorities need to be set. Resources from low priorities need to be reallocated to higher academic priorities.

Why do universities slowly adopt new technology-based strategies to reduce costs and improve efficiencies in the delivery of their services? Economists, such as Downs (1967), Johnson (1975), Buchanan (1965), Olson (1965), and Ostrom et al. (1973), suggest the answer: Because higher education institutions are not market-based, there are no market incentives to cut costs or improve efficiencies in order to survive. Based on the assumption of rational choice for individuals, one cannot expect the leaders of the college admissions office or other campus support units to propose reductions or elimination of their staff. That would amount to a reduction in their base of power or the elimination of their position. In addition, without market incentives to keep functions efficient and effective, central university administrators need evaluation criteria they can use comparatively to judge the relative worth of disparate functions. They do not have such criteria. They could use such evaluation criteria to set priorities for nonacademic functions, including assisting them in deciding whether to outsource functions that may be fulfilled by education-technology-based organizations.

Setting academic priorities is also rarely practiced. Instead, when faced with budget reductions, university administrators over the past 40 years have limited salary increases and reduced the hiring of tenured or tenure-track faculty. Meanwhile, the proportion of the budget accounted for by administrative staff has grown dramatically. Non-tenure-track faculty now account for "three-quarters of the instructional faculty at non-profit colleges and universities" (Kezar and Maxey, 2013, cf. Schuster and Finkelstein, 2008). The most important impacts of the decline of permanent faculty to less than 25% of instruction are that many departments no longer have the critical mass to carry out their responsibilities or they have been eliminated altogether.

Because governance of undergraduate education is delegated to the department in the university, absence of a critical mass to sustain the teaching and learning model of public colleges and universities is a major challenge. This issue is rarely discussed or analyzed. This hollowing out of the permanent faculty may be contributing to lower learning gains for undergraduate students and lower absolute learning outcomes overall. However, we do not know whether this is the case; no one to my knowledge has produced credible empirical-based evidence that might answer the question.[29]

Nonacademic Priorities: Support Services

Possible services to outsource range from student housing and maintenance of all facilities to power plants for heat and electricity to healthcare, police protection, and social welfare functions such as childcare. Whether or not the service is provided appears wholly correlated with sheer size—the larger the postsecondary institution, the more likely it provides the service itself instead of contracting it out.

Universities have no comparative advantage for provision of these services—the majority of these functions should be considered for privatization, for example, sharing of infrastructure. Free-standing, separate physical plants are an apparently unquestioned requirement for most large, individual higher education institutions and, if they are public, for the system administrations that govern them. Why so? In the Knowledge Economy, physical space assumes less importance than mental space. Combining all or parts of physical plants of state teaching universities, community colleges, and, in many cases, high schools could save substantial resources. Large states such as Florida, Texas, California, and New York are unlikely to have the resources to build the individual campuses necessary to support projected enrollment growth over the next two decades based on current conventions of space requirements.

New Models for Incentive Systems for Faculty

One cannot expect a continuous improvement model for teaching and learning to be added to the model we have for research until the incentive system governing faculty is changed to stimulate a greater faculty focus on teaching and learning. The research productivity metric used for faculty merit increases, promotions, and tenure is currently the principal driver of faculty behavior.

Of course, there are different schools of thought about how to define research productivity. However, there is no doubt about the importance of the research metric in determining the direction and outcomes of individual faculty careers in research universities. Moreover, this model governs the rest of the higher education sector, if only through the absence of a credible teaching and learning metric that is used as the basis for providing incentives for faculty as well. The impact of the research metric on faculty behavior trumps well-meaning reforms aimed at improving teaching and learning because there are no concrete incentives for faculty to focus on improvements in the classroom. What is most striking is how little attention is paid to this issue. Why is this the case?

Key premises underlying highly institutionalized organizations such as universities are not typically questioned. The current incentive system for faculty is a good example of this. It is also a good example of why the use-inspired approach to research on higher education makes sense. Historically, researchers have noted the costs of the research-based metric on diverting meaningful attention to teaching and learning. However, they usually have not had the background or expertise in economics or educational assessment that would enable them to judge whether or how new models of faculty incentive systems that favor teaching and learning can be developed and piloted. In addition, this research would need significant resources to implement, which neither universities, from their internal operating budgets, nor foundations, through grants, have provided.

Competency-Based Education (CBE) Degree

> CBE refers to instruction, assessment, grading, and academic reporting that are based on students demonstrating that they have learned the knowledge and skills they are expected to learn as they progress through their education. Competency-based programs allow students to advance through courses, certifications and degrees based on their ability to master knowledge and skills rather than time spent in the classroom. All students are held to clearly defined and rigorous expectations, but each follows a customized path to success that responds and adapts based on individual learning strengths, challenges and goals. And students can earn credit for prior learning and move at their own speed.
>
> (Glossary of Education Reform, 2014)

Instead of spending four years of seat time to obtain, for instance, the necessary 120 course credits to graduate, time to degree is no longer the primary metric used to certify students to graduate from college as seniors. Although most traditional colleges have not created CBE degree programs, the number of institutions that are implementing these programs is rapidly increasing. In fact, large university systems (e.g., University of Texas) and prestigious institutions (e.g., Harvard University) have created their own CBE programs. In addition to the benefits of the CBE degree, the new degree cuts costs for colleges and universities significantly. Time to degree is shortened and many CBE courses are conducted online, reducing the need for brick-and-mortar campus delivery systems. Faculty for these programs are also not limited to physical locations and may be specialists in their fields who teach a course online for the program. The move to the CBE degree is a major innovation in undergraduate and graduate education.

There is not yet much discussion or research on the extent to which the student-learning outcomes produced by CBE programs are equal, superior, or inferior to their on-campus, traditional, credit-hour-based four-year programs. There is a need to undertake evaluation research to answer the question of whether the efficacy of CBE programs equals or surpasses the traditional four-year, credit-based, on-site programs. This will require the use of standardized assessments, data mining, and cooperation between leaders of CBE and traditional four-year B.A. and B.S. programs. There is also the issue of gathering the resources necessary to conduct research on this policy issue.

Implications

The principal conclusion of framing the higher education institution as a major UIR target is that the value system of science should be the premise of the research paradigms used to develop objective tools that can assist participants and leaders of the institution to preserve and enhance the institution so as to improve student learning. That leads to several inferences.

Higher education produces two principal public goods, research and undergraduate education (Benjamin, 2012a, pp. 4–9). All the stakeholders involved in research accept the principle of peer review as the key fulcrum of the research process—recommendations for or against the award of research grants, review of draft articles, and book manuscripts submitted for publications, among others. The research grant awards and the publications of articles and books are public and are, therefore, transparent as well. Unless the research is deemed proprietary, it is a public good as soon as it is published. The intellectual property produced is available to anyone who wants to use it. Moreover, in the arts and sciences, engineering, and professional schools, the amount of externally funded awards is also made public for the principal investigators and their department, program, college, and university.

Second, undergraduate education of each student is a joint product of all the courses and out-of-class experiences the student has at the higher education institution. The result is a certified degree, which the institution stands behind. The whole of the student experience is designed to be greater than the simple aggregation of the students' courses. In this sense, undergraduate education is a public good with significant benefits to society based on the collective human-capital skills attained by the graduating students and a private good with benefits to individual students that they and their parents should pay for.

Third, it is not easy to define what the private-good verses public-good benefits are to students. The content and quality of the instruction students receive is based on the amount of knowledge their instructors bring to the classroom, including their pedagogical skills. The financial support instructors receive when they are graduate students includes grants and scholarships from government and private foundations. Other important support to them is by way of state-of-the-art research facilities, paid for in large part by overhead from research and public funding, library collections that feature the published scholarship on research, etc. The amount the students and parents should pay for these benefits should be based on empirical research.

Fourth, the accreditation process exists to monitor the quality of the production of undergraduate education. However, while undergraduate education may also reasonably be called a public good, there are no counterparts to peer review or transparency—the criteria featured for monitoring the research outputs of individual researchers and institutions. For example, all course syllabuses could be required to be made public, which would provide important information about the courses. Assessment could be provided for the student learning, produced for every student in each course, each major, or at the point of graduation. Moreover, institutions should be required to show third-party evidence based on standardized education assessments to benchmark these points in the education experience at each institution.

Fifth, most faculty and knowledgeable observers should be comfortable viewing undergraduate education as a public good with significant private good benefits as described here. The implication of Pasteur's Quadrant in higher education is that the value system of science should be used to analyze key elements of the institution and evaluate determinants of teaching and learning in particular. Due to its nature (i.e., qualities of transparency, application of peer review, replication possibility), principal stakeholders in the institution of higher education, such as faculty, should not object to its application in principle. Because undergraduate education is largely a public good, the implication is that results of the analyses and recommendations stemming from such work should be made public. Moreover, the fundamental criteria used to evaluate the research on the inputs, internal processes, and outputs featuring, in this case, student-learning outcomes, should be:

- No harm to the public good
- Actionable improvement of the public good
- Credible cost/benefit analysis that shows the differential impact of the projected changes from the research on stakeholders involved in the production or consumption of the good

Sixth, I define governance as the decision-making units, policies, and procedures, written and unwritten, that control resource allocation in colleges and universities (Benjamin, 2012a). Boards of Trustees are the ultimate authority but devolve authority to the administration, faculty senates, and department-based governance, which is still important for the top 40 or so research universities. It is difficult to generalize how education-measurement results should be used, but there are at least three guidelines to consider for all circumstances:

1. Single scores from standardized tests should not be used alone for college ranking purposes or for decisions with stakes attached for institutions or departments or programs within them (Benjamin, 2012b).
2. If public-based accountability systems are anticipated, the colleges and universities involved should be consulted about the purposes and intended content of the proposed accountability protocol (Benjamin and Klein, 2006).
3. Respect for the traditional norms of relative autonomy of departments and individual faculty should be maintained.

Governance may be strengthened in certain institutions of higher education if the institution is improved over time with results from a research program that succeeds in providing improved decision-making on how to improve teaching and learning.

Conclusion

Just as the history of the development of agriculture and medicine into science-based enterprises documents the growing benefits to Americans over the past 156 years, history shows that the research achievements of postsecondary education have been a critical part of that record of achievement. However, today the higher education institution and the higher education sector face serious issues that threaten their ability to effectively contribute to the Knowledge Economy.

First, the cost problem requires attention before the common pool problem freezes the ability of postsecondary education leaders to address the student loan, and corresponding debt, issue. In order to cut costs, administrators need to set academic and nonacademic priorities. However, they do not have the research tools needed to engage in priority setting. In addition, the cost problem is correlated with the increase in reliance on adjuncts to teach undergraduates, particularly in less-selective colleges. This change appears to have a negative effect on the quality of instruction and learning. It is important to determine whether this is correct and what might be done about it.

Second, the problem of inequality has become a critical public policy issue. The skill levels attained by graduating college seniors are critical to their job prospects in today's Knowledge Economy. Postsecondary education is central to the economic prospects of all Americans. Equal opportunity is an important principle, widely shared by citizens in a liberal democracy (see Chapter 6). If the sector presents barriers to equal opportunity for all graduating seniors through a market failure between college and career, then there is a major public policy challenge to solve. Recent significant social and economic advances in the United States have followed major changes in postsecondary education. The progress in science and technology over the past several decades—including the transistor, the invention of the Internet followed by the personal computer and establishment of Silicon Valley, and molecular biology's contribution to medicine—came after the federal government adopted the recommendation of the Vannevar Bush, a president-appointed committee on the future of science recommendations (Bush, 1945), to conduct most of the nation's research and development through the research universities. The long economic expansion of the U.S. economy from the late 1940s to the mid-1960s benefited from the additional millions of Americans who went to college aided by the GI Bill and subsequent local and state subsidies.

Today, the higher education sector faces challenges caused in large part by its past successes. Many more millions of citizens also want to attend college, graduate, and pursue the American dream. In the Knowledge Economy, however, these students need to be able to demonstrate they have attained the skills demanded by employers. The elimination of many jobs through globalization and the substitution of robots for humans are major threats to economic growth and stability. Finally, over time, as the higher education sector has grown and matured, it has fallen prey to the cost disease problem, just as other public-sector enterprises have. How can the cost problem be solved while simultaneously increasing the access, retention, and graduation of millions more low-income students from underrepresented groups with the skills they need to succeed in the Knowledge Economy?

To survive in the Knowledge Economy, the university as well as the corporation needs to restructure from a largely centralized silo structure to a structure that is flatter with more horizontal networks that are able to better disseminate and receive information within their separate structures—in this case, the colleges and departments within the institution.

What is most distinctive about use-inspired research applications of each field of inquiry introduced here is that all the research by the representatives of these fields is premised on asking and answering questions that bear on higher education's improvement only. Once this model of performance is accepted over time, a critical mass of research will accumulate in which the whole of the research program will be greater than the sum of its parts. This is so for the following reasons.

1. Research conducted by economists, cognitive scientists, education technologists, and measurement scientists will increasingly be informed by the research of the other several fields of study involved. For example, teaching and learning specialists will integrate the research results of cognitive scientists on transfer into their pedagogy. Teaching and learning specialists will also respond to recommendations of cognitive scientists about how much time should be devoted to lecture formats versus interactive presentations of students in class.
2. The newly emerging positive relationship between assessments, such as CLA+, and returns to education as measured by the level of jobs and wages obtained after graduation (Zahner and James, 2015; Arum and Roksa, 2011) should be corroborated by additional studies.
3. The positive relationship between test scores and jobs and wages should be disaggregated to better understand (a) what academic majors contribute the most to this relationship and (b) what types of pedagogy explain more variance in these relationships.

Just as in the case with the use-inspired research examples of agriculture, health, and national security, interdisciplinary research teams will form to mount sustained research programs on such issues as the cost and quality of undergraduate education. Another example of interdisciplinary research is likely to focus on the question of advancement of members of underrepresented groups related to the quality of students' college readiness at entry to college and the quality of their skill levels obtained as certified by appropriate standardized tests.

Controversial topics should and will inevitably be addressed as well. Adelman (2016) well states the position many faculty take that they will not accept or use the results of third-party, standardized tests. They will only accept the results of assessments they control themselves. The equally strongly held view of measurement scientists and many policy-makers is that only third-party standardized tests can be seen as objective measures of student-learning outcomes. These two contrary positions can and must be bridged through the UIR model.

Notes

1. See Benjamin (1982) for applications of this political economy approach. Important contributors to the political economy research program include Downs (1967), Olson (1965), Buchanan (1965), Niskanen (1971), Williamson (1981, 1990), V. Ostrom and E. Ostrom (1971), E. Ostrom et al. (1973), and E. Ostrom (1990). The premise of the collective-goods approach is the methodological assumption of individual rational choice (Harsanyi, 1969). This deductive method emphasizes point predictions rather than the inductive statistical-based method of explanation, which is more prevalent in the social sciences.
2. See Benjamin (1982) for a more complete description and several applications of the collective-goods approach. See also Benjamin et al. (1993) Benjamin and Carroll (1998).
3. Benjamin (1982, pp. 14–5). I also note that the concept of the cost disease, developed by Baumol (1967, 2012) and applied to postsecondary education by Bowen (2012), is an important explanation of why costs in higher education increase at rates higher than the CPI. However, as Bowen notes, the explanation itself does not offer a solution (Bowen, 2012, p. 4). The collective-goods approach augmented by more effective tools of decision-making offers solutions (see pp. 21–5 below).
4. Commonfund Institute (2016). For the description of the Higher Education Price Index (HEPI) see Griswold (2006).
5. As further evidence of the negative effect of the tuition increases, economists are beginning to tie the slow housing recovery to the inability of recent college graduates to afford home ownership because of their student loan debt (Brown and Caldwell, 2013; Gale et al., 2014).
6. The concept of critical mass of the permanent faculty is, to my knowledge, not defined precisely. However, if the size of a department faculty is below 10, it becomes challenging for a group of this size to execute their department-based teaching responsibilities, especially in larger public and private universities of more than, say, 15,000 students. In many of the larger universities, adjunct faculty are hired by the dean or provost's office and not by the faculty in the department.
7. For the SAT and ACT see the annual reports by the College Board and ACT. For NAEP see US Department of Education, Institute of Education Sciences, National Center of Education Statistics, National Assessment of Educational Progress (NAEP), various years, 1971–2008.
8. There are three nationally recognized standardized tests of critical thinking that are used widely: Proficiency Profile, Education Testing Service; College Assessment of Academic Proficiency (CAAP), ACT; and the Collegiate Learning Assessment (CLA+), CAE. These three tests were analyzed by measurement scientists from the three educational assessment organizations and validated in a study that compared the tests (Klein et al., 2009). I used CLA+ data for estimating the market failure between college and career because of my familiarity with that protocol and access to the large data set of CLA+ test results. CAE encourages researchers to use its database.
9. The focus here on the role and responsibility that the higher education sector has in shaping and providing the human capital to the private sector does not replace the other principal roles of the university, namely, to provide a liberal education to its students and to be a source of criticism and recommendations on the major public policy issues of the day. (See Brighouse and McPherson (2015) for classic and contemporary definitions of the aims of higher education).

10. Attempts at accountability systems from the state and federal level continue, the most recent being the Department of Education's College Ratings System, but none have or are likely to be accepted by higher education administrators or faculty unless clear incentives to encourage faculty to focus on the improvement of student learning are provided (see discussion of incentive system, pp. 39–40 below.) In addition, discontent with accreditation as the quality-assurance mechanism is high, but nothing is in the works to replace it.
11. Ostrom (1972) argued for transparent performance metrics about outcomes and key processes in nonprofit institutions that are not clearly subject to the discipline of the market. Simply putting the spotlight on performance indicators causes changes in attitudes and behavior of the participants, in this case higher education institutions. This is an example of what Mayo (1949, pp. 60–77) called the Hawthorne Effect.
12. Cook and Hartle (2012), based at the American Council on Education, the leading membership organization for higher education, dispute this argument.
13. The original argument about the invisible hand is by Adam Smith (1776), Book 1, Chapter 7.
14. Samuelson (1954) defined the public good as a good that if provided to one individual cannot be excluded from all other individuals in the same catchment, which is usually defined as the nation. National defense, health, energy, and "good" or "bad" economic policies all qualify as public goods under his definition.
15. The distribution by a local public utility of water that is pure for drinking purposes would seem to meet the criteria for a pure public good. However, in the winter of 2016 Flint, Michigan's public water supply was deemed not drinkable, and recriminations and law suits are a likely long-term consequence as the legal system attempts to sort out the causes of the collapse of this public good into a public "bad."
16. I thank Ken Norrie, who called my attention to the relevance of the common pool approach to the underinvestment issue facing postsecondary education (Benjamin, 2013). The common pool approach, an extension of the collective goods approach, was pioneered by Elinor Ostrom (1990), who won a Nobel Prize for her work on the CPP. For additional applications of the commons pool approach see Keohane and Ostrom (1995).
17. Stokes (1997, p. 73). Names in italic added by author.
18. In higher education, we have a continuous system of improvement model for research but not for undergraduate education. Research is evaluated through peer review, and the results are made transparent via the publication of research, with funding secured by a principal investigator, department, or college. Quality of research is evaluated by a number of quantitative and qualitative metrics. We do not have similar agreed-upon metrics to measure and report about the quality of undergraduate education.
19. Education assessment is a branch of statistics that has long been recognized as an important and highly legitimate field of inquiry. The standardized tests fielded by major testing organizations in the U.S. are subjected to rigorous scrutiny to determine whether they are reliable. The validity of the tests is also continuously examined. Often the validity-based argument made by opponents of standardized tests is about face validity. See Banta and Pike (2012) and Rhodes (2012) versus Miller (2012) and Davies (2012) in a symposium, edited by Peter Ewell, about the role of standardized assessment versus formative assessment in higher education (Benjamin, 2012b).

20. See discussion of the innovations of Keynes, Manheim, and Weber (Benjamin, 1982).
21. The Rand Health Insurance Experiment (HIE), funded by the Department of Health, Education, and Welfare (now the Department of Health & Human Services) conducted the largest and longest health policy study undertaken in U.S. history (Brook et al., 2006). The randomized experiment, the gold standard in social science research, cost tens of millions. Its findings have significantly shaped the subsequent discussions of the healthcare insurance industry. Imagine if the U.S. Department of Education had carried out a similar research study on the implications of the Common Core, the move toward deeper learning in K–12 education, before the Department of Education and Chief State School Officers, with support from the Gates Foundation, uniformed by the findings of a serious scientific-based study, simply attempted to implement the Common Core program. The broader question is why education has yet to attract the support for funding policy research on education issues at levels similar to that of health policy problems.
22. Neuroscience, in particular, appears to be advancing rapidly. See Wexler (2006 and Wexler et al., 2016) for who is developing evidence-based cognitive skills training programs.
23. See Von Eckardt (1996); cf. Resnick et al. (2005) for descriptions of cognitive science. CF Singley and Anderson (1989); Elman et al. (1996); Haskell (2000); and Bransford et al. (2000). There are over 100 departments of cognitive science in U.S. colleges and universities.
24. On the returns to education, see Heckman and Krueger (2003); Hanuschek and Woessmann (2011); Hanaschek et al. (2015); and Hoxby and Avery (2012). On the design and redesign of institutions, in particular analyses of the effectiveness and efficiency of centralized versus decentralized organizational arrangements, see Buchanan (1965); Johnson (1975); Olson (1965); Ostrom and Ostrom (1971); Ostrom et al. (1973); Samuelson (1954); Williamson (1981 and 1990); and Besley and Ghatak (2003); On behavioral economics, see Thaler and Mullainnathan, 2007) and Tversky and Kahneman (1981). There are over 500 departments of economics in colleges and universities in the U.S.
25. Educause (2012) a nonprofit association, aims to advance higher education through the use of information technology. Education software companies are numerous in the start-up space. Amazon, IBM, Microsoft, and Apple are among the leading technology companies developing education-relevant software for research and teaching. For example, research and development by Authess, an M.I.T.-based education technology start-up that features an artificial intelligence (AI) machine learning platform, suggests one can create an enhanced digital version of performance-based critical-thinking assessments that are shorter in length, faster to administer, much more affordable, and able to be scored instantaneously. See Authess.com.

    There are also hundreds of education technology programs in colleges and universities at the undergraduate and graduate levels.
26. Data analytics is defined thus, "the science of examining raw data with the purpose of drawing conclusions about that information." See Data Analytics (2015, p. 1). Sociologists are also developing significant expertise in data analytics. See Burrows and Savage (2014) and Mutzel (2015).
27. Education assessment is critical to include as one of these fields of inquiry because it is necessary for shaping the other fields into an integrated UIR approach to improvement in higher education. Assessment can be used to benchmark the learning outcomes of undergraduate education and therefore

can be an important dependent variable against which the analyses of the other fields of inquiry noted here can be evaluated. Because assessment is controversial, Part II and Chapter 13, the conclusion of the book, are devoted to further discussion of the topic. Key figures in the standardized education assessment field include Henry Braun, Boston University; Robert Linn, University of Colorado; Derek Briggs, University of Colorado; Larry Hedges, Northwestern University; Lydia Liu, ETS; Dan McCaffrey, ETS; Stephen Klein, former RAND research scientist and director of research emeritus, CAE; Paul Sackett, University of Minnesota; Richard Shavelson, Stanford University; and Jeffrey Steedle, Pearson. It is equally important to note the major roles of leaders of survey research and formative assessment in post-secondary education such as Peter Ewell, a seminal figure in several national assessment programs in the U.S. National Center for Education Management; George Kuh, founding director of the National Survey of Student Engagement (NSSE); Anthony Bryk, president of the Carnegie Foundation for Teaching; and Carol Twigg, president of the National Center for Academic Transformation (NCAT). Carol Schneider, past president of the Association of American Colleges and Universities (AAC&U), and her colleagues are developing Value Rubrics that assist faculty in focusing their strategies to improve teaching and learning in the classroom. The Lumina Foundation, under the auspices of Jamie Merisotis, has introduced the Degree Qualifications Framework, an important learning-centered framework for what college graduates should know and be able to do. The research of each of these groups should inform the work of their colleagues in the other group.

28. This estimate is based on Heckman and LaFontaine (2010). For an example of the use of data analytics for education policy issues, see the appendix.
29. Comparative evaluation criteria also could benefit from UIR. Such criteria often include categories such as quality, centrality, demand, workload, comparative advantage, and cost. The College of Liberal Arts of the University of Minnesota was faced with significant budget cuts occasioned by an economic recession. These general comparative evaluation criteria were used to evaluate and rank academic and nonacademic support activities (see CLA, 2006; Clugston, 1986).

References

ACT. 2014 and various years. *Annual Report*. Iowa City, IA: ACT.

Adelman, Clifford. 2016. Comment on "Separating Education From Credentialing," *Inside Higher Education*, August 1.

Aris, Rutherford. 1999. *Mathematical Modeling: A Chemical Engineer's Perspective*. New York, NY: Academic Press.

Arum, Richard and Josipa Roksa. 2011. *Academy Adrift, Limited Learning on Our Campuses*. Chicago, IL: University of Chicago Press.

Authess.com

Banta, Trudi W., and Gary R. Pike. 2012. "Making the Case Against—One More Time." *Occasional Paper 15*, National Institute of Learning Outcomes, September 24–30. www.NILOA.org.

Barran, Paul. 1964. *On Distributed Communications: I. Introduction to Distributed Communications Networks*. Santa Monica, CA: Rand Corporation.

Barron's Profiles of American Colleges. 2014. New York: Barron's.

Baumol, William. 2012. *The Cost Disease: Why Computers Get Cheaper and Health Care Doesn't*. New Haven, CT: Yale University Press.

———. 1967, June. "Macroeconomics of Unbalanced Growth: The Anatomy of Urban Crisis." *American Economic Review* 57: 415–26.

Becker, Gary. 1993. *Human Capital: A Theoretical and Empirical Analysis with Special Reference to Education* (2nd edition). Chicago, IL: University of Chicago Press.

Benjamin, Roger. 1982. "The Historical Nature of Social Scientific Knowledge: The Case of Comparative Political Inquiry." In *Strategies of Political Inquiry*, edited by Elinor Ostrom, 69–82. Beverly Hills, CA: SAGE Publications.

———. 2012a. *The New Limits of Education Policy: Avoiding a Tragedy of the Commons*. London: Edward Elgar.

———. 2012b. "Seven Red Herrings About Assessment in Higher Education." *Occasional Paper #15*, September, National Institute for Learning Outcomes Assessment: 7–14.

———. 2013. "Teach, Learn, Assess." In *Measurement of Student Learning Outcomes*, edited by Ken Norrie and Mary Catharine Lennon, 123–40. Montreal, QC: McGill-Queens University Press.

Benjamin, Roger, and Steve Carroll. 1996, December. "Impediments and Imperatives in Redesigning Higher Education." *Educational Administration Quarterly*: 705–19.

Benjamin, Roger, and Steve Carroll. 1998. "The Implications of the Changed Environment for Governance in Higher Education." In *The Responsive University: Restructuring for High Performance*, edited by William Tierney, 92–119. Baltimore, MD: Johns Hopkins University Press.

Benjamin, Roger, Steve Carroll, Mary Ann Jacobi, Cathy Krop, and Michael Shires. 1993. *The Redesign of Governance in Higher Education*. Santa Monica, CA: RAND, Institute on Education and Training, MR-222-LE.

Benjamin, Roger, and Steve Klein. 2006. "Assessment versus Accountability: Notes on Reconciliation." *Occasional Paper, No. 2*: 19.

Besley, Timothy, and Maitreesh Ghatak. 2003. "Incentives, Choice, and Accountability in the Provision of Public Services." *Oxford Review of Economic Policy* 19 (2): 235–49.

Bishop, John. 1995. "Adam Smith's Invisible Hand Argument." *Journal of Business Ethnics*, Vol 14, Issue 3, (March): 165–180.

Bransford, John D., Ann L. Brown, and Rodney R. Cocking. 2000. *How People Learn: Brain, Mind, Experience, School*. Washington, DC: National Academy Press.

Brighouse, Harry, and Michael McPherson. 2015. *The Aims of Higher Education*. Chicago, IL: University of Chicago Press.

Brook, Robert, Emmet Keeler, Kathleen Lohr, Joseph Newhouse, John Ware, William Rogers, Allyson Davies, Cathy Sherbourne, George Goldberg, P. Camp, Caren Kamberg, Arleen Leibowitz, Joan Keesey, and David Reboussin. 2006. *The Health nsurance Experiment: A Classic RAND Study Speaks to the Current Health Care Reform Debate*. Santa Monica, CA: RAND Corporation, RB 9174.

Brown, Meta, and Caldwell Snydnee. 2013. "Young Student Loan Borrowers Retreat from Housing and Auto Markets." *Liberty Street Economics*. Federal Reserve Bank of New York, April 17, 2013. http://libertystreeteconomics.newyorkfed.org/2013/04/young-student-loan-borrowers-retreat-from-housing-and-auto-markets.html.

Buchanan, James. 1965, February. "An Economic Theory of Clubs." *Economica* 32: 1–15.

Burrows, R. and Mike Savage. 2014. "After the Crisis? Big Data and the Methodological Challenge of Empirical Sociology." *Big Data & Society* 1 (1): 1–6.

Bush, Vannevar. 1945, July. *Science the Endless Frontier: A Report to the President*. Washington, DC: United States Government Printing Office.

Casner-Lotto, Jill, Linda Barrington, and Mary Wright. 2006. *Are They Really Ready to Work? Employers' Perspectives on the Basic Knowledge and Applied Skills of New Entrants to the 21st Century Work Place*. Washington, DC: Report of the Conference Board.

CLA. 2006. www.cae.org/cla.

Clugston, Richard. 1986. "Strategic Organization in an Organized Anarchy: The Liberal Arts College of a Public Research University." PhD Thesis, College of Education.

Commonfund Institute. www. commonfund.org.

Consumer Financial Protection Bureau. 2015. *Financial wee-being: The Goal of Financial Education*. Iowa City, IA, January.

Cook, Bryan J., and Terry W. Hartle. 2012. *Myth: Increases in Federal Student Aid Drive Increases in Tuition*. Washington, DC: American Council on Education, spring.

Data Analytics (DA). 2015. "What Is Big Data Analytics? The Science of Examining Raw Data with the Purpose of Drawing Conclusions about that Information." www.datamanagement.techtarget.com/definition/data-analytics.

Davies, Gordon. 2012. "Three Ruminations on Seven Red Herrings, National Institute of Learning Outcomes." *Occasional Paper 15*, September, 31–3. www.NILOA.org.

DeSilver, Drew. 2014. *The Ever-accelerating Rate of Technology Adoption*. Philadelphia, PA: Fact Tank, Pew Research Center, March 14.

Downs, A. 1967. *Inside Bureaucracy*. Boston, MA: Little, Brown & Co

Dresher, Melvin. 2007. *Games of Strategy: Theory and Applications* (2nd ed.). Santa Monica, CA: Rand Corporation.

Educause.edu. 2012. *Seven Things You Should Know About Badges*.

Elman, Jeffrey L., Annette, Karmiloff-Smith, Elizabeth A. Bates, Mark H. Johnson, Domenico Parisi, and Kim Plukett. 1996. *Rethinking Innateness: A Connectionist Perspective on Development*. Cambridge, MA: M.I.T. Press.

Enthoven, Alain C., and Wayne K. Smith. 1970. *How Much Is Enough? Shaping the Defense Program, 1961–1962*. Santa Monica, CA: Rand Corporation.

Finkelstein, Martin, Valerie Conley, and Jack H. Schuster. 2016. *The Faculty Factor: American Academy in a Turbulent Era*. Baltimore, MD: Johns Hopkins University Press.

Flexner, Abraham. 1910. *Medical Education in the United States and Canada: A Report to the Carnegie Foundation for the Advancement of Teaching*, Bulletin, No. 4, New York: The Carnegie Foundation for the Advancement of Teaching, p. 346.

Frolich, Norman, Joseph Oppenheimer, and Oran Young. 1971. *Political Leadership and Collective Goods*. Princeton: Princeton University Press.

Furniss, Norman. 1978, June. "The Political Implications of the Public Choice-Property Rights School." *American Political Science Review* 72: 399–410.

Gale, William G., Benjamin H. Harris, Bryant Renaud, and Katherine Rodihan. 2014, May 14. *Student Loans Rising: An Overview of Causes, Consequences, and Policy Options*. Washington, DC: Tax Policy Center, Urban Institute and the Brookings Institution.

Geiger, Roger, and Nathan M. Sorber. 2013. *The Land-Grant College and the Reshaping of American Higher Education*. New York: Transaction Press.

Gertner, Jon. 2012. *The Idea Factory: Bell Labs and the Great Age of American Innovation*. New York, NY: Penguin Group.

Giller, Andrew. 2012, February. *Introducing Bennett Hypothesis 2.0*. Washington, DC: Center for College Affordability and Productivity.

Glossary of Education Reform. 2014, May. www.edglossary.org/competency-basedlearning.

Godzich, Wlad. 1994. *The Culture of Literacy*. Cambridge, MA: Harvard University Press.

Goldfarb, Daniel. 2010. *Biophysics Demystified*. New York, NY: McGraw-Hill.

Griswold, John. 2006. *Higher Education Price Index (HEPI) Report*. Available at: http://www.commonfund.org.

Hanuschek, Eric A., and Ludger Woessmann. 2011. "How Much Do Educational Outcomes Matter in OECD Countries?" *Economic Policy* 26 (67): 427–91.

Haskell, Robert E. 2000. *Transfer of Learning, Cognition, Instruction, and Reasoning*. New York, NY: Academic Press.

Hardin, Grant. 1968, December 13. "The Tragedy of the Commons." *Science* 162: 1243–8.

Harsanyi, John C. 1969. "Rational-Choice Models of Political Behavior vs Functionalist and Conformist Theories." *World Politics* 21 (4): 513–38.

Hart Research Associates. 2014. *It Takes More than a Major: Employer Priorities for College Learning and Student Success*. Retrieved from http://www.aacu.org/leap/documents/2014_EmployerSurvey.pdf

Heckman, James J., and Alan Krueger. 2003. *Inequality in America: What Role for Human Capital Policies?* Cambridge, MA: MIT Press.

Heckman, James J., and Paul A. LaFontaine. 2010. "The American High School Graduation Rate: Trends and Levels." *Review of Economics and Statistics* 92: 244–62.

Hirsch, Fred. 1976. *Social Limits to Growth*. Cambridge, MA: Harvard University Press.

Hoxby, Caroline, and Christopher Avery. 2012. *The Missing "One-Offs": The Hidden Supply of High-Achieving, Low-Income Students (NBER Working Paper No. 18586)*. Cambridge, MA: National Bureau of Economic Research.

Johnson, Harry. 1975. *On Economics and Society*. Chicago: University of Chicago Press.

Kelchan, Robert. 2015. *The Landscape of Competency-Based Education*. www.AEI.org/wp-content/uploads/2015/01/Landscape-of-CBE.pdf.

Kerr, Clark. 1995. *The Uses of the University* (5th ed.). Cambridge, MA: Harvard University Press.

Kezar, Adrianna, and Daniel Maxey. 2013, May/June. "The Changing Academic Work Force." *Trusteeship*, American Governing Board.

Klein, Steve, Lydia Ou Liu, James Sconing, Roger Bolus, Brent Bridgeman, and Heather Kugelmass. 2009. *Test Validity Study (TVS) Report*. Supported by the Fund for the Improvement of Postsecondary Education, U.S. Department of Education. Retrieved from http://www.voluntarysystem.org/docs/reports/TVSReport_Final pdf.

Kobrin, Jennifer L., Brian F. Patterson, Emily J. Shaw, Krista D. Mattern, and Sandra M. Barbuti. 2008. *Validity of the SAT for Predicting First Year College Grade Point Average* (College Board Research Report No. 2008–5). Accessed the College Board website: https://professionals.collfegeboard.com/profdownload/Validity_of_the_SAT_for_Predicting_First_Year_College_Grade_ Point_Average.pdf.

Kuhn, Thomas. 1970. *The Structure of Scientific Revolutions* (2nd ed.) Chicago: University of Chicago Press.

Kurth, James. 1979. "The Political Consequences of the Product Cycle: Industrial History and Political Outcomes." *International Organization* 33 (1): 1–34.

Lakatos, Imre. 1970. "Falsification and the Methodology of Scientific Research Programmes." In *Criticism and the Growth of Knowledge*, edited by Imre Lakatos and Alan Musgrave, 91–196. Cambridge: Cambridge University Press.

Lambeth, Matthew T. 2014. *Privatization and the Public Good.* Cambridge, MA: Harvard Education Press.

Leef, George. 2015. "Does Privatizing Higher Education Undermine the Public Good?" *John W. Pope Center for Higher Education Policy*, October 23rd blog.

Light, Jennifer. 2003. *From Warfare to Welfare: Defense Intellectuals and Urban Problems in Cold War America.* Baltimore, MD: Johns Hopkins University Press.

Light, Paul 2005. *The Four Pillars of High Performance: How Robust Organizations Achieve Extraordinary Results.* New York, NY: McGraw-Hill.

Liu, Yujia, and David B. Grusky. 2013, March. "The Payoff to Skill in the Third Industrial Revolution." *American Journal of Sociology* 118: 1330–74.

Lucca, D., Nadauld, T., and Karen Shen. 2015. *Credit Supply and the Rise in College Tuition: Evidence from the Expansion in Federal Student Aid Programs.* New York, NY: Federal Reserve Bank of New York Staff Report No. 733.

Keohane, Robert O., and Elinor Ostrom, eds. 1995. *Local Commons and Global Interdependence.* London, UK: Sage Publications.

Maxwell, Nicholas. 1974, September. "The Rationality of Scientific Discovery, II, An Aim Oriented Theory of Scientific Discovery." *Philosophy of Science* 4: 227–47.

Mayo, Elton. 1949. *Hawthorne and the Western Electric Company: The Social Problems of Industrial Civilization.* London: Routledge.

Miller, Ben. 2013, June 11. *Is Technological Change Speeding Up? How Can You Tell?* Innovationfiles.org.

Miller, Margaret A. 2012. "Demonstrating and Improving Student Learning: The Role of Standardized Tests." *Occasional Paper 15*, National Institute of Learning Outcomes, September, 14–18. www.NILOA.org.

Mutzel, Sophie. 2015, December. "Facing Big Data: Making Sociology Relevant." *Big Data and Society* 2 (2): 1–5.

National Research Council. 2009. *A New Biology for the 21st Century.* Washington D.C.: The National Academies Press.

National Research Council. 2012. *Education for Life and Work: Developing Transferable Knowledge and Skills in the 21st Century.* Washington, DC: National Academies Press.

Niskanen, William. 1971. *Bureaucracy and Representative Government.* New Brunswick, NJ: Transaction Publishers.

Olson, Mancur. 1965. *The Logic of Collective Action.* Cambridge, MA: Harvard University Press.

Ostrom, Elinor. 1990. *Governing the Commons: The Evolution of Institutions for Collective Action.* Cambridge: Cambridge University Press.

Ostrom, Elinor, Robert Parks, and Gordon Whitaker. 1973, September–October. "Do We Really Want to Consolidate Urban Police Forces? A Reappraisal of Some Old Assertions." *Public Administration Review* 33: 423–33.

Ostrom, Vincent. 1972, September. "Polycentricity." In Paper delivered at the annual meeting of the *American Political Science Association*, Washington, DC.

Ostrom, Vincent, and Elinor Ostrom. 1971, March–April. "Public Choice: A Different Approach to the Study of Public Administration." *Public Administration Review* 31: 203–16.

Peer Review. 2016. *Integrating Evidence: The STIRS Approach* 18 (4), Fall.

Pickering, F. P. 1970. *Literature and Art in the Middle Ages*. Miami, FL: University of Miami Press.

Popper, Karl. 1959. *The Logic of Scientific Discovery*. Translation of Logik der Forschung, (1934) London: Hutchinson. London: Routledge.

Resnick, Lauren B., Alan Lesgold, and Megan W. Hall. 2005. "Technology and the New Culture of Learning." In *Cognition, Education, and Communication Technology*, edited by Peter Gardenfors and Petter Johanssen, 77–107. Mahwan, NJ: Lawrence Eribaun Associates Publishers.

Rhodes, Terrell. 2012. *Getting Serious about Assessing Authentic Student Learning*. National Institute of Learning Outcomes, *Occasional Paper 15*, September: 19–23. www.NILOA.org.

Rojstaczer, Stuart, and Christopher Healy. 2012. *Where a Is Ordinary: The Evolution of American College and University Grading, 1940–2009*. Teachers College Record: The Voice of Scholarship in Education.

Samuelson, Paul. 1954. "The Pure Theory of Public Expenditures." *Review of Economics and Statistics* 36 (4): 387–9.

Samuelson, Paul. 1967. "Indeterminacy of Governmental Role in Public Good Theory." *Papers on Non-Market Decision Making* 3 (Fall): 39–45.

Schuster, Jack H., and Martin Finkelstein. 2008. *The American Faculty*. Baltimore, MD: Johns Hopkins University Press.

Singley, Mark K., and John R. Anderson. 1989. *The Transfer of Cognitive Skills*. Cambridge, MA: Harvard University Press.

Smith, Adam. 1776. *The Wealth of Nations*. London: W. Strahan & T. Cadell.

Smith, Bruce. 1965. *The RAND Corporation: Case Study of a Non Profit Advisory Corporation*. Cambridge, MA: Harvard University Press.

Stokes, Donald E. 1997. *Pasteur's Quadrant: Basic Science and Technological Change*. Washington, DC: Brookings.

Thaler, Richard and Sendhil Mullainnathan. 2007. *Behavioral Economics, The Concise Encyclopedia of Economics* (2nd ed.). The Library of Economics and Liberty, online.econlib.

Tversky, Amos, and Daniel Kahneman. 1981. "The Framing of Decisions and the Psychology of Choice." *Science* 211 (4481): 453–8.

Von Eckardt, B. 1996. *What Is Cognitive Science?* Cambridge, MA: M.I.T. Press.

Wexler, Bruce. 2006. *Brain and Culture: Neurobiology, and Social Change*. Cambridge, MA: MIT Press.

Wexler, Bruce, Markus Iseli, Seth Leon, and William Zaggle. 2016. "Cognitive Priming and Cognitive Training: Immediate and Far Transfer to Academic Skills in Children." *Science Report* 6, 32859; doi: 10.1038/srep 32859.

Williamson, Oliver. 1981, November. "The Economics of Organization: The Transactional Cost Approach." *American Journal of Sociology* 87 (3): 548–77.

———. 1990, March. "A Comparison of Alternative Approaches to Economic Organization." *Journal of Institutional and Theoretical Economics* 146: 61–71.

Woodhouse, Kellie. 2015. "Closure Rates of Small Colleges and Universities Will Triple in the Coming Years and Mergers Will Double." *Inside Higher Education*, September 23.

Zahner, Doris, and Jessalynn James. 2015. *Predictive Validity of a Critical Thinking Assessment for Post-College Outcomes*. New York, NY. www.CAE.org

Part II

Evidence-Based Applications to Policy Questions

3 The Future Higher Education Policy Landscape From the Pasteur's Quadrant Perspective[1]

Is there a possibility that such a mandatory testing requirement for postsecondary education will be required by federal or state mandates? If assessment in postsecondary education should remain voluntary, who will provide these assessments, and can they ensure validity?

Despite the vision the Common Core leaders had—to establish higher national standards—most of the tests used to satisfy NCLB requirements focus on low- to medium-level reading and math skills, the skills seen as important for success in college and work. NCLB requires public release of test results by district and school, and the results are reported for all students. The high-stakes nature of these tests has led to corruption in testing and results reporting in several districts. Unfortunately, because the states use different tests, assess different abilities, and set their own cut-off standards for proficiency, it is not possible to compare results across states and, as a result, no national norms can be established.

In addition, many districts use tests that control for entering student ability in an attempt to give credit to districts for their value-add to student scores. Some districts also use these value-added student scores as part of their teachers' annual evaluations. Measurement scientists do not believe the methodologies being used for such purposes are credible (see McCaffrey et al., 2004).

In comparison, at least three assessment organizations, Educational Testing Service (ETS), ACT, and Council for Aid to Education (CAE), offer national education assessments of critical-thinking skills that both faculty and employers consider essential requisites for success in college and the workplace. These assessments provide both the college and its students participating in the testing with confidential information that the students or colleges can make public if they choose. At least one of these testing organizations publishes national norms and a variety of analyses based on the testing results (while not identifying institutions or students.) Furthermore, at least one organization provides certificates and/or badges for the mastery level students have reached, enabling students to claim badges for use with potential employers and as additional diagnostic insight about their skill attainment and how to improve in college and work.

Who Will Provide These Assessments, and Can They Ensure Validity? How Involved Should Faculty Be in Developing These Assessments?

First, it is important to understand the tension between formative and standardized assessments. Faculty, understandably, rate assessments like portfolios and value rubrics as having a high degree of face validity because they present the work of students. Standardized tests, on the other hand, are not seen as adding any value and are, therefore, considered unnecessary. Measurement scientists, however, are skeptical about claims that only formative assessments are warranted because there is no systematic evidence showing that formative tests are reliable or valid (see Chapter 8, p. 6 for a discussion of the concepts reliability and validity). Standardized assessments, in the view of measurement scientists, are preferable for any tests that have stakes attached to them. When stakes are attached, it is critical that students take the assessment under the same conditions and in the same amount of time. Moreover, the tests must be scored the same way by scorers who use scientific-based rubrics.

The interest in formative and standardized tests is growing rapidly in higher education. Interest in value rubrics, degree qualifications, and tests that faculty and students can use in the classroom is soaring. So, too, is interest in using standardized tests for any student-learning outcomes that have stakes attached. Boards of trustees and administrators want to know how well their institution is doing (on the kind of tests noted above) compared to institutions that are similar in student characteristics, financial support, size, and other characteristics. Reviewers of the claims of competency-based education programs want to know if these programs are as strong as traditional on-site, four-year colleges. Employers who receive badges or certificates from job applicants want to know how to interpret them. All these examples have stakes attached to them. Therefore, it is essential that test data for these purposes be based on the transparent criteria measurement scientists have developed for standardized tests.

Testing organizations have the resources—measurement scientists, Internet-based platforms, scoring and analysis capabilities, experience, and sunk costs—that translate into lower costs for high-quality standardized tests. Individual colleges or systems of colleges do not have the resources of these organizations. However, faculty should be the lead partners to their measurement scientist colleagues in providing content for the design of standardized test items, evaluation of the standardized test results, and the development of formative test items that are aligned with the standardized tests (see Chapter 11).

Measurement scientists, the statistical-based tools they use, and the test analyses they produce are often challenged by faculty. Why? Faculty are housed within departments that are granted relative autonomy by the university to recommend what to teach, who to teach it, and how students should be assessed. Education assessment test results and analyses are typically isolated, one-off research activities that are not related to either faculty engaged in teaching or to researchers in other fields relevant to improving student learning. Independent experts, no matter how talented, are not considered to have the standing necessary to contribute to department affairs. However, measurement science, including its education assessment subgroups, is a branch of statistics that has been in good standing in the Academy for hundreds of years.

Should These Assessments Stand on Their Own or Be Used in Conjunction With Other Metrics?

Science-based research is essential to address any policy problem in education that has stakes attached to it. Researchers in cognitive science, macro- and microeconomics, educational assessment, educational technology, and data analytics—to name a few examples—share a commitment to the logic and strategy of scientific inquiry. The premises of the value system of science, peer review, transparency, and the ability to replicate results are familiar to faculty and administrators. Most faculty should accept assessment-related work based on these core principles. When paired with a coherent and compelling use-inspired basic research strategy, it is possible to imagine a more integrated, interdisciplinary approach to the challenges that higher education faces.

How Can These Standardized Assessments Include All Subject Matters?

The initial effort has already been launched. The Gates Foundation's Measuring College Learning (MCL) project (Arum et al., 2016) is a collaboration of six national disciplinary associations to define the core learning outcomes of their fields. Prospects for success of this endeavor are good. If this group of six associations succeeds in creating attractive, reliable, and valid tests, other disciplines will follow. It will be important to develop standardized tests for the arts and sciences that form the basis for general education curriculum; other professional schools and applied subjects should and will follow.

This does not mean that critical-thinking tests will no longer be needed. The case for these meta domain tests is strong in today's Knowledge Economy when college graduates need to know how to access, structure, and use information—not only remember facts. Employers see these skills as the most important requisite for success in the workplace, and faculty see them as necessary for participation in civil society (Hart Research Associates, 2014).

What Role Will These Assessments Play in the Accountability Debate?

Increasingly, private and public leaders understand that human capital is the nation's most important asset. The K–16 education system is the formal venue to preserve and enhance that capital, and NCLB is the mandated accountability measure. But so far, the efforts to create federal accountability—from the Spellings Commission to the recent College Scorecard—have not gained traction. Efforts to create federal mandates are likely to continue. And, because of the tradition of relative autonomy of higher education in the United States, the best way forward is for leaders of higher education and state and federal policymakers to work together as partners to develop accountability metrics that both sides agree are appropriate.

Conclusion

Postsecondary education is the anchor of the K–16 education system charged with preserving and improving the nation's human capital and the knowledge, skills, and experience of all its citizens. As noted in Chapter 2, the higher education sector faces many challenges.

We need to develop a continuous system of improvement in teaching and learning combined with solutions to the other major issues noted. Use-inspired interdisciplinary research on higher education, stimulated by a book by D. Stokes (1997), is the best way forward. Higher education should follow the path taken by other major policy domains in the United States, such as agriculture, healthcare, and national security. In each of these major policy arenas, there came a critical historic juncture where a commitment was made to create an integrated, multidisciplinary research program that brought researchers and practitioners together to create new tools for decision makers to make better decisions. Such a commitment is long overdue for higher education. (See Chapter 2 for the complete argument and a description of how CAE is transforming its standardized tests into education technology tools.)

Note

1. This chapter builds on arguments made in Benjamin (2016).

References

Arum, Richard, Josipa Roksa, and Amanda Cook. 2016. (eds.) *Improving Quality in American Higher Education*. San Francisco: Jossey-Bass.

Benjamin, Roger. 2016. "Why Higher—ed's Standardized Assessments Can Work toward Progress." Symposium Entry, ECampus News, May 31.

Hart Research Associates. 2014. *It Takes More than a Major: Employer Priorities for College Learning and Student Success*. www.aacu.org/leap/documents/2013_EmployerSurvey.pdf

McCaffrey, Dan, J. Lockword, Dan Koretz, Laura Hamilton. 2004. "Models for Value-Added Modeling for Teacher Effects." *Journal of Educational and Behavioral Statistics* 29: 67–101. https//doe.org/10.3102/10769986029001067.

Stokes, Donald E. 1997. *Pasteur's Quadrant: Basic Science and Technological Change*. Washington, DC: Brookings.

4 The Focus on Critical-Thinking Skills for the Classroom, the Instructor, and New Sources of Content

> The extent to which the institutions in the post-secondary sector enable students to improve their creativity, skill, and productivity becomes the question not whether the institutions produce more graduates.
>
> (David Brooks, *New York Times*, May 8, 2012.)

Introduction

It seems impossible to be optimistic about the future of undergraduate education. Beleaguered from all sides—unprecedented financial challenges, access deficits of record levels, and institutional practices, built up over many decades to pursue growth in budgets through increases in the size of faculty and number of new academic programs—postsecondary institutions face the need to confront the problems created by that growth. This shift from growth to dealing with the implications of that growth has been a theme for our major social and economic institutions over the last several decades. Now it is a principal preoccupation of leaders of postsecondary institutions. The list of issues is headed by Baumol's cost disease problem (Baumol, 2012), personified in the $1.3 trillion student loan debt and retrenchments at colleges across the country. It appears inevitable that the postsecondary sector faces deep contraction. How can it successfully respond to the emerging imperative to improve the quality of the learning of its students?[1] One potential answer rests with the new, promising information-technology-based education solutions (see the publications of Educause). However, a question to address is why are these solutions not being adopted more quickly? The answer to that question rests in the black box of faculty governance that is not well understood. One needs an understanding of why department-based governance exists and how it works in order to answer this query. I address these issues to lay the groundwork for the following argument: Flip the classroom from the lecture format to an instructor-as-coach model, embrace information-technology-based education solutions, and provide the necessary incentives for faculty and administrators needed to encourage use of the new information technology for the reformed classroom.

Background

In The *New Limits of Education Policy* (2012), I describe the constellation of problems that add up to a set of policy challenges in postsecondary education that exceed the healthcare issue—approximately 50 million high school dropouts, 40% of the entering college students not ready for college, unacceptable retention and graduation rates, and increasing evidence that student learning is not adequate for the requirements of today's knowledge economy (Benjamin, 2012, Chapter 2). To make matters worse, cost increases continue to rise well above the consumer price index, as measured by the higher education price index, while funding to public and private higher education are have not returned to previous levels in the aftermath of the financial crisis.

In short, administrators and faculty can no longer assume that the sources of funding will increase at rates commensurate with needs. Nor can they assume that students will show up ready for college or leave prepared for life and work.

However, I also have described the governance system of the university and the incentive system that guide faculty behavior (see Chapters 2 and 11). The incentive system, now oriented to encourage research, needs to be adapted to encourage faculty to improve teaching and learning. Most interpret this to mean negative incentives (meaning sanctions), but there is a way to create positive incentives to encourage faculty and administrators to focus on teaching and learning in a new way and, at the same time, cut costs and increase revenues. Positive incentives are the preferred strategy to choose. How is this possible? The short answer is that the digital education content is rapidly catching up with the promise Internet-based technology platforms present. Here is the argument.

It's not hard to develop a short list of significant tools for information that bear on postsecondary education—androids; tablets and personal computers; Google; the Google book project; courses now led by the major new entrants, MIT, Harvard, Stanford, Princeton, Michigan, and Penn; hundreds of thousands of blogs; single-purpose educational content; and the move to digitize textbooks by major publishers such as Pearson and McGraw-Hill. All this is happening with dramatic speed. Yet the model for the classroom at the university in nonprofit colleges and universities remains largely unchanged. The instructor lectures to students sitting taking notes on the content provided. The opportunity is to flip the classroom[2] from a focus on content dissemination to a focus on sharpening the abilities of students to use content to improve their critical-thinking abilities to access, structure, and use information. This would mean the teaching and learning model will shift from the teacher lecturing and the student passively receiving the content to a student-centered approach many have demanded. It also is aligned with the changes occurring in the curriculum and publishing industry which involve (1) the move from print to digital[3]and (2) a move from focusing mainly on content to concentrating on case-based and problem-based materials that encourage students to apply what they know to new situations. The opportunity, then, is to embrace the new stream of content made available and encourage use of tools such as tablets and iPhones in the classroom to bring information thought relevant instantly into the classroom to provide material the students and instructor can use for oral and written arguments in an interactive environment.

The Importance of Keying Innovations to the Academic Governance System

Perhaps if one takes a standard MBA casebook approach to our subject, one would expect the traditional university to be swept away just as Kodak, the Walkman, and travel agents have disappeared. However, there are cogent reasons for the way the governance system of the American university developed. Centralization of institutional arrangements when it comes to the production and consumption of information-sensitive goods is problematic for a host of reasons. Devolving authority to experts to decide what is to be taught in their field, by whom, how to teach, and whether and how to assess makes sense. And, in any event, the department-based governance system this system comprises will be with us for the foreseeable future. The traditional nonprofit part of the postsecondary education sector accounts for about 89% of the sector today. If the challenges noted above are as urgent to address as I and others believe, we must find creative ways to engage the faculty anchored in their governance system.

What Will the New "Flipped" Classroom Look Like?

The reform movement in postsecondary and K–12 education can be divided into three parts. The evolution of the "flipped" classroom permits the three reforms to be aligned and achieve a sufficient critical mass to "take off." First, the era of education-through-lecture is over. It is no longer necessary or even reasonable for the instructor to stand before the class and impart content-based knowledge to the students passively absorbing it. Instead, the format will shift to a student-centered approach; the instructor becomes more of a coach, lecturing much less but leading discussions, encouraging students to apply what they know in new situations, and making oral and written presentations. Courses themselves are moving from focusing on content to applying that content to new problems. Thus, a case-based or problem-based approach is encouraged.

Finally, the Internet is encouraging a next generation of assessments such as performance assessments, e-portfolios, interactive simulations, and games that give promise of moving assessment away from multiple-choice tests that are not optimal for today's knowledge economy to more open-ended assessments that can also be used as instructional tools. The goal of the new flipped classroom is to improve the analytical, problem-solving abilities of the students. The classroom, then, becomes the venue for teaching the higher-order skills prized in the Knowledge Economy where one can Google for facts, but this means one needs critical-thinking skills to access, structure, and use information.

This new paradigm for the classroom is possible because it is cheaper and better (meaning of high quality) for instructors to assign the task of learning much of the content through OER-based online courses and digital text material.

How Might Performance Assessments Be Used in This New Classroom?

Because there are no "right" answers to CAE's performance assessments, it is possible to teach to these "tests." Instructors may wish to use performance tasks in the classroom. Students might interact with each other by doing what are called think aloud activities as they work through the questions. Alternatively, they might assign them as practice tools to assist in the improvement of the critical-thinking skills for which the teacher aims in the class. Scoring manuals for the performance tasks might be provided to the instructor to permit her to score the results of students taking the test. The performance assessments might also be scored almost instantaneously through computer-assisted scoring. In these ways, among others, performance assessments can be used as part of instruction and for diagnostic purposes.

The Black Box: Faculty Governance

Although many of the technology-based solutions described by Educause and others appear promising, the rate of their adoption has been slow at best. Why is this the case? It is due to a lack of understanding of why department-based faculty governance exists and how it operates. The role of faculty governance is unlikely to be eliminated. Moreover, it should not be eliminated if colleges and universities are expected to improve the quality of student learning while these same institutions are also expected to cut costs if they are to survive.

Why Does Faculty Governance Exist?

The American university grafted the German graduate school onto its undergraduate four-year institution in the late 19th century. U.S. higher education leaders agreed with the idea that the preferred way to organize colleges and universities was to train able graduates of undergraduate programs in disciplines for graduate degrees and devolve authority research and teaching to department-based faculty to carry out these two key missions. This remains the preferred option of organizing faculty in the nonprofit traditional university sector. While devolved faculty governance has declined for the research enterprise, it remains central to teaching and learning for the following:

- Deciding what curriculum is taught
- Choosing the pedagogy used
- Determining what departments and fields within them exist and their size and emphasis
- Deciding individually what research is stressed
- Defining and implementing the criteria and evaluation for determining the quality of faculty
- Defining functionally the standards of admissions and graduation for students.

Because these factors define much of the activities of the university, without collective faculty support, explicit or at least tacit, deans, provosts, and presidents struggle or are ineffective.

The Importance of the Incentive Structure for Faculty

The current incentive system anchored in departments is aligned with the goal of producing and consuming research, particularly in the research universities, the apex institutions in the postsecondary education sector. Once an incentive system is set up, it will be resilient. This is so because individuals will not question the parameters of the existing incentive system unless they begin receiving substantial negative externalities produced by the incentive system in place. Individuals are content to operate within the routines of the professional lives because they do not wish to have to reinvent the nature, time, and place of their daily routines. This accounts for the institutional inertia extant in all our major social institutions. Therefore, any model developed to integrate information-technology-based improvements to teaching and learning into the classroom must contain incentives the faculty find acceptable or, more importantly, attractive to endorse. That is why I put forward the subject of revenue sharing next. Revenue sharing of some sort comprises a solid way to engage the present incentive system of faculty.

Thesis: education reform will be the next big innovation involving a primary change from reliance on the lecture to (1) a student-centered approach, (2) a shift in curriculum and textbooks from a focus principally on content to a focus on applying what one knows to new situations (thus the case approach and problems focused on critical-thinking skills), and (3) open-ended assessments that are better aligned with the other two parts of the reform model than multiple-choice tests.

The flip-the-class concept brings the three parts of the education reform movement together, and revenue-sharing ideas comprise a useful set of positive incentives that will encourage faculty to invest in their shifting from a reliance on lectures that deliver content to the Socratic method that emphasizes sharpening the critical-thinking skills needed to access, structure, and use content now largely supplied by information-technology-based providers.

Revenue Sharing

Revenue sharing is a familiar model for colleges and universities in the administrative functions such as energy generation, catering services, building of dorms, and joint production of hundreds of services not core to the academic mission such as international travel centers, bookstores, and, yes, even airports. Recently, technology platforms have been built to aid the admissions function (ConnectEdu), marketing for the recruitment of new students (Academic Partners), and digitization of library material (www.turnthepage.org). The college and the provider share the profits from these functions.

A method of payment for performance assessments and other instructional tools is in the space currently occupied by hard-copy textbooks. Textbooks typically cost over $100. If a student is full time, meaning they take four or five courses per semester, they spend at least $1,000 per year. As textbooks are digitized and often turned into very low-cost pdfs or offered free on open-education source platforms, it would seem reasonable to ask students to pay for, say, $500 worth of instructional aids during the year. Performance tasks would be part of a basket of such tools that the instructor might require students to use in class or point out their availability for access by the student to practice with or access. In other words, instructors might ask the students to pay up to the agreed-upon amount of $500 during the academic year. The student could choose to access no instructional aids beyond this or access them at their discretion. Probably the best way to deal with making sure the student pays up to $500 is to add this amount as part of the student fees at the start of the academic year. That might be controversial to do in a time of recession and high tuition (see below for a short discussion on this point.) Five to ten instructional tools might be chosen to be part of a basket of such tools for use in the classroom. If all providers were asked to accept the revenue sharing concept to enter this space, that would help remove any perception of conflict of interest involved. The idea of an additional revenue stream of a few hundred dollars per student would be welcome to faculty and administrators who have few attractive revenue sources to use (see Appendix 1 for a discussion of one incentive model).

The Prediction of Cost Reductions

I make the assumption that the cost problem in higher education identified for 2012 (Figure 2.1, Chapter 2) is severe enough that boards and presidents are going to reduce costs significantly over the next five years. They will focus on the nonacademic functions that have (by some estimates) doubled in staff size over the past two decades, while tenure and tenure-track faculty have declined from 50% plus to about 25% today. They will outsource functions where possible. Already the list of tech-savvy providers is growing rapidly. One example is ConnectEdu, which assists high school students and their parents to fill out admissions forms and carries out the entire process right up to the point where the admissions office makes its enrollment decisions. The cost is a few dollars rather than the estimated $600 per admissions candidate for the current admissions offices at colleges. There are many other examples (the acquisition budget of libraries, for instance) that would place colleges on a much better financial footing; in turn, this will induce aggressive presidents and their boards to lower tuition rather than raise it. Alternatively, they may provide more financial aid.

The rate of tuition increases is probably close to a ceiling. It appears that administrators are getting serious about cost reduction because their survival depends on them getting serious about reducing costs. They are starting to understand that the downturn in their funding sources is due to structural changes and they cannot expect funding to return to prerecession levels.

Practice Versus Theory

Even if this position statement makes theoretical sense, implementation of parts or all of the model sketched here will not be instantaneous. Situations on the ground will dictate whether academic leaders grasp the potential of this new approach to teaching and learning. Some faculty leaders will begin to think about how to take the information-technology-based ideas to scale in their departments and institutions. Similarly, provosts and presidents will develop their own take on the nature of the cost problems they face and come up with interesting combinations of approaches to solving their cost issues. The hope is they realize how much easier change will be if they create positive incentives for the faculty to participate actively in solving the problems while improving teaching and learning at the same time. Once there are successful examples of institutions that are making progress on the shift to the new classroom and cutting costs, those successes will be emulated by others. This bottom-up model is always preferred in the diverse American postsecondary system to a top-down approach, which is unlikely to engage the interest of the faculty.[4]

Notes

1. While retrenchment of public subsidies for postsecondary education appears to be the future for the near term, I attempt to make the case for rethinking the balance between the public and private provision of postsecondary education in Benjamin (2012). However, additional public investment is unlikely to occur until the postsecondary sector gets the cost problem under better control.
2. I credit Adrian Sannier, senior vice president for product, Pearson Education for using this increasingly widely used concept in a recent presentation at the American Enterprise Institute Seminar.
3. For example, Course Smart, founded by McGraw-Hill, Pearson, and John Wiley in 2007 to provide digital versions of textbooks to students, has a rapidly expanding library of more than 1,000 college textbooks offered at 60% less than print versions of the textbooks.
4. Centralized to down solutions are not preferred when major institutional reforms are needed. Indeed, disruptive changes that emanate through market forces are what typically destroy or transform existing economic and social institutions. The goal is to design solutions that create sustainable changes that reduce costs and improve the quality of undergraduate education but are aligned with the norms of faculty governance.

References

Baumol, William. 2012. *The Cost Disease: Why Computers Get Cheaper and Health Care Doesn't*. New Haven, CT: Yale University Press.

Benjamin, Roger. 2012. *The New Limits of Education Policy: Avoiding A Tragedy of the Commons*. London: Edward Elgar.

Appendix 1
An Example of Revenue Sharing

What is needed is a model that is faculty centered and provides incentives for them to adopt technology-based instructional tools. For example, many universities give the principal investigator one-third of the overhead created by the grant she wins, one-third goes to the department or college, and one-third goes to the central administration. One could promote this same model for teaching and learning. The metrics might be savings created by substituting technology-based productivity improvements for their administrative functions, digital textbooks and digital instructional materials substituting for print materials, and improvements in graduation rates and student-learning outcomes based on agreed-upon metrics decided upon jointly by the departments or colleges on the one hand and central administrators on the other.

5 Recreating the Faculty Role in University Governance

Introduction

It is not clear that the parts of the university add up to a greater whole. One of the problems is the fragmentation of faculty who are distributed in departments, schools, and colleges isolated one from the other. This fragmentation has led to the virtual collapse of governance in public universities, which causes a variety of serious problems. I will consider whether and how governance and faculty participation might be redefined in the public research university in a way that encourages more faculty participation (Benjamin, 2003; Benjamin and Carroll, 1997, 1998; Benjamin et al., 1993) The public research university seems ideal for this subject because it is where most graduate education takes place and thus develops the future professorate that teaches in other sectors of higher education (Steck, 2003).

It should be clear at the outset that this chapter rests on a set of assumptions that lead to a possible scenario; it adopts the public choice approach (Benjamin, 1980; Harsanyi, 1969; Lindblom, 1990). Public choice adherents assume that institutional change is driven by the presence of mixes of incentives and sanctions that persuade individuals to respond. Conversely, they view cultural arguments as useful descriptions but not explanations of behavior. How do individuals and the institutions they inhabit change if they are not forced to make choices about the costs compared to the benefits of taking new action? Given these assumptions, public choice adherents (Hirschman, 1970; Hirschman and Rothschild, 1973) posit an ideal type, a synthesis gleaned from the "real" world that if realized would create the imperatives for change in individual and, hence, institutional behavior.

This chapter proceeds in the following manner. After restating the problem of the decline of shared governance in universities, I develop a set of distinctions between research and undergraduate education. My thesis, noted elsewhere in this book, is that centralized institutions that produce services fall prey to significant information distortion. The greater the number of bureaucratic levels through which information passes, the greater the likelihood the information will be distorted. Flatter, horizontal designs are needed in such institutions to create more effective information flows between groups (in this case academic departments) so that they can work together more productively.

My argument here is that the research enterprise, especially sponsored research, has become too complex for consideration by the traditional structure of faculty senates. Apart from anything else, these bodies include the "have" and "have-not" professors when it comes to getting large research grants. Professors in the humanities, much of the social sciences, and several professional schools lack the opportunities for lucrative funded research. However, all faculty units do participate in undergraduate education, with the humanities and social sciences in featured roles. If faculty interest in undergraduate education can be raised from the department to the institutional level, it could revive a renewed interest by faculty senates in discussing and recommending university-wide policies on improving undergraduate learning, especially general education.

For this result to occur, there must be strong incentives and/or the prospects of sanctions that entice or compel faculty to set their sights on improving teaching and learning at the institutional level. The positive incentives relate to the benefits accruing from raising the quality of undergraduate education—better retention and graduation rates and better incoming students over time. The potential negative sanctions in this case flow from the accountability movement in higher education that increasingly demands real evidence of student learning. I create an argument based on my understanding of the direction of this accountability movement and the probable or possible responses by the faculty in public research universities. It offers a plausible model—not a description—of the accountability and assessment literature in higher education. To be plausible, the model reflects my thinking about the intersections between accountability and assessment requirements. The utility of this chapter will depend on how much it encourages readers to think about the problem of spurring greater faculty participation in university-wide governance.

Governance

Elsewhere, I define governance as the decision-making units, policies and procedures, written and unwritten, that control resource allocation in universities and colleges (Benjamin et al., 1993). This characterization focuses on all the actors, both internal and external to the institution, who influence resource allocation. Resource allocation is not limited to financial resources but also includes the distribution of prestige, goal setting, and development and maintenance of the vision and mission of the institution.

Why Faculty Participation in University Governance Is Important?

Faculty remain the critical lynchpin because they determine the criteria for the evaluation of teaching and research at their institution (see also page 87 above for a more detailed list).

Because these factors define much of the activities of the university, without faculty support, explicit or at least tacit, deans, provosts, and presidents struggle or are ineffective. Another critical consideration is the public assumption by the collective faculty of the equality of all fields of knowledge within the university (Benjamin and Carroll, 1996). Though few individual professors may actually believe all fields are equal, they are reluctant to argue publicly that any one field is less important than another. In part, professors want to avoid alienating colleagues in other departments. In addition, the salience of fields has shifted historically. Physics was dominant in the early 20th century, and microbiology grew in importance near the end of that century. Obscure fields in veterinary biology dealing with retroviruses became vital with the discovery of AIDS. Despite shifts in demands and importance of fields, professors are reluctant to recommend restructuring or cutbacks in other departments or colleges. After all, they may be next in line. The administration and trustees must therefore take the lead in reallocations as well as reductions because of the faculty's reluctance to participate in cutting their colleagues' programs.

Despite this faculty reluctance, the administration cannot provide direction to public universities without persuading the faculty of the necessity for reductions and reallocation. The faculty need not participate in making cuts and shifts, but they must accept their necessity if the recommendations have any chance of being implemented. A second point is that the board of trustees and the central administration formally set standards for admission and graduation, but the faculty implements and interprets the meaning of those standards. If there is not congruence between the definitions of those standards by the faculty and the administration, the goals of the administration and board of trustees are not achievable. In the end, the faculty implements the vision and mission statements of the institution they serve. If the faculty does not accept the vision and mission statements of the institution, they remain paper documents only. Finally, the developments in new and old fields of knowledge, as practiced by the faculty of a research university, create the sparks of innovation that produce paradigm shifts. Therefore, if the faculty is not involved in the governance of the university, the institution is diminished greatly because the administration is only a bureaucratic infrastructure dedicated to enabling teaching, research, and service. Any university becomes a hollow structure without the rich advice of its faculty about the university's goals based on their diverse knowledge from a range of fields.

The Challenge of the Changed Environment

There was a time, from before World War II until the early 1980s, when the increases in demands on colleges and universities roughly matched the growth in resources. In retrospect, growth in student enrollment and faculty positions seemed orderly and slow. Under these conditions, each of the three major internal partners of university governance—trustees, administration, and faculty—played well-understood and mutually reinforcing roles. The three actors may have operated in rough concert because of a general agreement about the nature and goals of teaching and research—two of the central functions of the university (the other being service). The era before World War II preceded the compact between the federal government and the university that generated the extraordinary growth in large-scale research in the health sciences, engineering, and several applied areas. It also predated the focus of universities on externally funded research. Under these conditions, professors across the university had an interest in seeing resources distributed somewhat equitably across fields. In undergraduate education, a campus consensus at least tacitly existed that students needed a common core of liberal education to graduate. Faculty had an interest in participating in the senate that oversaw the terms of engagement for undergraduate curriculum across the university.

Faculty played a strong role, through the faculty senate, along with the administration and trustees and the trustees at the institutional level. This process became known as shared governance (American Association of University Professors, 1996). "As essential participants in the governance process, each acts as a checks-and-balance mechanism by which the power of the other is counterbalanced. Both better decisions and broader decision acceptance can be anticipated as a result" (Del Favero, 2003, p. 906). Measures of success of the ideal include achievement of consensus and widespread acceptance of decision-making (Benjamin and Carroll, 1998). Where did this ideal occur? The answer is where memberships of faculty senates consisted of distinguished faculty at the institution and where administrations developed university policy in close collaboration with the faculty senate. The assent of most top administrators from prominent roles in faculty senates exemplified this close cooperation.

In fact, a strong possibility of the breakdown of this ideal always existed. The reason is that at least two of the participants—the faculty and the administration—could and did claim the same piece of the governance pie: control of the allocation of resources in the broadest sense. For example, administrators controlled the financial resources. Faculty controlled the curriculum, who taught it, and who should be recommended to teach it. Why did cooperation rather than conflict characterize the relationship between these two groups? The "traditional" environment in which supply and demand factors remained in reasonable equilibrium, growing at roughly the same rate until the 1990s. But such stasis, if it ever really existed, has changed dramatically. Growth had become exponential and diverse in demands for more research, both theoretical and applied; in student enrollment, especially a more heterogeneous student body; and in fields outside the traditional arts and sciences.

By comparison, the growth in the share of resources for public universities from state budgets has steadily declined. In the early years of the 21st century, acute budget cuts in many states have left public universities in the position of having to reduce funding for some programs. Moreover, the volatility of budgets and new demands for instruction and research make the classic shared governance model slow, inefficient, and inadequate to meet the demands of this competitive, dynamic world of public research universities. Under these conditions, state boards of higher education demand greater control (Carlin, 1999), the accountability movement grows, and apathy toward participation by professors in university governance increases (Lazerson, 1997). Shared governance appears, says Breneman (1995, p. 1), poorly suited "to the sorts of wrenching challenges that lie ahead." The question remains, what should replace it?

Over the 1950s and 1960s, the typical public research university grew substantially, and the "multiversity" became the unquestioned organization (Kerr, 1995). With size come economies of scale (so it is thought), greater efficiency, and greater effectiveness. Another term for this is *critical mass*. With great size comes a large faculty with differentiated skills and interests that, in turn, means that many more interests of students for instruction and potential clients for research can be accommodated. With great size also comes economies of scale regarding the development of one physical plant design team, say, for an entire state's higher education system, the facilities management group, the finance office, and so on. Moreover, the size and complexity of the faculty and ancillary enterprises grow dramatically as well (Benjamin et al., 1993). Outside the institution, accrediting agencies, coordinating and system boards, the state legislature, and a variety of special interest and advocacy groups exert pressure, sometimes requiring the college to respond to demands ranging from the context and rigor of the curriculum to the number of books in the library.

Such size and complexity could only exist by ceding much of the academic governance to the academic departments. The concept, fully developed by the early 20th century, claimed that specialists in the fields of knowledge know best what to teach, who should teach what subjects, and what to do in research. Senior members of the departments know best what quality means in their fields and which professors deserve recommendations for promotion, tenure, and merit increases. Of course, deans and vice presidents had to agree, but they really held only the power to block, not initiate. In any event, the department typically reports to a dean within a college, another separate unit in the university. These colleges in research universities stand in isolation. Campus governance arrangements promote a departmental and not a university view of the critical issues of research focus and undergraduate education, especially that part accenting the liberal arts and sciences for all undergraduates. In most public research universities, the concept of a core curriculum as the venue for a liberal education has disappeared. Under such conditions, professors argue that their courses or their department major is the appropriate level of analysis for undergraduate education.

Incentives and rewards for professors are also department based in the research university. A primary reason is that research productivity determines the merit pay of faculty and their recommendations for promotion and tenure. The senior members or chair of one's department determine the criteria to make judgments about the level of research productivity of individual professors. Multi- and interdisciplinary research centers increasingly join in this role of judging research. They are often formed to receive the external funding that drives many research programs and, in turn, the careers of scientists and engineers. Deans and provosts can confer on and deny promotion, tenure, or merit increases, but departmental specialists who can best judge research results initiate the recommendation. Under these conditions of departmental or college dominance, the university becomes an abstract notion not of practical relevance to the day-to-day activities of professors. Departments, colleges, and multidisciplinary centers constitute the real world of recommendations and resources for professors.

The New Governance Challenges and Possibilities

In a number of key areas today, university leaders find themselves in uncharted territory. For example, priorities in research have shifted. Multidisciplinary research increasingly replaces single, department-based research at the frontiers of knowledge. The infrastructure for large-scale science has become so great that several entities must fund these projects. Increasingly, those partnerships link universities and industry. The latter provides equipment, researchers, and funding, morphing such assets into virtual labs that allow both industrial and university scientists to work jointly on research programs. The leaders of such projects become successful scientific entrepreneurs who make their own arrangements and commitments with the central administration of universities and businesses and federal research agencies. Under these conditions, it is difficult—if not impossible—to figure out how to set research priorities for the faculty at the university level. However, undergraduate education—especially general education—may well be a different matter.

Undergraduate education in most public research universities has a bewildering number of majors and distribution requirements in general education. The concept of a core curriculum is typically absent. Under such conditions, faculty representatives on college- or university-wide curriculum committees engage in logrolling when voting on the new courses submitted for approval by other departments. They tend to vote yes in the hope and expectation that the other department representatives will reciprocate when their turn comes to submit proposed courses for approval. The result is a factionalized curriculum with no real incentive for faculty to focus on setting the institutional learning goals for undergraduates. Hence, faculty no longer focus on the quality of undergraduate education, and faculty senates no longer consider it a critical issue.

As noted earlier (Chapter 2, pp. 35–77), the absence of comparative evaluation criteria for setting priorities for resource allocation constitutes a special challenge for university governance. In addition, a seemingly limitless number of internal and external actors have some claim, role, or influence on resource allocation. The net result is that the degrees of freedom for action in the university are reduced. The faculty role in governance becomes problematic because the institution no longer clearly governs itself in terms of the definition offered earlier. It is not surprising that the distinguished professors do not participate in faculty senates, whose influence withers away. Indeed, fragmentation raises the question of whether it is even appropriate to speak of a university. The whole of the university is no longer clearly more than the sum of its parts.

The fall in state funding has not helped the unity of the university since it encourages the production of self-generated income from research, tuition, and gifts at the college, school, and department levels. My prediction of the steady decline in the percentage of state budgets allocated to higher education turned out to be conservative. The decline has accelerated in the first two decades of the 21st century (Benjamin, 1998). All indications are that this trend will continue. Universities have attempted to make up the difference with tuition increases. These annual increases have been at or above 10% from 2002 to 2004, followed by stabilization of public university budgets in most states. There is increasing concern that upper limits exist to tuition growth because they increase student debt and threaten access to postsecondary education by underrepresented groups. Faced with the prospect of continued financial erosion, all parties in public research universities have an incentive to maximize their claims on the university budget.

Higher Education as a Public Good

Higher education, particularly undergraduate education, is a public good that has been eroded (Chapter 2, pp. 35–8). The concept public good means if the good is supplied to one individual it is supplied to all members of the community or class. Classic public goods are such items as national defense or K–12 education—if supplied to one American, they are supplied to all. Similarly, the environment (good or bad), health, and education are thought of as public goods. In the real world of the 21st century, we know that the classic distinction formulated by Samuelson (1967) is not so clear. Public goods also produce private benefits. Private goods such as airlines produce public goods if a single airline serves a small community in a rural state.

Undergraduate education has been and should be treated as a public good served by a set of institutional arrangements called the university. We will explore the consequences of the collapse of this understanding of public goods. The obverse—private goods—are market-based and the product of a simple transaction. Party A desires good B and party C supplies good B to party A at an agreed price. Both parties are presumably satisfied, otherwise they would not agree to the transaction. Public goods are not easily partitioned into sets of well-defined producers and consumers. That is why we call them public goods in the first place. We agree to tolerate ambiguity of production and consumption in public goods precisely because the good they bring is thought to be so critical to all members of society.

Differences Between Faculty Research and Undergraduate Education

- The contribution of the individual to research can usually be ascertained, for example, by the quantity and quality of research papers, the size and number of research awards, and the number of citations.
- The contribution of the individual faculty member or even the individual department to the knowledge and skills acquired by graduates is not easy to ascertain, for example, because standards for grades for students vary from one faculty member to another, from department to department, and across colleges and because general education skills in student learning are not generally assessed; courses and majors are, but these are difficult to compare.

University-wide research priorities can be established. However, based on the assumption of the equality of knowledge and department-based governance, it is understandably difficult for the faculty collectively through senates to contribute effectively to this process. Funding requirements to mount successful efforts in area A of science detract from the possibility of doing so in area B of science. Such conflicting interests may be why scientific entrepreneurs make their own arrangements with provosts and presidents. Although the public position of these officers claims the importance of undertaking research in all fields of knowledge, externally sponsored research gets most of the attention from the administration. The stability of funding of public as well as private research universities now increasingly depends on it. The administration may not resist research and scholarship in the social sciences, humanities, and some professional schools, but the provision of funding is where the assumption of the equality of knowledge stops for the central administration. Large-scale science projects, which generate significant external funding, dominate the decisions of presidents and provosts. Those decisions provide matching funds; commit faculty positions; and allocate money for laboratory equipment and space mainly for science, engineering, and medicine. In contrast, faculty senates, which represent the collective faculty, cannot realistically deal with research because it divides their constituency into haves and have-nots. As a result, faculty as a whole have a disincentive to participate in governance related to the research mission on a university-wide basis.

Undergraduate Education

Undergraduate education currently does not attract the attention of the university faculty. Little incentive exists for participation on a university-wide basis in deliberating on matters, such as the knowledge and skills graduates should possess and the means of assessing their achievement. But this neglect could change, for the following reasons.

Most university mission statements insist that their institution exists to improve critical thinking, analytic reasoning, and communication skills (Stevens, 2010), or what may be called the skills of liberal or general education. These skills exhibit public good-like qualities. No one department, course, or major produces them, and all graduates should have them.

Individual faculty may and do argue that, since they do not teach these skills in their departments, they should not be evaluated for their achievement by students. Nor should assessment of student learning be focused on their acquisition. This position has carried the day until very recently. Now, employers, commentators, and observers of higher education increasingly argue that it is these public good-like skills that are precisely what undergraduate education should improve. That narrow content or specialization should not be the major focus of undergraduate education. Undergraduate education should teach students how to think and not only train them to be proficient in a specific academic field. From this perspective, the institution, not the department, becomes the focus of assessment because no one department produces or improves these skills. Such a shift would prove surprising given the history of the fragmenting university over the past 70 years.

The Case for the Whole

Departments are important. The majors they offer students are essential. But it may be time to also consider the institution as the key unit of academic analysis. Outsiders are certainly calling for it. Education is not only about specialized content; it is about teaching students how to think. All institutions commit to improving the critical-thinking skills of their students. These sentiments are etched in most mission statements of colleges and universities (Stevens, 2010). Employers increasingly call for improvements in the critical thinking, analytical reasoning, and communication skills of the graduates they hire. Surveys of the informed public indicate the same desire. It is the promise of the institution to improve these general education skills. In this sense, undergraduate education may be considered a candidate to be a public good again, if a way can be found to provide a discourse that faculty and administrators can use for communicating across departmental boundaries.

Undergraduate Education and University Governance

How can focusing on improving undergraduate education unite the faculty and renew university governance and faculty senates? First, we must view undergraduate education as a public good that produces improvements in the general education skills of critical thinking, analytical reasoning, and written communication. Next, to make faculty comfortable in focusing on improving undergraduate education, we must encourage the development of an assessment system that gives faculty the information needed to make effective changes in the curriculum, pedagogy, and other internal processes affecting undergraduate education.

It is admittedly a tall order to convince faculty to focus on improving undergraduate education and to create an appropriate assessment system to support that effort. How can we focus faculty attention on the quality of undergraduate education? And how can we promote the faculty senate as the venue for decision-making that fosters institutional improvements in undergraduate education? My approach is based on the public choice assumptions that incentives and sanctions (existing or the prospect of) drive individuals who make up collectives such as faculty to change their behavior.

What follows is a sketch of an argument for focusing faculty thinking in a more systematic way on the quality of the general education component at the institutional level. I am not arguing this scenario will be played out tomorrow. We will see whether and when the argument gets played out in real time in public research universities.

Putting aside the questions of timing, I believe that undergraduate education will be gradually more differentiated from research and that faculty will increasingly focus on the quality of undergraduate education at the institutional level. This result may occur initially because of real and perceived accountability pressures but also because of the rewards associated with improving teaching and learning. I make the case for using an assessment approach to provide the discipline and common language necessary for the quality of undergraduate education to become a focal point of a strengthened role of faculty in university governance. This argument uses assessment as a method of reviving faculty governance.[1]

The Argument

The "public" (taxpayers, legislators, and governors) wants to be assured that their college students are receiving a quality education. This interest in accountability is fueled by the same factors that have led to higher tuitions, shrinking state budgets, and the increasing cost of higher education (Jones, 2003). In the past, institutions relied on accreditation reviews and various types of actuarial data, such as graduation and minority access rates, to demonstrate quality. That approach is no longer adequate for colleges, just as it no longer sufficient for K–12 education (as evidenced by No Child Left Behind legislation and the emphasis on statewide testing of students).

The public wants to know whether its education institutions are helping students acquire the knowledge, skills, and abilities they will need when they graduate (Immerwahr, 2000). In addition, policymakers increasingly want to know how much students actually have learned, not how much they believe that they have learned. Forty-four states have established accountability systems (Burke and Minassians, 2002) for higher education.[2] Seat time, course grades, and graduation rates are no longer sufficient. In short, the public is increasingly asking its colleges and universities to show that acceptable progress has been made in student learning.

To satisfy this demand for accountability, higher education institutions need to demonstrate that their students have acquired important skills and knowledge in addition to achieving other goals such as graduating, achieving necessary prerequisites for professional schools, and gaining employment. The only credible way to show such learning is to test them on what they are supposed to know and be able to do. Institutional ratings, student and faculty surveys, and other indirect proxies are just not sufficient. Instead, direct measures of outcomes are needed. Colleges and universities already assess students but hardly ever for the purpose of demonstrating the value the institution adds to a student's knowledge and skills. At least until recently, their reasons for testing have had nothing to do with accountability. Instead, colleges and universities have tested incoming students to make sure they have the skills needed for coursework. Students with insufficient skills are generally placed in remedial programs. In addition, some colleges administer tests at the end of the sophomore year to make sure students are ready for their upper-division studies. These so-called rising junior exams, like the initial placement tests, focus on basic reading, writing, and math skills. They focus on the individual student without attempting to measure the contribution of the institution to student learning.

Some colleges are now expanding their testing programs to include assessing other abilities, such as critical-thinking skills, that are central to the college's mission but cut across academic majors. College administrators see this as a way to demonstrate the beneficial effects of the educational experiences at their institutions to prospective students and their parents.[3] Nevertheless, most institutions continue to rely on their faculty—individually, not collectively—to assess their students' content knowledge and skills.

This approach satisfies the faculty, who generally believe professors already provide sufficient and appropriate assessments of student learning. They use midterm and final exams, term papers, classroom participation, and other evidence to assign grades. And they feel these grades reflect how much students learn in their courses.[4]

Unfortunately, professor grades are idiosyncratic. Two courses with the same title may cover different content, even at the same college. There are also large differences in grading standards among professors across colleges. What constitutes B work at one school may correspond to A or C work at another institution. The same is true across professors within an institution.[5] There also has been substantial grade inflation over time.[6] Hence, professor-assigned grades cannot be relied on to provide a valid measure of whether the students in one graduating class are more or less proficient than those in another class or at another college. Value-added comparisons are not made of the contributions of institutions to growth in student learning from entry to exit. Some other metric is needed.

The search for another index has led some colleges to experiment with portfolios, grades in capstone courses, or other institution-specific indicators of learning (Banta and Pike, 2012). However, all these measures have the same fundamental limitation as regular course grades, namely, the absence of a way to interpret reliably and validly scores outside the context of a particular course or school at a given point in time. To correct that problem, the measures have to be administered under the same standardized conditions to everyone, and the scores obtained have to be adjusted for possible variation in average question difficulty, reader leniency, and other factors. Locally constructed measures, such as course grades or portfolios, do not have these essential features and therefore cannot be used for making valid comparisons within institutions over time or for comparisons among institutions at a single point in time.

Those limitations are not present with the measures that are used for statewide K–12 testing (such as the Stanford-9, Iowa Tests of Basic Skills, and the National Assessment of Educational Progress), college and graduate school admission decisions (such as the SAT, ACT, GRE, and LSAT), or licensing exams in the professions (such as accountancy, law, medicine, and teaching). Thus, when results really matter, such as for high-stakes decisions about individuals, procedures are used that help to eliminate the effects of extraneous factors, such as who drafted the questions or scored the answers.

The Role of the State

States have a legitimate and critical role in assuring accountability in their higher education institutions. Many states set objectives for educational levels to be achieved by entering students; participation rates by ethnic/racial groups; minimum passing scores for law, medicine, and other professional schools; and numbers of graduates to be achieved in particular fields such as teaching, nursing, and technology.[7]

The states also provide the instructional budgets for public undergraduate education and infrastructure support, including buildings, libraries, and scientific equipment. States clearly have a right and a responsibility to require accountability from the institutions they support. Why, then, are we not further ahead in developing assessment systems of student learning that work from the point of view of the institutions and the states?

The problem is that the assessment measures used at the institutional level differ from most of the accountability indicators favored by states. First, the concept of accountability must be specified. Most broadly, in the context of higher education, accountability can be defined as the extent to which public higher education institutions meet the goals set for them by the state. (In the best case, these goals are mutually agreed to by both parties.) Just as faculty and institutions set assessment goals for a variety of purposes, states set accountability goals for different purposes. Most states desire accountability for prudent use of resources or, at the very least, absence of fraud. Some state leaders demand evidence of increased participation, retention, and graduation rates for underrepresented groups. An increasing number want to be assured that students have gained knowledge and skills from their educational experiences. Approaches and measures of student learning favored by faculty differ from those preferred by state leaders. Here we focus on this last goal of state-based accountability, evidence of student-learning outcomes (Naughton et al., 2003).

Approaches to student-learning outcomes by faculty have the following characteristics:

- Their goals are to improve curriculum and pedagogy as well as set targets for students.
- They focus on individual students, departments, or—to a lesser extent—institutions but not on interinstitutional comparisons.
- They are content rich, tailored to the context of the institution, generated by faculty themselves, and often time intensive and costly.
- Because the emphasis is on content, they tend not to be replicable from one institution to the next.

In comparison, state-based approaches are:

- Focused on accountability objectives
- Aggregated at the regional or state level and ideally replicable and comparable across institutions
- Centered on indirect proxies of student-learning outcomes such as the percentage of passing rates for teaching examinations
- Inclusive of teacher, nurses, and other professional school examinations; number and percentage of students that take the GRE; and retention and graduation rates
- Poor in content or tailored to the context of the individual institutions and not developed by faculty
- Based on cost-effective methods, making use of existing data

The result is a disconnect between the faculty and institutions on the one hand and the state on the other.

Assessment Principles

The assessment principles adhered to by institutions need to be comparative based in some manner and focused on general education skills to respond to the accountability requirements. Here is what that would entail.

Measures whose scores are interpretable across professors, colleges, and time allow relevant comparisons to be made within and between institutions. For example, the scores on such measures can be used along with grades on other tests (such as the SAT or ACT) to assess whether the students at a school are doing better or worse on an outcome measure than would be expected given their entry-level skills. Measures that are applicable across institutions also may serve as benchmarks for interpreting the results with similar but locally constructed instruments or course grades. Measures that are designed to permit comparisons across institutions thus provide a signal of academic performance (and are therefore a motivator for change). Such signaling can indicate whether the faculty and administrators need to take a closer look at the resources, curriculum, pedagogy, and programmatic structure underlying undergraduate teaching and learning. In short, such measures may help colleges document the progress they are making in fostering student learning. The measures also may contribute to improving academic programs by providing institutions with baseline and outcome scores to help identify the effects on learning of programmatic and curricular changes.[8]

To accomplish these ends, cross-institutional measures must have certain essential characteristics. The scores must be reliable in the sense that they are not overly affected by chance factors. If the results are aggregated to the university level (such as to providing information about programs), then the degree of reliability required to identify effects is much less than would be needed for making decisions about individual students. The scores must be valid in the sense of providing information about student characteristics that are important to the institution's goals, such as improving their students' ability to communicate in writing and to think critically about issues. The tests themselves must be fair to all takers, that is, regardless of the students' demographic or other characteristics. Finally, results must be reported to students and institutions promptly and in a way that is understandable to the recipients and facilitates decision-making.

The process of implementing such measures at the university level is fraught with land mines. For instance, any top-down effort to impose them on faculty and students is likely to run into trouble. Norms ceding power to faculty on key issues remain strong. These norms were developed over time in the wake of the construction of the modern American university during the last quarter of the 19th century. Graduate research functions were married to the undergraduate mission. That move created the basis for the professional development of the doctorate as the final degree for faculty. With that development came the recognition that only those who received the PhD in their field should make decisions about the fields of specialization on which to focus, the curriculum, who to recommend to teach, etc.

Instead, it will be essential for the academic community to see them as a valuable adjunct to its own measures or even embed them into capstone courses. Similarly, attempts to use the results to punish institutions for having less than stellar or even average improvement scores would stop the assessment effort in its tracks. Instead, the results need to be used to identify best practices that other institutions could try as well as to spot potential problem areas where additional support is needed. In addition, the measures themselves must be intrinsically interesting and engaging so that students will be motivated to participate in the assessment activities and try their best to do well.

It is not feasible to measure all or even most of the knowledge, skills, and abilities that are central to college or university learning goals. Much of what is learned takes place outside the classroom. This situation leads to the concern that what is tested will be overly emphasized in the institution's instructional programs. In short, some will say that the only abilities that count are the ones that are measured. This position is akin to saying, "You shouldn't measure anything unless you can measure everything." This concern can be addressed by varying the types of measures used over time and by augmenting the measures that are used across institutions with local program-specific instruments.

States are increasingly developing assessment systems that emphasize accountability. Resistance by faculty to accountability-oriented systems of assessment (that are focused on indirect, proxy measures of student learning) also continues and is unlikely to change. This reaction is unfortunate, even problematic, if, as I believe, the state-level demand for accountability is only going to grow. We should reject the argument that the unit of analysis for accountability must be only the state (Callan et al., 2001; Callan and Finney, 2003; National Center for Public Policy in Higher Education, 2000) or the argument that the unit must only be the institution (Banta and Pike, 2012).

How might we reconcile the implications of the two units of analysis? The prime focus of accountability should be on student learning. It is the growing insistence on the part of the state that institutions be held accountable for the quality of their student learning that, I predict, will drive faculty to implement the principles of assessment noted above in the service of an increased focus on the quality of general education at their institution.

If the growing pressure convinces faculty to focus more attention on the quality of general education, representatives of the state and institutions will need to work out the equivalent of a legal agreement that both parties will implement. These rules of engagement must give both parties incentives to cooperate. What should the rules of engagement be? There must be agreement on the measures to be used. The measures must meet faculty objectives but the ability for interinstitutional comparison should be built in to satisfy the needs of the state. Although the two parties need to agree on common measures to be used, their goals are different. Since faculty are primarily interested in assessment for educational improvement while the state is primarily interested in assessment for external accountability, the two parties will need to reach agreement on what information from the assessments may be aggregated at the regional or state level.

Relations between the institution and the state will improve significantly if there is agreement that the initiative should focus on increasing the value-added contribution of the institution to general education skills over time rather than on absolute levels achieved. Indeed, if there is agreement that the value-added approach is appropriate, there can be a time lag built in during which institutions identified as being below minimum levels of quality can be asked to show improvement over a several-year period. Since institutions, as well as the state, are interested in demonstrating that they are improving, this strategy should provide common ground between the two groups.

Bridging the Disconnect Between Assessment and Accountability

There is a disconnect in assessment and accountability goals focused on student learning between the institution and the state. Can it be overcome by the state exerting control through its levers of power—that is, the power of the purse or regulation? Probably not, or, to put it another way, the result would certainly be a pyrrhic victory with no winners on either side. Can the disconnect be bridged?

The answer is yes. It appears that, increasingly, state leaders will be judged on how well they improve the skills of their workforce to make their states more competitive economically. Faculty and administrators will come to recognize the right of state political leaders to be concerned about the quality of undergraduate education. As a result, they will accept the right of states to set goals for improvement in student-learning outcomes at their public colleges and universities. Eventually, along with the growing recognition that the role of the state in setting goals is reasonable, there should also flow state-based incentives, accepted by higher education leaders as appropriate, to encourage their public higher education institutions to meet those goals. This result will occur because of the growing recognition, by all parties, that human capital is the most important asset possessed by a region, state, or nation (Krueger, 2003). However, in the case of higher education, reliance on the experts (the faculty) to define the most appropriate methods of assessment is, necessarily, a prerequisite to success. This recognition of the need to work together by faculty and administrators at the university on the one hand, and state leaders on the other, may well take some time, and the road getting there will likely be bumpy. However, if human capital is as important as we believe, state and national leaders will ultimately be entrusted with the task of setting standards for improvement in student learning. If we reach a wider consensus on how to implement this principle, we will be able to develop policies and practices in assessment that benefit the institution and the state and, most importantly, the citizens both serve.

A New Role for the Faculty Senate

If public universities start down this road, a number of important policy questions must be answered. These questions, I believe, will call for substantial faculty input, again, on an institution-wide basis.

1. *Assuming the assessment done uncovers the need for improvements, what, if any, assessment data should be made public to outside agencies and on what terms?*

This question enters uncharted territory. State commissions and departments of higher education are calling for evidence of performance. To date, faculty have generally resisted their requests, or the data collected has been sufficiently far from the classroom that faculty can ignore the process of data collection and the results. Faculty might well react differently if data on direct measures of cognitive learning, as discussed earlier, are assembled. Faculty will probably wish to use the information for formative assessment purposes. State officials will want to use the information for summative, evaluative purposes.

The rules for what data should be reported publicly and to whom can be sorted out, but there must be a real bargaining process, with faculty involved in this negotiation. Where else would the faculty make their case than in a representative assembly such as the faculty senate?

2. *Assuming the assessment results cover all the programs, departments, and colleges in the public research university, what role, if any, should they play in resource allocation?*

For example:

- Should more funding go to units that have lower results from the assessment of student learning to improve them?
- Should units that do well on the same measures get more resources to reward them?
- Should instructor/student ratios be lowered in order to improve student-learning outcomes?
- Should there be fundamental changes in the curriculum on a university-wide basis, for example, establishment of a core curriculum?
- Should there be changes in pedagogy?

These and related questions need the input of the faculty if the university is to respond to them properly. What other venue makes sense than the faculty senate? Since there are a variety of questions, there would be increased business for the senate education committee, the budget committee, and the committee on facilities and instructional equipment. Since the humanities and social sciences faculties, by definition, play an important role in the undergraduate curriculum, heightened attention to improving teaching and learning should raise the profile of these parts of the faculty.

If the movement to focus on general education skills in addition to courses and majors succeeds, institutional forums will again become the venue for deliberation and recommendations by faculty across the university. If the faculty senate is nonexistent or moribund, it will have to be recreated to provide such a venue. If this comes to pass, there will be a variety of side benefits that will reconnect the faculty and the administration in public research universities. And that will be a good thing.

A Not-So-Modest Proposal

The time has come to offer a proposal that could not only revive university-wide faculty governance in faculty senates but also the central importance of the arts and sciences faculty on campus. It could also breathe new and needed life into student-learning assessment.

1. *Faculty or university senates should once again take charge of the goals, courses, content, and outcomes of general education.*

   No single move could do more to fix the fragmented university at the undergraduate level, answer the complaints of external critics about learning outcomes of graduates, or restore the arts and sciences faculty to their appropriate role in university governance and undergraduate education. The proposal focuses on general education because that is the collective responsibility for the faculty—especially in the arts and sciences—while academic majors belong to the diverse departments.
2. *Senates should appoint a blue-ribbon faculty commission of leading professors—largely from the arts and sciences—to propose the goals, content, and outcomes of general education.*

   Such a step would end the common practice in public research universities of leaving general education requirements to the determination of colleges and schools for their own majors. These commissions should draw heavily on the excellent work in general education of the Association of American Colleges and Universities (AAC&U). This group notes that employers and academics already agree on the desirable outcomes of general education (AAC&U, 2005). It includes the intellectual and practical skills of written and oral communication; inquiry and critical and creative thinking; quantitative and information literacy; teamwork; and the integration of learning. The knowledge derived from general education should also involve an appreciation of the arts and humanities, the social sciences, and the sciences and mathematics.
3. *That commission—with assistance of faculty and staff experts in evaluation and institutional research—should develop the multiple methods for systematically and periodically assessing the extent to which graduates actually acquire that knowledge and those skills and propose how to use the results to improve institutional performance.*

Reliable information and evaluation techniques are the hallmarks of scholars. This proposal would ask leading scholars in the arts and sciences to bring the same tools they use in research to evaluating the knowledge and skills acquired by students during their college years.

Not Probable, but Possible and Desirable

Academic skeptics will sneer at both the possibility and the desirability of this proposal. Even campus realists, looking at the record, may well deny the possibility of this proposal, while perhaps accepting its desirability. Both will doubtless pose that fateful question: What will make faculty senates and the faculty in the arts and sciences tackle now what they have assiduously avoided for decades—addressing and assessing general education?

The answer is simple. Taking charge of general education and assessing its results is now in the self-interest of the arts and sciences faculty, especially those from the arts, humanities, social sciences, and the sciences with limited opportunities for funded research and less-than-burgeoning demands for undergraduate enrollments.

Four potent forces are coalescing to make the adoption of this proposal possible, if not probable: pressure, power, prestige, and payoff.

Pressure

The pressure, especially on public research universities, to both demonstrate and improve the knowledge and skills of undergraduates has never been stronger. State, business, civic, and now federal leaders are demanding it. Faculty leaders probably accept the skills and knowledge listed earlier as the goals of general education, but they have clashed over the methods or courses that best achieve those objectives and have resisted assessing learning outcomes, especially those that require or encourage institutional comparisons. Clearly, the faculty, especially in public research universities, does not want to assess student-learning outcomes.

One prospect may well change the faculty's position. That is the growing probability that outsiders will impose the goals of undergraduate learning and the methods of assessing their achievement. Either the faculty will do it, or outsiders will do it for them. Faced with that choice, the faculty should decide to do it.

Power

The faculty in most of the arts, humanities, social sciences, and even some science disciplines cannot be happy with the way that the professional schools have hijacked general education or dismissed its importance in the name of job training. (That unhappiness hides their own preference for specialized courses in their disciplines over their responsibility for general education.) How it must grate on professors in those areas to read on their university websites that students should look at the listings of their colleges and schools to discover the course requirements of general education.

Taking charge of general education and its assessment is not only self-defense against outside imposition; it is the way to power in faculty governance. The move to have faculty senates and arts and sciences faculty take charge of general education and assessment will win strong support from trustees, presidents, and provosts. Given the numbers of professors in the arts and sciences, they represent clear majorities in the faculty senates. The way to power is clear. Arts and sciences faculty have the numbers and the expertise. All they need is the will.

Prestige

Once, the prestige on campus went to the liberal arts and sciences for their special contribution to undergraduate education. Now the shift of prestige mostly to sponsored research has diminished the position of professors especially in the arts, humanities, and the social sciences, where large research grants are scarce.

The fragmentation of general education, along with the university, has ended that special position of the arts and sciences. It has prevented the arts and sciences faculty from getting the benefits from their natural accent on synthesis and connections across the disciplines, which should bring prestige when problems both theoretical and applied fall increasingly in the connections among the disciplines. Prestige in an age of collaboration, cooperation, and connection should go to the faculty in the arts and sciences, but first that group must ensure that the general education conveys those connections and that graduates can use them to solve complex problems.

Payoff

Even the most idealistic professors at this point might well say, "Power and prestige are fine, but what about the financial payoff?" There is money in taking charge of general education. Governors and legislators would reward well a public university that identified the knowledge and skills expected of its graduates and assessed the extent of their achievement. In turn, trustees, presidents, and provosts would happily provide funding for a program that responded in an academically responsible way to those demands for accountability. Presidents and provosts know that only the faculty can and should develop such a program. They would reward the effort.

Another possible result is that a new metric for faculty rewards other than research productivity may emerge. The way it might work is that financial incentives are offered to faculty participating in general education in response to their achieving demonstrated improvements as measured by value-added growth, answering the question of how much improvement in the growth in general education skills of students occurs. Thus, the arts and sciences faculty could receive some part of their merit pay increases based on the contribution to general education.

Another funding benefit is not so obvious. Not all departments in the arts and sciences can attract large research grants or increasing student majors, which these days produce the lion's share of departmental funding. Tuition is a rising source of income in public research universities as they increase enrollment to close the gap in revenues from the fall in state funding. To encourage such self-generated income, many universities have adopted variations of Responsibility Center Management or budgeting that allow colleges and schools to keep most of their earned income. Some of these systems give most of the tuition income to the units that register the majors. The University of Michigan has taken a different tack that could increase the financial payoff to colleges, schools, and presumably departments in the arts and sciences enrolling general education students. It allocates 75% of the tuition income to course enrollments rather than major registrations (University of Michigan, College of Engineering, 2004). Such a provision could prove a real boon to arts and sciences departments offering attractive courses that fulfill the general education requirements.

A Final Thought

Daniel Burnham, a Chicago architect at the end of the 19th century, challenged his colleagues "to make no small plans." Now is the time for public research universities to once again think big with the breadth, style, and verve that once characterized governance proposals from the faculty in the liberal arts and sciences. This not-so-modest proposal seeks to save general education from specialized training, silence the external critics on student learning, and revive academic senates as centers of university governance. Even in this age that glorifies multitasking, that is no small plan, but perhaps it is a proposal big enough to interest the arts and sciences faculty in public research universities.

Notes

1. This section of the chapter, the argument, owes much to Steve Klein.
2. Seat time, course grades, and graduation rates are no longer sufficient. In short, the public is increasingly asking its colleges and universities to show that acceptable progress in being made in improving student learning.
3. Nevertheless, most institutions continue to rely on their faculty—individually not collectively—to assess their students' content knowledge and skills.
4. Moreover, although attendance at meetings on higher education assessment held by groups such as the Association of American Colleges and Universities has increased in recent years, most faculty remain skeptical of standardized assessments discussed here.
5. For example, Klein et al. (2005) developed a method to deal with the problem of widely divergent grading patterns across institutions. They converted GPAs within a school to z-scores and then used a regression model (that included the mean SAT score at the student's college) to adjust the correlations with GPAs for possible differences in grading standards among colleges.
6. For example, Harvard University, where until 2005 90% of the undergraduate students were deemed honors students, is, like other institutions, attempting with the problem of grade inflation (Donadio, 2005).
7. See the master plans of state higher education coordinating commissions or governing boards, for example of Texas and Nevada.
8. With at least two noteworthy exceptions—the Cooperative Institutional Research Program and the National Survey of Student Engagement

(NSSE)—efforts at higher education assessment have focused on developing approaches and instruments that deal with individual courses or majors that are often diagnostic in nature. However, one needs assessment data that permits comparison to successfully conduct formative assessment within institutions. The variation in learning goals and teaching approaches is enormous across American higher education. How can one know how well an institution is faring unless one compares the performance of the institution with that of other institutions on agreed-upon benchmarks of student-learning performance?

References

American Association of University Professors. 1996. *Statement on Government of Colleges and Universities*. Accessed August 9, 2006. www.aaup.org/statements/Redbook/Govern.htm.

Association of American Colleges and Universities (AAC&U). 2005. *Liberal Education Outcomes*. Washington, DC: Association of American Colleges and Universities.

Banta, Trudi W., and Gary R. Pike. 2012. "Making the Case Against—One More Time." *Occasional Paper 15*, National Institute of Learning Outcomes, September 24–30. www.NILOA.org.

Benjamin, Roger. 1980. *The Limits of Politics: Collective Goods and Political Change in Postindustrial Societies*. Chicago, IL: University of Chicago Press.

Benjamin, Roger, Steve Carroll, Mary Ann Jacobi, Cathy Krop, and Michael Shires. 1993. *The Redesign of Governance in Higher Education*. Santa Monica, CA: RAND, Institute on Education and Training, MR-222-LE.

Benjamin, Roger, and Steve Carroll. 1996. "Impediments and Imperatives in Redesigning Higher Education." *Educational Administration Quarterly*, December: 705–19.

Benjamin, Roger, and Steve Carroll. 1997. *Breaking the Social Contract: The Fiscal Crisis in California Higher Education*. Santa Monica, CA: RAND.

Benjamin, Roger, and Steve Carroll. 1998. "The Implications of the Changed Environment for Governance in Higher Education." In *The Responsive University: Restructuring for High Performance*, edited by William Tierney, 92–119. Baltimore, MD: Johns Hopkins University Press.

Benjamin, Roger. 2003. "The Environment of American Higher Education: A Constellation of Changes." *Higher Education in the Twenty-First Century, The Annals of the American Academy of Political and Social Science*, edited by Paul Rich and David Merchant, 585, January: 8–29.

Breneman, David. 1995. *Higher Education: On a Collision Course with New Realities*. Washington, DC: Association of Governing Boards of Colleges and Universities.

Burke, Joseph C., and Henrik P. Minassians. 2002. *Performance Reporting: The Preferred "No Cost" Accountability Program*. Albany, NY: The Rockefeller Institute of Government.

Callan, Pat M., William Doyle, and Joni E. Finney. 2001, March/April. "Evaluating State Higher Education Performance." *Change* 33 (2): 10–9.

Callan, Pat. M., and Joni E. Finney. 2003. *Multiple Pathways and State Policy: Toward Education and Training Beyond High School*. San Jose, CA: National Center for Public Policy and Higher Education.

Carlin, J. F. 1999, November 5. "Restoring Sanity in an Academic World Gone Mad." *The Chronicle of Higher Education*, p. A76.

Del Favero, Marietta. 2003, March. "Faculty-Administrator Relationships as Integral to Higher-Performing Governance Systems." *American Behavioral Scientist* 46: 903–22.

Donadio, Rachel. 2005, March 27. "The Tempest in the Ivory Tower [Review of the Book *Harvard Rules* and *Privilege*]." *The New York Times*: 12.

Harsanyi, John C. 1969. "Rational-Choice Models of Political Behavior vs. Functionalist and Conformist Theories." *World Politics* 21 (4): 513–38.

Hirschman, Albert O. 1970. *Exit, Voice, and Loyalty: Responses to Decline in Firms, Organizations, and States*. Cambridge, MA: Harvard University Press.

Hirschman, Albert O., and Michael Rothschild. 1973, November. "The Changing Tolerance for Economic Inequality in the Course of Economic Development." *Quarterly Journal of Economics* 87 (4): 544–66.

Immerwahr, John. 2000, August. *Great Expectations: How the Public and Parents of White, African-American and Hispanic Students View Higher Education*. San José, CA: National Center for Higher Education Public Policy.

Jones, Dennis. 2003. *State Shortfalls Projected throughout the Decade*. San Jose, CA: National Center for Public Policy and Higher Education.

Kerr, Clark. 1995. *The Uses of the University* (5th ed.). Cambridge, MA: Harvard University Press.

Klein, S., George Kuh, Marc Chun, Laura Hamilton, and Richard Shavelson. 2005, May. "An Approach to Measuring Cognitive Outcomes across Higher Education Institutions." *Research in Higher Education* 46 (3): 251–76.

Krueger, Alan B. 2003. *Education Matters: A Selection of Essays on Education*. London, England: Edward Elgar.

Lazerson, Marvin. 1997, March/April. "Who Owns Higher Education? The Changing Face of Governance." *Change* 29 (2): 10–15.

Lindblom, Charles E. 1990. *Inquiry and Change: The Troubled Attempt to Understand and Shape Society*. New Haven, CT: Yale University Press.

National Center for Public Policy and Higher Education. 2000. *Measuring up 2000: The State-by-State Report Card for Higher Education*. San Jose, CA: National Center for Public Policy and Higher Education.

Naughton, B. A., A. Y. Suen, and R. J. Shavelson. 2003. "Accountability for What? Understanding the Learning Objectives in State Higher Education Accountability Programs." *A Paper Presented at the Annual Meeting of the American Educational Research Association*, Chicago.

Samuelson, Paul. 1967, Fall. "Indeterminacy of Governmental Role in Public Good Theory." *Papers on Non-Market Decision Making* 3: 39–45.

Steck, Henry. 2003, January. "Corporatization of the University: Seeking Conceptual Clarity." *The Annals of the American Academy of Political and Social Science* 585 (1): 66–83.

Stevens, A. 2010. "Summary of Mission Statement Research." Unpublished, New York: CAE.

University of Michigan, College of Engineering, Division of Resource Planning and Management. 2004, August. *Understanding the UM Budget Model and CoE's Operating Budget*. Retrieved from the University of Michigan College of Engineering, Resources Planning and Management web site.

6 Leveling the Playing Field From College to Career

Preface

There is much to discuss and debate about the sources and effects of inequality on economic growth and social mobility, and the relationship between education and economic growth. However, an undergraduate degree from a highly selective and elite college gives students a strong advantage in gaining employment in jobs that promise greater lifetime earnings. The widely held assumption is that the prestige of the college is a useful proxy for the quality of the graduates of that institution. Irrespective of the relationship between education and economic growth, postsecondary education is imperative to the enhancement of human capital and a rich source of talent for employers. If there are significant bottlenecks, or structural impediments, that block equal opportunity for students of high ability that do not go to elite colleges, we should identify the problem and attempt to reduce or eliminate it (Fishkin, 2014).

In the United States, achieving equal opportunity in postsecondary education is typically described in terms of enrolling more underrepresented groups in selective colleges. The belief is that if this step is accomplished, it will have a fundamental impact on the problem of inequality at the national level. However, what if there are not enough places for students in selective colleges to accomplish this goal? What if selective colleges do not have enough capacity to make a significant impact on the problem of serving students from underrepresented groups with demonstrated high abilities? The rest of this chapter will address these questions.

Introduction

The postsecondary education sector is beset by a number of severe headwinds. Cost issues now elicit comparisons with the healthcare sector's cost problem. Access deficits continue to rise, and retention and graduation rates are unacceptable. Questions about the quality of education are increasing as well. Moreover, the rise of online and competency-based undergraduate programs, emerging across the for-profit, nonprofit, and public sectors, constitutes a disruptive force that threatens the business model of the traditional brick-and- mortar, postsecondary education sector.

However, it is important to remember that higher education was formed to achieve two principal objectives: 1) to provide education for students, encouraging them to achieve their highest intellectual potential and 2) to encourage faculty to teach and produce scholarship and research to their highest level of ability. A principal role, introduced by Thomas Jefferson, is for higher education to be the major source of social mobility for all citizens. This ideal was institutionalized as the Morrill Land Grant Act of 1862. It is this principle on which I focus here.

Today, the college that students attend largely determines their economic and social chances in life. The question is whether the level of prestige granted to a select group of institutions unduly restricts the ability of all students to benefit equally from the educational attainments they demonstrate. Do all graduating college seniors secure jobs commensurate with their skills?

If the answer is no, can we identify innovations that assist in leveling the playing field for all citizens?

Equal Opportunity, Not Equal Results

> [. . .] if Smith and Jones have the same native talent and Smith is born of wealthy, educated parents of a socially favored ethnicity and Jones is born of poor, uneducated parents of a socially disfavored ethnicity, then if they develop the same ambition to become scientists or Wall Street lawyers, they will have the same prospects of become scientists or Wall Street lawyers if equal fair opportunity prevails
>
> (Rawls, 2001, "A Theory of Justice," heading of section 13).

This statement captures how the concept of equal opportunity is used here.

Since the premise I am beginning with is that there is not a level playing field for all graduating college seniors, a basic question is: Why have we not attempted to create and implement innovations to deal with the problem until now? Here is a good answer:

> Goldman Sachs doesn't intrinsically care about Harvard. They care about finding the best person for the job. Elite brand degrees have just traditionally been the best proxy metrics for that because precise metrics weren't heretofore available.
>
> (Ferreira, 2013)

We now have more precise metrics that can be used to offset the power of the proxy of elite brand institutions. The rest of this paper suggests how we can benefit from using them. I will use the Collegiate Learning Assessment (CLA), in particular the recent next generation of this protocol, CLA+, for my illustrative argument because I am most familiar with this assessment.[1]

The Context for the Problem

If the absence of equal opportunity is the problem, can higher education be altered to create a more level playing field for all graduating college seniors? What is the premise behind this question? My argument is that, as in most countries, a set of selective colleges can be described as a positional good that determines the life chances of most students. The concept of positional good (Hirsch, 1976) describes goods that fall under the category of "zero sum," which means there are upper limits to their consumption. Only a finite number of people can attend a chamber music concert before it ceases to be one. The same thing is true about many other goods in life, including top positions in the private and public sector. The places at highly selective colleges are limited; by definition, a selective college would cease to be one if it grew beyond perceived enrollment limits. (This itself is a contentious point for some.) I will attempt to provide empirical evidence that selective colleges do not enroll the vast majority of high-ability students. If this hypothesis is borne out, we have a mal-distribution of our human capital at the societal level and an unequal playing field in the college-to-career space.

Second, are significant innovations in major social institutions, such as higher education, possible? The institution of higher education itself is rightly thought to be one of the major social institutions in American society, highly institutionalized and thus not easily transformed by outside disruptive forces. However, it is important to remember that humans create institutions and not the other way around (Harsanyi, 1969). Since the education system is the only venue we have to preserve and enhance human capital, it is prudent to audit it from time to time to judge whether it is in need of redesign. This is particularly true for U.S. postsecondary institutions because they have greater importance in today's Knowledge Economy, where national economies that strive to stay at the forefront of the new product-innovation cycle and the ideas that generate the highest economic value-added are the winners.

Finally, does educational technology provide new ways to innovate in postsecondary education? The reason this question is important is because education technology now provides a cornucopia of potential innovations for higher education institutions.

There are now technology-based solutions, including open-education resources, flipping classrooms, and adaptive and personalized instruction.

Advances in education-assessment tools, the reason for the innovation suggested here, has been stimulated by recent investments of over $360 million by the U.S. Department of Education in 21st century tests, in support of the Common Core movement in K–12 education. As a byproduct, new ways to use educational technology have led to novel assessments—such as interactive games—that give promise of being widely implemented.

Significant innovation, in support of institutional redesign of important segments of higher education institutions, is possible. We appear to be at a moment when we can think practically about re-engineering key processes to make the higher education sector more efficient and more effective.

The Case for a Market Failure

Today, going to college is the principal means to success in the United States. However, all postsecondary education institutions are not equal; a few are viewed as selective colleges. These colleges, with the Ivy Leagues at the apex, are examples of positional goods. Only a small percentage of college students enter and graduate from these colleges. Many leading companies recruit only from this group of colleges. The most selective colleges and universities have strong barriers to entry. Students who win enrollment to these colleges tend to have the advantage of significant financial and social support from early childhood through high school.

Parents, with the appropriate financial means, are willing to financially support their children in gaining the skills needed for admission to Yale because that gives their children entry into the select circle of society's "winners," economically and socially. They have the resources to compete for top public and private leadership positions that, by definition, are finite, in short supply, and possess a zero-sum quality. There typically is only one CEO of a company; one dean and one president, respectively, of a university; and so on. Of course, selective colleges have scholarships and affirmative action policies that permit them to enroll minority students, but the resources devoted to these policies are not enough to have a significant impact on creating a truly diverse student body.

The gap between the per-student endowment of Yale versus a public university, such as the City University of New York, is so large that it is difficult not to conclude that education at Yale is a very different student experience, which gives graduates huge lifelong advantages in their individual human-capital assets.[2] No one should want to harm Yale's ability to deliver an education of the highest quality. However, as the support for public higher education wanes across the United States, we must be prepared for even greater economic and social inequality, less social mobility, less diversity, and, in all likelihood, less economic growth. Why? Because the selective colleges may not supply a sufficient critical mass of educated citizens to maintain the U.S. human-capital comparative advantage globally. We should examine what might be done about this issue.

The rich diversity of American postsecondary education is correctly cited as a unique strength. However, just as we made significant changes in admissions requirements for college applicants in the aftermath of World War II by creating admissions tests, such as the SAT and ACT, to complement the high school GPA, we now face the need to create a test to complement the graduating college senior's GPA. We should do so to reset the opportunity structure held in place by the positional-good world of postsecondary education (Hirsch, 1976). However, we should not attack selective colleges but design a way to widen the opportunity structure for students in less- selective colleges. Why should we do this now?

The positional-good system of selective colleges may have made sense in an earlier age of American development, but with a population of over 320 million (soon to be 400 million in three or four decades), the bulk of whom live well outside the geographic reach of most of the selective colleges, we need to dramatically expand the opportunity system created by postsecondary education. This is especially true for underrepresented high-ability students because they appear to attend less-selective colleges in overwhelming numbers. What follows is an attempt to justify this problem statement and suggest a way to attack it.

The Problem to Solve

Hoxby and Avery (2012) demonstrate that as many as 10–15 times the number of African-American and Hispanic students as previously thought have SAT or ACT scores that meet the admissions requirements of the most prestigious colleges in the United States. However, these students are often advised not to apply to selective schools and attend high schools not visited by college recruiters from elite institutions. If we did not have the SAT and ACT in place, admissions officers would only have students' high school GPAs to rely upon for admissions decisions. There likely would be even fewer students from underrepresented groups admitted to the most selective colleges because the SAT and ACT provides important additional information to students' high school GPAs (Kobrin et al., 2008).

College to work presents a more severe market failure because there are no tests to accompany students' college cumulative GPAs that could control for the grade inflation and variability of grades across colleges. Such a test could assist in leveling the playing field for students from less-selective colleges without damaging the prospects from selective colleges.

Students

Grade inflation has resulted in the national mean college cumulative senior GPA rising to 3.3 (on a four-point scale) (Rojstaczer and Healy, 2012).

This means that most graduating seniors do not have an objective way of distinguishing their skills from other students when they apply for jobs; they are all above average. Students who attend the top 150 selective institutions are likely to get a pass because many employers will choose students based on institutional prestige. However, what about the others, the 90+%of graduating seniors who attend less-selective institutions? Moreover, what about the most disadvantaged students? There are many low-income students who graduate from these colleges and universities that have the critical-thinking skills and abilities that employers cherish.

Colleges

Less-selective colleges produce many college graduates who achieve distinction in their careers. However, they face a branding problem. Since these colleges do not have reliable tools that make the case for their stronger graduating seniors, employers may never discover their students. Less-selective colleges, in particular, should consider recommending that their graduating seniors take CLA+. This should increase the number of their graduates at the peak of the value-added economic product cycle. If this turns out to be the case, less-selective colleges will change employers' preconceived notions about their graduates and the colleges that produce them.

In sum, the market failure between graduating college seniors in less-selective colleges seeking employment and employers is blocking hundreds of thousands of students from attaining employment appropriate for the high-ability skills they have attained. Too many students do not get to interview for jobs for which they have the skills because employers are unaware of them. This is bad for the students in question, their institutions, and employers. At the macro level, it means too much of our human capital is mal-distributed. And it also is a major block to opportunities for high-ability students from disadvantaged backgrounds who attain skill levels equivalent to their selective-college counterparts.

Employers

Employers spend much time and money interviewing potential applicants for jobs. Some employers give applicants assessments on the skills and abilities they require in their employees. However, in the age of grade inflation, how do hiring managers decide who to interview in the first place? If, in addition to résumés and college transcripts, hiring managers have the results of a valid and reliable critical-thinking test, their pool of potential applicants would be enlarged. The employment process would be more effective and efficient, and employers would be better equipped to tap the social, economic, and ethnic diversity of students reflected in all our colleges and universities.

Increasingly, employers have been forced to ask applicants to send their SAT/ACT scores or Graduate Management Admission Test (GMAT) scores along with their résumé because the high level of grade inflation means the transcripts of graduating seniors do not supply sufficient information about the job candidates' skills. This is unacceptable. The GMAT, a solid critical-thinking test, is targeted for a small population of students applying for business-school programs. The SAT is not an acceptable measure for the skill levels college seniors have achieved, for two reasons. First, reliance on a test that applicants took before they entered college means no credit is given to the effect of the college experience. This not only unacceptable, it is not credible. We know from analysis of the CLA database that the overall mean student-learning growth for college students from freshmen to seniors is .73 (a .44 standard deviation). This finding is based on analysis of all students taking the CLA in over 1,200 test administrations over the past eight years. This is a significant effect. College does matter to student-learning growth, and it matters a lot (see Benjamin, 2014). We should not assume that college does not matter. Moreover, we should not ignore the strong probability that many of these same students and their Hispanic and non-Hispanic white counterparts who attend less-selective colleges exhibit above-average growth in their critical-thinking skills as a result of their college experience, even if they do not attend highly selective colleges.

The Challenge

The results of a reliable and valid prescreening assessment of graduating college seniors might provide suitable information to enlarge the pool of potential applicants for employers. If less-selective colleges produce many college graduates that achieve high levels of the skills employers cherish and can overcome the problem of employers not knowing how to find these students, these institutions will change the perception of employers about their graduates and the colleges that produce them.

The hypothesis, then, is that less-selective colleges graduate a large number of high-ability students (as defined by appropriate standardized assessments), as many or more students than the selective colleges that serve as the proxy for excellence.

Validating the Market Failure Thesis

There is at least one data set that may be useful for this purpose: the data set of the Collegiate Learning Assessment (CLA and CLA+). There are two other reliable assessments in the graduating senior space, the ETS's Proficiency Profile and ACT's Collegiate Assessment of Academic Progress (CAAP), that are also potentially appropriate for this purpose.

What is CLA+? Is it reliable and valid? CLA+ measures critical-thinking skills, regarded as the top priority by employers (Hart Associates, 2013). The protocol incudes six subscores:

- Analysis and problem solving
- Writing mechanics
- Writing effectiveness
- Scientific and quantitative reasoning
- Critical reading and evaluation
- Argument critique

These cognitive skills are independent from academic disciplines and are teachable. They are thought to be particularly important skills in today's Knowledge Economy where one can Google for facts and, hence, the question becomes whether the student can access, structure, and use information, not just whether he or she can remember the content; these skills are highly prized by faculty and college leaders who, like their K–12 counterparts, are moving toward "deeper" learning (Benjamin, 2014).[3]

CLA, and the updated CLA+, has been used in over 700 colleges and universities in the United States, many testing on an annual basis since 2004–05. It has been used internationally in approximately 125 colleges in 12 different countries.

Figure 6.1 indicates that 68% of the students fall within one standard deviation of the mean score 1,159. The question is how many of the students scoring in the top 10%, 25%, and 50% are in selective versus less-selective colleges (see Appendix C).

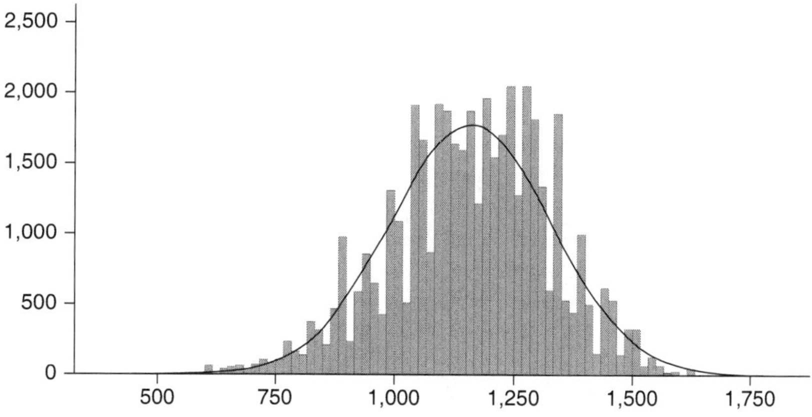

Figure 6.1 Distribution of Senior CLA Scores

CLA Score

Table 6.1 Proportion of Selective versus Less-Selective Institutions

	Colleges & Universities		*Student Enrollment*	
	1980	*2012*	*1980*	*2012*
Selective	143 (5%)	143 (5%)	762,248 (12%)	940,771 (9%)
Less-Selective	3,014 (95%)	3,014 (95%)	5,584,841 (88%)	9,823,718 (91%)
ALL	3,157 (100%)	3,157 (100%)	6,347,089 (100%)	10,764,489 (100%)

Table 6.1 was constructed to set the context for our test of whether a market failure exists. Over the past 30-plus years, the number of students in the 143 selective colleges has grown by 171,000. Over that same time period, the number of students attending less-selective colleges has grown by over 4,200,000. The largest growth in four-year college attendance is in the less- selective colleges.

The list of selective colleges is based on Barron's selectivity college index (see Appendices C and D), the same index used by Hoxby and Avery (2012). Of course, any division of colleges and universities into selective and less-selective categories can be challenged. For example, today Indiana University, the University of California, San Diego, and private liberal arts colleges such as Earlham College and Kalamazoo College would appear to warrant the label selective. Barron's selectivity index reflects judgments based on past performances that may not capture recent trends. Based on the analyses here, the list of selective colleges itself should be widened. See Appendix C for information on the data sources. Note that the numbers above for the Colleges and Universities column do not necessarily reflect all four-year, degree-granting colleges and universities in existence in 1980 and 2012; these numbers come from an enrollment data set from the Integrated Postsecondary Education Data System (IPEDS), so there may be institutions not included here simply because they did not provide enrollment data to IPEDS.

Using the percentages of students above 1,400, above 1,300, and above 1,200, Table 6.2 shows that selective colleges produce a higher percentage (24%) of students above 1,400 than the less-selective colleges (6%). However, there are almost twice as many high-ability students graduating from less-selective colleges above the 1,400 level. The proportion of high-ability students in the less-selective colleges grows for students testing above 1,300 and 1,200 (see Graph 6.1). The less-selective colleges have large percentages of low-income (Pell Grant) and moderate-income students from diverse backgrounds.

The map shows that the selective colleges are isolated from most students in the United States. The 143 selective colleges, largely in the

Table 6.2 Projected National CLA Performance

A *Actual* *CLA Performance*	*Exiting Seniors at CLA Institutions*		
	Selective Institutions	*Less-selective Institutions*	*ALL*
Above 1,400*	395 (24%)	2,631 (6%)	3,026 (7%)
Above 1,300	841 (52%)	8,001 (18%)	8,842 (20%)
Above 1,200	1,284 (79%)	17,956 (41%)	19,240 (43%)
ALL	1,627 (100%)	43,352 (100%)	44,979 (100%)

* These scale points are based on the CLA scale, which, like the "old" and upcoming SAT, ranges from 400 to 1,600.

B *Projected National CLA Performance*	*Bachelor's Degree Recipients Nationally (2011–12) and Projected CLA Performance*		
	Selective Institutions	*Less-selective Institutions*	*ALL*
Above 1,400	53,307 (24%)	95,295 (6%)	148,602 (8%)
Above 1,300	113,497 (52%)	289,796 (18%)	403,293 (23%)
Above 1,200	173,282 (79%)	650,365 (41%)	823,648 (46%)
ALL	219,572 (100%)	1,570,207 (100%)	1,789,779 (100%)

* Note that the total national percentages differ somewhat from the percentages of students at all CLA institutions scoring at given levels, due to a slight underrepresentation of selective colleges taking the CLA.

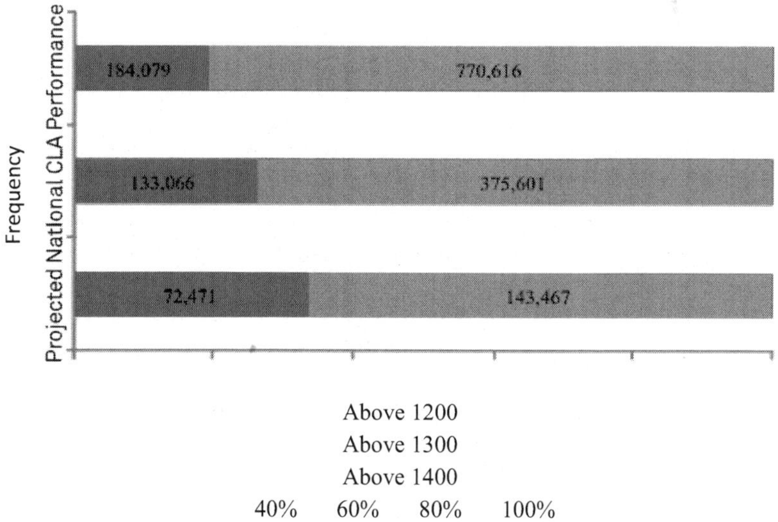

Graph 6.1 Projected National CLA Performance

Graph 6.2 Geographic Distribution of Selective and Less-Selective Colleges

Table 6.3 Distribution of Students' Race and Ethnicity by Institutional Selectivity, 1980 and 2012

	Students		*1980*		*2012*	
	ALL 1980	*ALL 2012*	*Selective Institutions*	*Less-Selective Institutions*	*Selective Institutions*	*Less-Selective Institutions*
Non-Hispanic White	81%	56%	86%	81%	58%	56%
Hispanic	5%	13%	3%	5%	9%	13%
Black or African-American	9%	13%	5%	10%	5%	13%
Asian or Pacific Islander	2%	6%	4%	2%	13%	5%
Other	3%	13%	3%	3%	15%	12%

northeast, form a positional-good gatekeeper system that overly determines the life chances of all students across the country. We know most students attend college within commuting distance. The location of the selective colleges means there is a disconnect with large and growing ethnic/racial and income groups throughout the United States.

Table 6.3 provides further evidence of the market-failure challenge. First, there has been a significant change in distribution of race and ethnicity by institutional selectivity from 1980 to 2012. The selective colleges are more diverse. The main point, however, is that the increasingly small proportion of total college enrollment made up by selective colleges reinforces the market-failure thesis. The major growth of enrollment is in the less-selective college group.

Possible Solution

The goal is to develop tools that allow for the demonstration of skills that are important for both employers and students and to make that information accessible to students and employers.

CAE has developed a data mining tool, labeled "CLA+ as a Work Readiness Prescreening Tool in the College-to-Career Space" (see Appendix A). It is being piloted to see if it can reduce the market failure.

Each student receives a score report that indicates the level of mastery for skills measured by CLA+. Qualifying students (those with proficient or advanced-mastery levels) may claim a certified badge through a secure vault hosted by Pro Exam. Students will be able to store their score reports with online transcript service providers and place their CLA+ scores on employment boards. In a pilot, qualifying students (those with top scores) were invited to a virtual career fair, hosted by Brazen Careerist in May 2014, to meet with selected employers. Employers who attended the virtual career fair did so knowing that the students they met possess the mastery level critical-thinking skills they regard as requisites for an interview. Moreover, they knew that they met many students who have

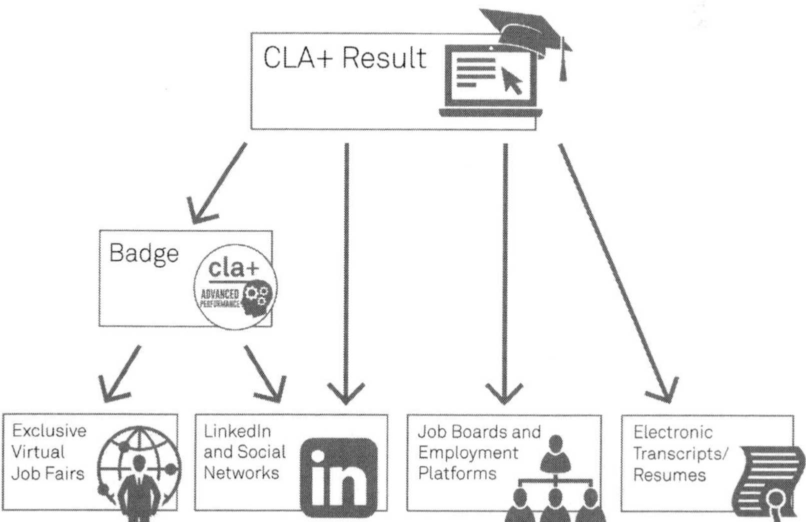

Figure 6.2 The CLA+ CareerConnect System Between Graduating Seniors and Employers

the diverse backgrounds they are seeking to diversify their workforce. Both employers and students saved time and money through the virtual career fair meeting.

The steps outlined above are possible for graduating seniors who take CLA+ and elect to add the additional information to their transcript; secure a certified badge, if eligible; and send their results to respected jobs boards accessed by employers. If students qualify, they can also attend a virtual career fair, all of which will improve the odds of high-ability students in less- selective colleges obtaining a good job and starting a promising career.

Benefits of a More Level Playing Field

When groups do not believe the playing field is level, they become discouraged and drop out. If enough students, enough colleges, and enough employers embrace the innovation outlined here, then the market failure will be reduced. Most economists agree that an open, transparent market brings greater benefits to buyers and sellers. Ways to reduce the "noise" between college and career should thus be encouraged. This would result in a better distribution of human capital and a more level playing field.

Conclusion

Olson's collective action model (1965) suggests that new innovations are needed to help create a more level playing field. We cannot expect stakeholders at the selective colleges to deal with the problem alone. New innovations are needed to reset the rules of the game that students, employers, and colleges operate within. There is a strong case for use of an appropriate standardized assessment to provide graduating college seniors and employers with additional information about their critical-thinking skills. Such an assessment could be used as a sourcing tool by employers, which would be of assistance to them and the students they identify assisted by the measurement tool.

The "tunnel effect," formulated by economists Hirschman and Rothschild (1973), suggests why a more level playing field for careers encourages members of all ethnic/racial groups to compete/work hard. Imagine you are in the left-hand line of two lanes of traffic held up in the Lincoln Tunnel. Frustration builds. Finally, cars in the right-hand lane begin to move. What are your emotions then? Hirschman posits that you are excited and now positive about the possibility that your lane of traffic is next to move. You see light at the end of the tunnel. However, what are your reactions when your lane does not move forward? You realize that while cars in lane 2 moved forward, your lane is stuck. You are stuck. That is when feelings of anger or despair set in. The United States is only one example of the market failure. Based on countries in which I have lived, many countries probably exhibit significant disconnects between their higher education systems and employment. Because many countries may face similar market failures between college and career, as outlined in this case study of the U.S., research programs should be formed to refute or corroborate the points I have made and create new evidence-based findings on the topic across nations.

Most importantly, the principle of equal opportunity is widely shared in liberal democracies (Hartz, 1955). "Equality has always been the most radical and potent idea in American history" (Wood, 2014, p. 38). If it is problematic in the college senior-to-career space for many students to find jobs appropriate to their skills, then that is a serious problem that we need to fix. Today, we have metrics to measure the quality of the skills that colleges and employers indicate they covet.

We also have education-technology-based tools to more quickly inform employers and students about the cognitive skills required for jobs and the skills that students have that appear to meet those requirements.

The market failure problem between graduating college seniors and employers should be very high on the policy agenda to solve by both private and public stakeholders involved. It is a matter of significant national interest to more efficiently allocate the nation's human capital, the only resource any nation has, and to improve equal opportunity, which is key to improving economic and social equality.

Appendix A

The Case for CLA+ CareerConnect as a Work Readiness Prescreening Tool in the College-to-Career Space

CLA+ CareerConnect has three distinct but interrelated purposes for the three principal stakeholders in the college-to-career space: employers, students, and colleges. All three goals are intended to reduce the market failure that has resulted in a disconnect between colleges and employers and between graduating college students and employers. The first purpose is to provide a prescreening tool for employers. The second purpose is to validate, augment, and frame the growing number of credentials, organized as digital badges, for students. Colleges and their instructors may also use CLA+ to validate the badges they produce. The third purpose is to validate the crucial role colleges have in producing students with the proficiency in critical-thinking skills that professors and employers agree are requisites for success in the workplace.

The premise of utilizing CLA+ CareerConnect as a prescreening tool is that additional credible information about the overall critical-thinking skills of students is needed to accompany the information provided by college transcripts. Only a standardized test that measures critical-thinking skills, such as CLA+, which is widely seen by the measurement science community as reliable and valid, is appropriate for this purpose. It is crucial for tests that are built by measurement scientists to be reliable and valid in scientific terms to accompany the rich, granular information provided by digital badges and workplace assessments.

CLA+ as a Prescreening Tool for Tests for Employers

A large amount of time and energy has been spent designing assessments employers can use to make hiring decisions. Therefore, most of the attention devoted to assessments for work readiness is focused on the human resources department. Although assessment protocols for human resource departments may be tailored to meet a specific employer's needs, the assessment categories may be divided as follows:

Aptitude tests—predictive of job success in specific fields and focus on abilities, such as spatial visualization, verbal conceptualization, and math aptitude. These tests are expensive, time consuming, and must be updated frequently to remain aligned with changing job requirements.

Personality tests—"instruments for the measurement of emotional, motivational, interpersonal and attitudinal characteristics as distinguished from abilities" (Anastasi and Urbina, 1997). For example, characteristics such as one's openness to experience, extroversion, agreeableness, conscientiousness, emotional stability, wellbeing, and/or happiness are measured.

Academic discipline tests—tests of content knowledge for particular fields and domains. For example, these tests help answer questions like: Does an applicant for a position in accounting have the requisite content knowledge to do the job?

Cognitive abilities tests—assess critical-thinking or cognitive skills (see below), but these tests are also extended to soft skills such as persistence, collaboration, entrepreneurship, creativity, collaboration, and moral or ethical reasoning (Kraiger et al., 1993).

The most prominent example of a work readiness assessment is ACT's WorkKeys (2014), which comprises a combination of these types of tests. This test, crafted to predict job success in thousands of occupations, most of which are in the sub-baccalaureate market, requires applicants to demonstrate familiarity with the skills needed for success in the occupation, but the test also predicts the ability of applicants to succeed.

The Criteria for the Evaluation of Tests

No matter what combination of test items make up an assessment protocol, reliability and validity, along with time and cost, are always the basic criteria used to evaluate the test.

Validity concerns the extent to which the test measures the knowledge, skills, and abilities it is designed to measure. Reliability refers to the degree of consistency of students' scores across a test's questions, the consistency of scores across different assessors, and whether the tests are given to students under the same conditions and over the same time period and therefore meet the essential criterion of fairness (Klein, 2002). The measurement science community views these two criteria as necessary for an effective assessment.

Time and cost are also crucial. Assessments that require more than two hours are restricted to high-stakes tests, such as the SAT, MCAT (medical school), and LSAT (law school). Tests that cost more than $75 to $100 are products for niche markets; for example, certification tests for specialized professional fields such as piloting an airplane.

The types of tests listed above vary on the criteria noted. Aptitude tests are costly and time consuming to administer. Academic discipline tests, geared toward specific fields, are possible to administer, but it is not easy to compare potential applicants across diverse fields. Personality tests are used widely but are not considered highly reliable by the measurement science community (Stabile, 2002).

Cognitive abilities tests are not only considered a significant requisite for employment success, they are the only tests with sufficiently high levels of reliability and validity (as defined by measurement scientists) that permit wide comparisons across all graduating college seniors and are also efficient in testing time and cost. Cognitive abilities can also be defined as critical- thinking skills, which are regarded as the top priority by employers (Hart Research Associates, 2013). Faculty surveys also place these cognitive abilities at the top of requirements for graduating college seniors (Hart Research Associates, 2013). Moreover, most colleges feature these skills in their mission statements or general education goals.

Three assessment organizations, ETS, ACT, and CAE, cooperated in a test validity study of the two multiple-choice tests that assess these critical-thinking skills developed by ETS and ACT, respectively, and the performance-based assessment developed by CAE. All were judged reliable and valid by the measurement scientists at these three education assessment organizations. However, this does not mean, necessarily, that all of the assessments measure the same criteria (Steedle et al., 2010).

Many have suggested that measures of soft skills, such as entrepreneurship, collaboration, creativity, and moral or ethical reasoning, should be added to the above list of prioritized cognitive skills. These additional measures have not yet received the endorsement of the measurement science community in regards to reliability and validity (see Hersh et al., 2008). Therefore, adding the soft cognitive skills to the above listed cognitive skills must wait for the research and development process to prove their reliability and validity. Therefore, development and implementation of combinations of the above types of tests for use by human resources departments to make hiring decisions will remain a long-term, perhaps ongoing, set of issues to solve.

The Case for a Prescreening Assessment

Given the numerous combinations of work-readiness assessments and the difficulties involved in designing assessment protocols that meet the minimum conditions required by the four criteria of reliability, validity, time, and cost, it is understandable that a healthy debate is underway to clarify which strategy, or strategies, make the most sense for developing assessments that meet the needs of human resource departments. However, the implication of the market failure argument presented here suggests the emphasis on assessments for human resource departments is not the most urgent problem on which to focus.

Employers indicate there is a significant skills gap in the United States. There are an estimated 10–20 million vacant jobs in the U.S. (Economic

Modeling Specialists International, 2014). The number of places for students in selective colleges remains static at under one million (see Baron's selectivity index, 2014). Employers need methods to distinguish the large number of students from less-selective colleges that display the requisite skills to succeed in the professional world. A significant increase in hiring high-ability students from less-selective colleges for competitive jobs would increase the motivation for additional students in these colleges to work harder to succeed.

Meeting the Occam's Razor Test

CLA+ CareerConnect is built upon the foundation of the Collegiate Learning Assessment (CLA+), an assessment subjected to more than a decade of critical scrutiny by members of the measurement science community (see Chapter 9). The result is a test that is viewed as reliable and valid. The time (90 minutes) and cost (less than $50) required to take CLA+ are reasonable. The CareerConnect system, based on education technology innovations, brings employers and eligible students together efficiently at little or no cost to either party. CLA+ CareerConnect therefore meets the Occam's razor requirement that metrics should deal with the most significant problem and not be multiplied unnecessarily to deal with it.

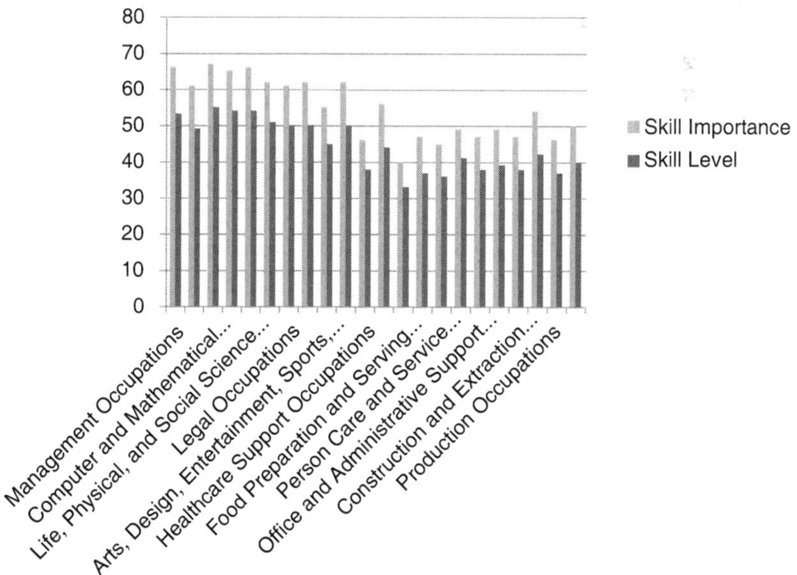

Figure 6.3 The Large Number of Fields That Require a Bachelor's Degree
(O*Net Data Base, Bureau of Labor Statistics)

The case to use a widely accepted critical-thinking test such as CLA+ as an additional tool to prescreen potential applicants to determine who employers should consider interviewing is compelling. Unlike suggestions that colleges and universities change their mission to focus on preparing students for jobs, the goal of CLA+ CareerConnect is to bring many more high-ability graduating seniors to the attention of employers. Since colleges and professors emphasize that critical-thinking skills are central to their mission, CLA+ CareerConnect is aligned to a central premise that the vast majority of colleges already embrace. The critical-thinking skills measured by CLA+ capture a large percentage of skills desired by employers in a large number of fields that require a bachelor's degree, as defined in the Bureau of Labor Statistics O*NET database (National Center for O*NET Development, 2014). CAE proposes using CLA+, then, as a prescreening tool to reduce the "noise" between the employer and the applicants, particularly the graduating college seniors starting their job searches.

CLA+ Can Be Used to Evaluate Digital Badges

Badges are secure, verified, Internet-based credentials that include information used to interpret the badge outcomes. Badge data include:

- The outcomes required to earn the badge and the evidence earners provided to demonstrate their competence
- Qualifications of the sponsor or sponsoring organization

CLA+ can be used to evaluate the efficacy of the badge by providing evidence about the student's skills as documented by a badge and CLA+ scores that measure larger skills sets such as critical thinking, problem solving, quantitative and qualitative reasoning, and writing skills. The CLA+ mastery levels attained by the student provides a verification of the student's badge because the CLA+ scores should be aligned with the skill levels documented by a badge. Here is the case for a third-party role for a standardized test such as CLA+ to help employers interpret badges.

Benefits of Badges

1. College degrees and their transcripts are difficult to interpret. The same B.A. degree can be conferred for very different courses of study at different schools and sometimes for different graduating students at the same school. In a college transcript, information about course outcomes is not specific or transparent enough to help employers understand how courses map to the specific knowledge or skills required for career success.
2. College grades are subjective and can be a low-quality indicator of actual competence. At best, they can provide a general idea of how well a student has performed. But there is a growing sense

that grade inflation is making the college GPA unreliable for employers. Competency-based criteria that map learning to job requirements effectively complement the grades on a college transcript, thus providing better information for employers evaluating candidates.

3. As noted previously, the reputation of the institution drives the value of a degree, not work readiness. Graduates of selective colleges benefit the most from the brand of their college. However, every college graduate in less-selective colleges stands to benefit from classroom learning outcomes directly connected to standardized work activities and job-related skills.
4. College transcripts and degrees do not include the skills or knowledge acquired outside the classroom at places such as part-time jobs, internships, or campus- related activities.

Benefits for Employers, Students, and Colleges

Employers, students, and colleges stand to benefit from the badge movement for a number of reasons. The information about the skill level a student obtains in a class on software or computer language, accounting, nonparametric statistics, or game theory can be directly interpreted by an employer. Students, perhaps especially in less-selective colleges, also can benefit significantly from the badges they achieve. They can show potential employers that they have the specific skills that align with career success. The colleges can also benefit from joining the badge movement. College instructors are already the source of many new badges based on the classroom learning their students are achieving. Colleges can aggregate the badges their instructors have developed to demonstrate how their institutions are directly impacting the workforce opportunities of their students.

In short, badges are an important emerging tool that will assist in reducing the "noise" the market failure produces, which, in turn, is leading to an increasing mal-distribution of human capital at the national level and greater inequality at the individual-student level.

The Problems Digital Badges Need to Overcome

The management of identity issues has been a hurdle. As colleges and others begin to issue digital credentials, they need to confirm earner identity and protect the integrity of the credentials they issue. How can the employer judge the validity of the student's badge? How can employers equate different badges that purport to measure the same skills? These and other issues for the burgeoning badge movement suggest a role for an appropriate standardized test that can be used to evaluate the efficacy of badges.

The Role of CLA+ CareerConnect

CLA+ CareerConnect was created as a prescreening tool to increase the pool of highly qualified talent for employers, controlling for the positional-good bias of the current system of higher education that overly benefits students who go to the most selective colleges but comprise less than 10% of all college students. CLA+ CareerConnect gives the large number of high-ability graduating college seniors in less-selective colleges—approximately 1.2 million each year—a greater opportunity to compete for the high value-added jobs for which their critical-thinking skill levels qualify them. CLA+ benchmarks the minimum standards of critical thinking that colleges and employers both regard as requisite for college graduation and success in the workplace. Moreover, CLA+ CareerConnect is well suited to verify the trustworthiness and authenticity of the badges students put forward to employers. Each student taking CLA+ is monitored by an Internet-based test security organization to verify the student taking the test is the individual supposed to be taking the test and does not cheat. Therefore, CLA+ results can be used to corroborate and verify the disparate badges for which authenticity and identity may be problematic.[4]

Appendix B

See numerous studies of reliability and validity listed and analyzed in Chapter 7. Also see Arum and Roksa (2014), which shows that students who did well on the CLA are in better financial situations and have much less unemployment five years after graduation than students who scored low on the CLA.

Appendix C

Data Sources:

National college data were obtained from the National Center for Education Statistics, IPEDS website (http://nces.ed.gov/ipeds/datacenter//), and represent institutional enrollment, bachelor's degrees awarded, and race/ethnicity data for all four-year, degree-granting institutions in the database for the years 1980 and 2012. Note that enrollment data are not available for all institutions; these data were reported for 1,826 institutions in 1980 and 2,806 institutions in 2012.

CLA performance data are from all U.S. four-year institutions that tested seniors in spring 2011, 2012, and 2013.

Selective institutions consist of those identified by Heller (2004). Note that three of the institutions in Heller's list—all part of Rutgers University—are considered a single institution by NCES, so the count of selective universities is smaller here (N=143 versus N=146). Heller's list is based on information provided by Barron's selectivity college index (Baron's Profiles of American Colleges, 2014).

Appendix D

Selective Colleges and Universities:

Amherst College, MA
Austin College, TX
Babson College, MA
Barnard College, NY
Bates College, ME
Beloit College, WI
Boston College, MA
Boston University, MA
Bowdoin College, ME
Brandeis University, MA
Brigham Young University-Provo, UT
Brown University, RI
Bryn Mawr College, PA
Bucknell University, PA
California Institute of Technology, CA
Carleton College, MN
Carnegie Mellon University, PA
Case Western Reserve University, OH
Claremont McKenna College, CA
Colby College, ME
Colgate University, NY
College of the Atlantic, ME
College of the Holy Cross, MA
College of William and Mary, VA
Colorado College, CO
Colorado School of Mines, CO
Columbia University in the City of New York, NY
Connecticut College, CT
Cooper Union for the Advancement of Science and Art, NY
Cornell University, NY
Dartmouth College, NH

Davidson College, NC
Drew University, NJ Duke University, NC
Emory University, GA
Franklin and Marshall College, PA
Furman University, SC
George Washington University, DC
Georgetown University, DC
Georgia Institute of Technology-Main Campus, GA
Gettysburg College, PA
Grinnell College, IA
Grove City College, PA
Hamilton College, NY
Hampshire College, MA
Harvard University, MA
Harvey Mudd College, CA
Haverford College, PA
Illinois Institute of Technology, IL
Illinois Wesleyan University, IL
Jewish Theological Seminary of America, NY
Johns Hopkins University, MD
Kenyon College, OH
Kettering University, MI
Knox College, IL
Lafayette College, PA
Lawrence University, WI
Lehigh University, PA
Loyola University Maryland, MD
Lyon College, AR
Macalester College, MN
Massachusetts Institute of Technology, MA
Miami University-Oxford, OH
Middlebury College, VT
Mount Holyoke College, MA
New College of Florida, FL
New York University, NY
Northwestern University, IL
Oberlin College, OH
Pennsylvania State University-Main Campus, PA
Pepperdine University, CA
Pitzer College, CA
Pomona College, CA
Princeton University, NJ
Providence College, RI
Reed College, OR
Rhodes College, TN

Rice University, TX
Rose-Hulman Institute of Technology, IN
Rutgers University-New Brunswick, NJ
Saint Louis University-Main Campus, MO
Santa Clara University, CA
Sarah Lawrence College, NY
Scripps College, CA
Sewanee-The University of the South, TN
Skidmore College, NY
Smith College, MA
Southwestern University, TX
St, Mary's College of Maryland, MD
St. Olaf College, MN
Stanford University, CA
Stevens Institute of Technology, NJ
SUNY at Binghamton, NY
SUNY College at Geneseo, NY
SUNY College of Environmental Science and Forestry, NY
Swarthmore College, PA
Syracuse University, NY
The College of New Jersey, NJ
Trinity College, CT
Trinity University, TX
Tufts University, MA
Tulane University of Louisiana, LA
Union College, NY
United States Air Force Academy, CO
United States Coast Guard Academy, CT
United States Merchant Marine Academy, NY
United States Military Academy, NY
United States Naval Academy, MD
University of California-Berkeley, CA
University of California-Davis, CA
University of California-Los Angeles, CA
University of California-Santa Barbara, CA
University of Chicago, IL
University of Florida, FL
University of Georgia, GA
University of Illinois at Urbana-Champaign, IL
University of Mary Washington, VA
University of Miami, FL
University of Michigan-Ann Arbor, MI
University of North Carolina at Chapel Hill, NC
University of Notre Dame, IN
University of Pennsylvania, PA

University of Puget Sound, WA
University of Richmond, VA
University of Rochester, NY
University of Southern California, CA
University of Virginia-Main Campus, VA
University of Wisconsin-Madison, WI
Ursinus College, PA
Vanderbilt University, TN
Vassar College, NY
Villanova University, PA
Wake Forest University, NC
Washington and Lee University, VA
Washington University in St Louis, MO
Webb Institute, NY
Wellesley College, MA Wesleyan College, GA
Wheaton College, IL
Whitman College, WA
Williams College, MA
Worcester Polytechnic Institute, MA
Yale University, CT

Notes

1. The other two national assessments are Proficiency Profile (Educational Testing Service) and The Collegiate Assessment of Academic Progress (ACT). These three critical-thinking tests were found to be reliable and valid in a test validity study sponsored by the Department of Education, Fund for the Improvement of Postsecondary Education. See Klein et al. (2009) cf. Steedle et al. (2010).
2. The per-student endowment at Yale University is $1,750,000 while the per-student endowment at the City University of New York ranges from a few hundred dollars at Medgar Evers College to $9,000 at Baruch College. Voluntary Support of Education, VSE Data Miner, cae.org
3. For evidence of reliability and validity, see the studies listed and analyzed in Chapter 9. For important new validity evidence see Arum and Roksa (2014), which shows that graduating seniors who do well on CLA+ are in better financial situations and are more likely to be employed than students who do poorly on CLA+
4. For more detailed information about the digital badge movement, see Educause.edu (2012). Seven Things You Should Know About Badges; cf. Pearson Vue.com. (2015).

References

ACT. 2014. *Work Keys*. Iowa City, IOWA: ACT.

Anastasi, Anne, and Susana Urbina. 1997. *Psychological Testing* (7th ed.). Upper Saddle River, NJ: Prentice Hall.

Arum, Richard, and Roksa. 2014. *Aspiring Adults Adrift: Tentative Transitions of College Graduates*. Chicago, IL: University of Chicago Press.

Barron's Profiles of American Colleges. 2014. New York: Barron's.

Benjamin, Roger. 2014. "Two Questions About Critical-Thinking Tests in Higher Education." *Change: The Magazine of Higher Learning* 46 (2), 24–31.

Economic Modeling Specialists Intl. 2014. *The Skills Gap: A National Issue that Requires a Regional Focus* (New Skills At Work Report). New York, NY: JPMorgan Chase & Co.

Educause.edu. 2012. *Seven Things You Should Know About Badges.*

Ferreira, Jose. 2013. *Disruptive Innovation versus Harvard: Who Will Win?* [Web log post]. Accessed September 5, www.linkedin.com/today/post/article/20130905152238-5048055-disruptive-innovation-vs-harvard-who-will-win.

Fishkin, Joseph. 2014. *Bottlenecks: A New Theory of Equal Opportunity.* Oxford: Oxford University Press.

Heller, Donald. 2004. "Pell Grant Recipients in Selective Colleges and Universities." In *America's Untapped Resource: Low-Income Students in Higher Education*, edited by R.D. Kahlenberg, 157–66. New York: The Century Foundation Press.

Hersh, Richard H., Matt Bundick, Richard Keeling, Corey Keyes, Amy Kurpius, Richard Shavelson, Daniel Silverman, and Lynn Swaner. 2008. "A Well-rounded Education for a Flat World." *Paper Presented at the Leadership Coalition: President's Symposium*, Washington D.C. https://www2.cortland.edu/dotAsset/197175.pdf

Hirsch, Fred. 1976. *Social Limits to Growth.* Cambridge, MA: Harvard University Press.

Harsanyi, John C. 1969. "Rational-choice Models of Political Behavior vs. Functionalist and Conformist Theories." *World Politics* 21 (4): 513–38.

Hart Research Associates. 2013. *It Takes More than a Major: Employer Priorities for College Learning and Student Success.* www.aacu.org/leap/documents/2013_EmployerSurvey.pdf

Hartz, Louis. 1955. *The Liberal Tradition in America: An Interpretation of American Political Thought since the Revolution.* Boston, MA: Harcourt Brace.

Hirschman, Albert O., and Michael Rothschild. 1973, November. "The Changing Tolerance for Economic Inequality in the Course of Economic Development." *Quarterly Journal of Economics* 87 (4): 544–66.

Hoxby, Caroline, and Christopher Avery. 2012. "The Missing 'one-offs': The Hidden Supply of High-achieving, Low-income Students." *NBER Working Paper No. 18586.* Cambridge, MA: National Bureau of Economic Research.

Klein, Steve. 2002. "2002Direct Assessment of Cumulative Student Learning." *Peer Review* 4 (2/3): 26–8.

Klein, Steve, Lydia Ou Liu, James Sconing, Roger Bolus, Brent Bridgeman, Heather Kugelmass. 2009. *Test Validity Study (TVS) Report.* Supported by the Fund for the Improvement of Postsecondary Education, U.S. Department of Education. www.voluntarysystem.org/docs/reports/TVSReport_Final pdf.

Kobrin, Jennifer L., Brian F. Patterson, Emily J. Shaw, Krista D. Mattern, and Sandra M. Barbuti. 2008. *Validity of the SAT for Predicting First Year College Grade Point Average* (College Board Research Report No. 2008–5). Accessed the College Board website: https://professionals.collfegeboard.com/

profdownload/Validity_of_the_SAT_for_Predicting_First_Year_College_Grade_ Point_ Average.pdf.

Kraiger, Kurt, J., Kevin Ford, and Eduardo Salas. 1993. "Applications of Cognitive, Skill-based, and Affective Theories of Learning Outcomes to New Methods of Training Evaluation," *Journal of Applied Psychology* 78: 311–28.

National Center for Education Statistics. IPEDS website http://nces.ed.gov/ipeds/datacenter//numerous years.

National Center for O*NET Development. 2014. O*ONET OnLine. Accessed March 25, www.onetonline.org.

Olson, Mancur. 1965. *The Logic of Collective Action*. Cambridge, MA: Harvard University Press.

Pearson Vue.com. 2015. "Unlock the Power of Badges in Credentialing." *Acclaim-badges*. Html Vue.

Rawls, John. 2001. *A Theory of Justice*. Cambridge, MA: Harvard University Press.

Rojstaczer, Stuart, and Christopher Healy. 2012. *Where a Is Ordinary: The Evolution of American College and University Grading, 1940–2009*. Teachers College Record, the Voice of Scholarship in Education 114 (7).

Stabile, Susan J. 2002. "The Use of Personality Tests as a Hiring Tool: Is the Benefit Worth the Cost?" *Journal of Business Law* 4: 279–317.

Steedle, Jeffrey 2012. "Selecting Value-added Models for Postsecondary Institutional Assessment." *Assessment & Evaluation in Higher Education* 37 (6): 637–52.

Steedle, Jeffrey, Heather Kugelmass, and Alex Nemeth. 2010. "What Do They Measure? Comparing Three Learning Outcomes Assessments." *Change: The Magazine of Higher Learning* 42 (4): 33–7.

Wood, Gordon. S. 2014, August 14. "A Different Idea of Our Declaration [Review of the Book *Our Declaration: A Reading of the Declaration of Independence in Defense of Equality*, by D. Allen]." *The New York Review of Books* 61: 37–43.

7 The Role of Generic Skills in Measuring Academic Quality

The Link Between the Human-Capital Approach and Generic Skills

Gary Becker and his colleagues in the University of Chicago economics department get credit for the human-capital approach (Becker, 1993). These scholars define human capital as the stock of knowledge and skills present in a nation's population. Such capital accrues through education, training, and experience. As the human-capital field matured, economists began to mine its implications for education (Kreidl et al., 2014). The analysis of the returns on the amount and quality of education achieved has become an important research program.

This body of research suggests that education should focus on the knowledge, skills, and experience required in the knowledge economy and society. This means focusing on the ability to access and structure information and applying it to solve new problems (Simon, 1996). Recent theories of learning reflect this change in emphasis from specific content domains to a focus on being able to find and use information. Bransford et al. agree that the goal now is to help students develop the intellectual tools and learning strategies needed to acquire the knowledge to think productively (Bransford et al., 2000). All societies must ensure their workforce can generate value-added ideas that can be a foundation for sustained economic growth and prosperity. These skills are seen as requisites for success in the workplace by college graduates. Therefore, this means teaching critical-thinking skills and measuring students' progress toward desired attainment levels. In today's Knowledge Economy, this privileges the ability to access, structure, and use information, which, in turn, places the focus on generic skills.

The Case for Standardized Assessments

Measurement scientists who work in the education assessment space have developed criteria to evaluate assessment protocols. They are particularly concerned about reliability and validity. Validity is about the extent to which the assessment measures the knowledge, skills, and abilities it was designed to measure. Reliability refers to the degree of consistency of students' (or schools') scores across different assessors and whether the assessments are given to students under the same conditions and over the same time period. The need for standardized assessments rests on the premise that decisions with stakes attached should be seen to be reliable and valid. If the assessment is not reliable and valid, how can stakeholders rely upon the test results when making decisions with consequences? For example, faculty understandably support student portfolios (Banta and Pike, 2012; Rhodes, 2012; AAC&U, 2005). However, most measurement scientists are skeptical of the claim that portfolios are equal to or better than standardized assessments because they have doubts about the reliability of portfolio-based assessments. I share their view and argue that any decision with stakes attached should use a standardized test along with or in addition to formative assessments.

What, then, are the major differences between standardized and formative assessments? Perhaps the central distinction between the two groups concerns the different assumption about what unit and level of analysis is appropriate for educational assessment. Adherents of formative assessment privilege the classroom and individual universities as the unit and level of analysis on which to focus. They do not believe comparisons between and among universities are possible or, in any event, necessary because they do not believe in standardized tests, and/or they do not believe it is possible to provide interuniversity comparisons. For example, one argument that is frequently expressed is that missions of colleges and universities are so different that it makes no sense to compare them. Furthermore, it is argued that research has shown no statistical differences between institutions on measures of critical thinking, which is the educational component measured most often (Banta and Pike, 2012). The second, often-repeated argument is that variance is much higher within institutions than between institutions, so between-institution comparison is not worth doing (Kuh, 2007, pp. 32–3). There are two responses to these assertions.

The first is that most higher education institutions commit to improving generic skills as a fundamental part of their compact with students. This commitment is enshrined in mission and vision statements of most colleges and universities. Second, the fact that there can be at least two standard deviations among similarly situated colleges and universities, including selective colleges on the CLA+ value-added protocol, means there is a substantial canvas of similar institutions where researchers may study best practices in teaching and learning (see Chapter 8).

Finally, it has been argued for some time that including performance assessments would encourage greater coherence between instruction, curriculum, assessment, and the complex decision-making tasks faced in life beyond the classroom.

Reliability and Validity Evidence of One Generic-Skills Measure: CLA+

Reliability

The Cronbach's alpha measures the internal consistency of a set of test items. The reliability coefficients for two forms of the CLA+ assessment (one performance task and 25 selected-response questions) are .87 (form A) and .85 (form B). These scores are reliable enough for making decisions about grading, admissions, placement, scholarships, etc. (Zahner and James, 2015). The reliability coefficient for CLA+ has been at or above .87 in four annual testing administrations, including 2017–18, and also in two test administrations of Teco, the Italian version of CLA+.

Second, CLA+ results can be compared within and between colleges. For example, value-add models can be used to estimate the growth in learning between freshmen and senior year. The average effect size reflecting differences in CLA+ performance between entering freshmen and graduating seniors has been .75 over several annual test administrations. There are significant intra- and intervariations in the effectiveness of efforts to develop generic skills. Going to college matters a good deal, and where students go to college is highly significant (see Chapter 10)

Validity

Construct validity refers to the degree to which test scores may be interpreted as indicators of the skills (or construct). Construct validity is often evaluated by examining the patterns of correlations between (or among) a test and similar or different tests. In a technical validity study that carried out this kind of analysis by comparing the tests of critical-thinking skills fielded nationally (e.g., ETS, ACT, and CAE), construct validity for all three tests was demonstrated (Klein et al., 2009).[1]

Are Generic Skills Independent?

In a summary of several studies, I find that generic skills are applicable over an array of academic disciplines and can be both assessed and improved by teaching. CLA+ is based on the belief, and supported by research, that learning is highly situated and context bound. However, through practice in one subject area, learned knowledge becomes sufficiently generalized to enable students to transfer it to the realm of enhanced reasoning, problem solving, and decision-making that can be demonstrated across content domains.

One additional validity question concerns the test paradigm itself. Multiple-choice assessments remain the dominant testing regime. There is a significant education reform movement underway in the United

States in both K–12 and postsecondary education. First, there is a shift from the longstanding lecture format to a student-centered approach. Second, there is a change in emphasis in text material, from a primary focus on content to a focus on case studies and problem-based materials. The significant changes underway in K–12 and postsecondary education in these two dimensions of education are ahead of the progress needed in creating assessments that measure generic skills of students. Assessments that are better able to measure how well students are learning—and how well institutions are teaching—these skills have become necessary. If the human-capital school demonstrates the importance of education, the implications of the knowledge economy and recent theories of learning place the focus on improving the generic skills of the next generation of students. These developments create an urgent need to generate and implement a testing paradigm that measures and simulates these skills. That paradigm is performance-based assessment, such as that provided by CLA+. However, one issue inhibiting the introduction of this or any external-based assessment to U.S. universities is the department-based governance model that is so critical to the success of the U.S. higher-education system.

Department-Based Barriers to Overcome

Department-based governance means professionals in each field of inquiry organize themselves in departments based on the premise that those qualified in a field of knowledge are equipped to govern themselves and, in turn, to decide which fields of inquiry within their discipline should be covered, what subjects should be taught, who should be hired and promoted, and how students should be taught and assessed. No matter how great their knowledge, skills, and/or accomplishments, outsiders are perceived to lack the shared understanding needed to contribute to these decisions in a meaningful way. Faculty is, therefore, typically not interested in whether their instructional methods produce acceptable results based on independent, third-party assessments. Their interests do not often extend to research findings that question the premise of department-based governance (Benjamin and Carroll, 1996).

As a result, department-based governance has led to a two-culture split within the academy. Too many faculty resist science-based research on higher education. Thus, there is a paucity of empirical research supported by the value system of science. Scholarship that is not based on the value system of science lacks transparency and clear peer-review standards and does not privilege the value of replication of research results. Without systematic, empirically based evidence, it will not be possible to propose, develop, and implement effective remedies to the two-culture division.[2]

Researchers in cognitive science, macroeconomics and microeconomics, educational assessment, educational technology, and data analytics—to name a few—toil in independent silos, isolated from each other. However, they share a commitment to the logic and strategy of scientific inquiry. The premise of the value system of science, peer review, transparency, and the ability to replicate results are familiar to faculty and administrators. When paired with a coherent and compelling use-inspired basic research strategy, it is possible to imagine a more integrated, interdisciplinary, scientific approach to the challenges that higher education faces.

Framing the Uses of Generic-Skills Tests

The following statement from the "Revised Scoping Paper for an AHELO Main Study" (2015) provides the challenge to which we need to respond: "In a globalizing world, governments want to have more profound knowledge about the education and skills pool at the upper end of the distribution. Economic arguments relating to productivity, innovation, competitiveness and growth, and social arguments relating to social cohesion, trust and various other social outcomes of education create a need for governments to assess the learning outcomes of their new cohorts of tertiary graduates" (OECD, 2015, p. 8).

Current Uses of Generic-Skills Assessment: The CLA+ Case

If leaders of colleges and universities are indeed at a tipping point—simultaneously facing rising costs, declining resources, and a decline in the quality of student-learning outcomes—new decision-making tools that assist college leaders in responding to this challenge would be useful and welcome. CLA+ attempts to provide one decision-making tool for this purpose. The following practical uses of the CLA+ generic-skills assessment, in the form of reports and data analytics offered to all test takers, are designed to assist the higher education sector improve the quality of student learning and to anchor interdisciplinary research conducted by researchers from the disciplines noted above. Because researchers in all these fields of inquiry share a commitment to the value system of science, which privileges peer review, ability to replicate research results, and public transparency of those results, department-based faculty should be reassured that the results are not controlled or manipulated by policymakers or administrators privately.[3]

Participants in CLA+ receive test results with student, institutional, region, and country-based reports with:

- Value-added results
- Certificates/badges with test results for qualifying students (students at the proficient to accomplished end of the distribution of generic skills) to showcase their levels of mastery to employers (CLA+ CareerConnect)

- Online results analysis tool, CLA+ Analytics, part of CLA+ Data Miner
- Online videos and interactive exercises to help students improve their generic skills
- Professional development seminars to train professors on techniques to improve their students' performance

These applications are designed to do the following:

- Permit employers to more easily identify students of high ability who warrant interviews for high, value-added jobs
- Permit graduating seniors to distinguish the level of generic skills they attained from that of other students
- Permit universities to identify departments and programs that contribute the most to the growth and attainment of generic skills
- Permit ministries of education to identify universities that produce the most value-added growth and/or the highest level of attainment of generic skills
- Permit graduating secondary-school students and their parents to know the level of value-added growth their potential university choice produces
- Provide the basis for research to understand the impact of resources on the value-added growth and the highest attainment levels universities provide their students
- Permit researchers to evaluate which academic disciplines contribute the most to student-learning success
- Provide diagnostic information about the generic skills of entering students and the retention and graduation rates of students from various demographic backgrounds, in particular underrepresented groups
- Provide the basis for cross-national comparisons of similarly situated students, universities, and national systems

Potential Uses and Interdisciplinary Roles of the Generic-Skills Measure

We know from the history of the development of empirical, evidence-based research in agricultural and health policy research that there can be an evolution from specific evidence-based results to major new research programs.[4] The question is whether the time is right for a similar transition to occur in higher education policy research. Two immediate possibilities present themselves.

The decline of productivity growth is an important puzzle to solve. Productivity, defined as the output per hour worked, adjusts for the contribution of capital and materials and provides a measure of the pace of technological change by tracking productivity growth year over year. From 1948 to 1973, the annual average growth in U.S. productivity declined from 2.5% to a stabilized rate of about 1.01% in the past decade.[5]

Why does this productivity slowdown, which appears to be similar for other advanced economies, matter? Little or no productivity growth for one or two years is not especially noteworthy. However, annualized year-over-year productivity growth is essential to a national economy and society. Lower economic growth accelerates the rise in social and economic inequality, which appears to be a growing problem in advanced economies today (Piketty, 2014). To examine the possible explanations of the slowdown in productivity growth, two subfields of economics appear most relevant for our purposes. They are both focused on the service sector.

The first subfield, returns to tertiary education, shows a net decline in the benefits of a BA degree. Kreidl et al. (2014),[6] reviewing occupational trends in education over labor-force entry cohorts in 42 nations over most of the 20th century and the beginning of the 21st century, find that occupational returns to education have been steadily decreasing (Carnevale, 2015; cf. Abel and Deitz 2014).

The second possible explanation is an error in measuring the productivity of the service sector. If we could more accurately measure the service sector (e g., health, social, and education), productivity growth would look much better (Baumol, 2012). The OECD defines the service economy as "a diverse group of economic activities, not directly associated with manufacture of goods, mining or agriculture. They typically involve the provision of human value-added in the form of labor, advice, managerial skill, entertainment, training, intermediation and the like" (OECD, 2000, p. 7).

Powell and Snellman state that the rise of the service economy involves "a shift in focus from the principal production and consumption of physical goods to today's principal focus on the production and consumption of services, in particular . . . knowledge intensive activities" (Pawell and Snellman, 2004, p. 199). Nordhaus writes, "the structural shift from high to low productivity growth sectors, from manufacturing to services)" is the most important contributor to slowing productivity growth, which requires further careful examination (Nordhaus, 2016, p. 3).

The service sector now accounts for over 80% of the GDP of the United States and more than 70% in the OECD member countries overall. Baily and Montalbano argue "if productivity growth were more accurately measured, particularly in health, education and other services, the growth rate would look better than it does currently" (Baily and Montalbano, 2016. This is a reasonable position, which leads to the need to reconceptualize the way we measure GDP (Beyond the Numbers, 2014). A generic-skills measure could be used to track the productivity growth year over year.

The OECD Findings Regarding the Skills Mismatch Problem

A generic-skills measure could also illuminate trends in the current debate over a skills mismatch. Is there is evidence of a skill mismatch? The OECD finds that more than 40% of European workers feel their skill levels do not correspond to those required to do their job. In parallel, many employers report that they face recruitment problems due to skill shortages. "The costs of persistent mismatches and shortages are substantial. For instance, skill shortages can constrain the ability of firms to innovate and adopt new technologies while skill mismatches reduce labor productivity due to the misallocation of workers to jobs. Individuals are also affected as skills mismatch can bring about a higher risk of unemployment, lower wages, lower job satisfaction and poorer career prospects" (OECD, 2016a, p. 7; Bol, 2015).

In the language of economics, this description is labeled as a maldistribution of human capital at the national level. This statement also describes the impact of a skills mismatch on individuals, which translates as a problem of unequal opportunities for individuals. Since the equality of individual opportunity is a fundamental tenet of liberal democracies, this also is a major policy issue with which most, if not all, countries must be concerned (see Chapter 6).

The OECD divides skills valued in every job, occupation, and sector into (a) cognitive and noncognitive skills and (b) job-specific skills such as technical knowledge associated with a job or occupation (i.e., practical competencies). Key cognitive skills are critical thinking, problem solving, qualitative and quantitative reasoning, and writing mechanics and persuasiveness. Noncognitive skills refer to persistence, teamwork, entrepreneurial ability, and moral or ethical reasoning ability. While it is recognized that noncognitive skills are important, it is also recognized that they are not yet measured in a reliable and valid way. Therefore, the immediate focus is on cognitive skills (OECD, 2016b).

Experts at the OECD offer two alternatives for moving the cognitive generic-skills agenda forward:

1. Create a comprehensive qualifications framework that would cover all jobs. The challenge here is the need to constantly update changes in each occupation and make sure that the occupations compared across countries are defined in the same way. The OECD experts recognize this alternative is complex; requires intensive, large-scale labor; and is cumbersome.[7]
2. The second alternative is to "focus on developing general (generic) skills in the education and training system so that workers can more readily adapt to different working environments and allows them to learn field or job-specific skills on the job" (Montt, 2015, p. 40).

This second alternative is aligned with and supports the rationale for focusing on generic skills. The problem, then, is whether we can advance our understanding of both the productivity growth issue and the skills mismatch problem by exploring the potential linkages between them.

The first task is to see whether declining productivity growth supports a closer look at the skill mismatch problem. Second, is there a compelling rationale to introduce a generic-skills assessment to assist efforts to improve measurement of productivity and aid research that attempts to explain economic growth, the skills mismatch problem, and the increasing inequality of individual opportunity in the workplace? If the generic-skills measurement supports the argument that there is a connection between productivity growth and the skills mismatch issue, this would also demonstrate an absence of a level playing field for many students at the high end of the distribution of generic skills.

Conclusion

The logic of the human-capital approach in today's Knowledge Economy privileges critical-thinking skills. The focus on the importance of generic skills in today's Knowledge Economy, which privileges the service sector, provides the fundamental rationale for exploration of a new interdisciplinary role for measuring generic skills. First, a generic-skills measure may be used as additional information to track the growth of productivity year over year. Second, the measure may illuminate the trends in the skills mismatch space.

In addition to the current and potential uses of generic-skills measures such as CLA+, quality-assurance agencies are interested in student-learning-outcome measures that clearly demonstrate whether the quality of student learning is improving. Because of the problematic history of efforts to develop accountability systems that compel universities and colleges to demonstrate the level of student learning attained by their graduating seniors, at least in the United States, it may be preferable to focus on measuring the generic skills of a representative sample of graduating seniors within a state, region, or country. This method is more likely to obtain a more statistically accurate picture of what the level of student learning for graduating seniors has reached on an annual basis. The National Assessment of Educational Progress (NAEP) represents one model for such an approach.

The premise of this approach differs from that of the current uses of CLA+ noted above. Instead of using the institution of higher education as the unit of analysis, the student is the focus. The advantage of this approach is that it bypasses the institution altogether. See "An overview of the NAEP" for the description of this approach, which has become the gold standard for the assessment of the quality of elementary and secondary education in the United States (National Assessment of Educational Progress, 2018. However, since individual universities would not be initially involved in this approach, quality-assurance groups would need to engage the colleges and universities to review the generic-skills assessment results for their state or region to understand the diagnostic results of the assessment and provide compelling evidence about the level of student-learning skills reached by graduating seniors at their institution. The quality-assurance agency might then request that the institution propose changes to its curriculum and pedagogy to improve its student-learning results to meet the state or regional requirements set by the quality-assurance agency. In such a model, the quality-assurance agency might recommend the best practices to improve writing, quantitative and qualitative reasoning, and problem solving (which are core subcomponents of generic skills) to levels negotiated between the institutional leaders and the representatives of the quality-assurance agency. The quality-assurance agency might also provide various positive incentives or negative sanctions to encourage the desired improvements.

Finally, the only way to find out whether the generic-skills measure proves to be a useful additional indicator of the productivity growth and skills mismatch issues is to try it out by a number of pilots. The proposition put forward here is that a collegiate measure of educational progress, C-NAEP, could serve as the generic-skill measure used to evaluate changes in the skills mismatch problem and the production growth issue.

Notes

1. Also see Benjamin (2012). Studies of the predictive validity of CLA+ include Steedle (2012), Zahner and James (2015).
2. Ostrom (1972) argued for transparent performance metrics about outcomes and key processes in nonprofit institutions that are not clearly subject to the discipline of the market. Simply putting the spotlight on performance indicators causes changes in attitudes and behavior of the participants, in this case higher education institutions. This is an example of what Mayo (1949, pp. 60–77) called the Hawthorne Effect.
3. Because of the importance of human capital, local, state, and national public leaders are likely to increase their interest in holding institutions accountable for the student-learning results they achieve. Of course, there is considerable debate about whether assessment results should be used for accountability purposes versus improvement. If the faculty and institutions do not have a credible voice in this debate, the department-based barriers will likely continue (Benjamin and Klein 2006, p. 19).
4. Ruttan and Hayami (1987) showed that because of the progress in scientific research on agriculture, agricultural economists were able to measure agricultural productivity growth. Following the Flexner Report, (Flexner, 1910), leaders of medical education decided to change medicine from a clinical to a science-based field.
5. The U.S. permits the most extensive post-World War II historical period to measure productivity growth in advanced economies. Other advanced

economies in Western Europe and Asia did not fully recover economically until the mid-1950s. However, OECD-based measures of productivity growth for these countries now presents similar trends to the U.S.

6. Other explanations of declining productivity growth include (a) mismanagement of new information-technology advances, (b) impact of artificial intelligence on investment, (c) decline in investment, and (d) slowdown in global trade due to national populism.
7. A precedent for this in the United States is ACT's WorkKeys, a comprehensive map of thousands of vocations.

References

AAC&U. 2005. *Liberal Education Outcomes*. Washington, DC: Association of American Colleges and Universities.

Abel, Jaison R., and Richard Deitz. 2014. *Do the Benefits of College Still Outweigh the Cost?* New York, NY: Current Issues in Economics and Finance, Federal Reserve Bank of New York, Vol. 20, No. 3. www.newyorkfed.org/research/currentissues

Baily, Martin, and Nicholas Montalbano. 2016, September. *Why Is U.S. Productivity Growth So Slow? Possible Explanations and Policy Responses*. Hutchins Center Working Paper #22. Washington, DC: The Brookings Institution.

Banta, Trudi, and Gary Pike. 2012. "Making the Case Against—One More Time." *Occasional Paper 15*, National Institute of Learning Outcomes. September 24–30. www.NILOA.org.

Baumol, William. 2012. *The Cost Disease: Why Computers Get Cheaper and Health Care Doesn't*. New Haven, CT: Yale University Press.

Becker, Gary. 1993. *Human Capital: A Theoretical and Empirical Analysis with Special Reference to Education* (2nd edition). Chicago, IL: University of Chicago Press.

Benjamin, Roger, and Steve Carroll. 1996, December. "Impediments and Imperatives in Redesigning Higher Education." *Educational Administration Quarterly*, 705–19.

Benjamin, Roger, and Steve Klein. 2006. "Assessment versus Accountability: Notes on Reconciliation." *Occasional Paper*, No. 2, Paris: UNESCO, p. 19.

Benjamin, Roger. 2012, September. "The Seven Red Herrings About Standardized Assessments in Higher Education, forward by Peter Ewell, commentaries by Margaret A. Miller, Terrel L. Rhodes, Trudy W. Banta, Gary A. Pike, and Gordon Davies." *Occasional Paper #15*, National Institute for Learning Outcomes Assessment (NILOA).

Beyond the Numbers. 2014, January. *Below Trend: The U.S. Productivity Slowdown, the Numbers Since the Great Recession*. www.bls.gove/opub/btn volume—6 (2): 1–10.

Bol, Thijs. "Has Education Become More Positional? Educational Expansion and Labour Market Outcomes, 1985–2007. 2015." *Acta Sociologica* 58 (2): 105–20.

Bransford, John, Anthony Brown, and Robert Cocking. 2000. *How People Learn: Brain, Mind, Experience, School*. Washington, DC: National Academy Press.

Carnevale, Anthony P. 2015. *Credentials and Competencies: Demonstrating the Economic Value of Postsecondary Education*. Washington DC: Center on Education and the Workforce, Georgetown University.

Flexner, Abraham. 1910. *Medical Education in the United States and Canada: A Report to the Carnegie Foundation for the Advancement of Teaching*. New York: The Carnegie Foundation for Teaching, Bulletin No. 4, p. 346.

Klein, Steve, Lydia Liu, James Sconing, Roger Bolus, Brent Brideman, and Heather Kugelmass. 2009. *Test Validity Study Report*. Fund for the Improvement of Postsecondary Education, U.S. Department of Education. www.VoluntarySystem.org/docs/reports/TVSReportFinalpdf.

Kreidl, Martin, Harry B. Ganzebow, and D.J. Treiman. 2010. *How Did Occupational Returns To Education Change Over Time?* Los Angeles, CA: California Center for Population Research, University of California, Los Angeles, October 10. PwP-CCPR-2014-017.

Kuh, George. 2007. "Risky Business." *Change*, September/October: 30–5.

Mayo, Elton. 1949. *Hawthorne and the Western Electric Company: The Social Problems of Industrial Civilization*. London: Routledge.

Montt, Guillermo. 2015. "The Causes and Consequences of Field-of-study Mismatch: An Analysis using PIAAC." Working Papers, No. 167. Paris: OECD Social, Employment and Migration, OECD Publishing.

National Assessment of Educational Progress (NAEP). 1983–2018. *National Center for Education Statistics*. Washington, D.C.: United States Department of Education.

Nordhaus, William J. 2016, August 18. "Why Growth Will Fall." *The New York Review of Books*: 1–3.

OECD. 2000. *The Service Economy*. Paris: OECD Publishing, Business and Industry Policy Forum Series.

OECD. 2015, April. *Revised Scoping Paper For An AHELO Main Study*. Paris: OECD, Directorate for Education and Skills.

OECD. 2016a. *Getting Skills Right: Assessing and Anticipating Changing Skill Needs*. Paris: OECD Publishing.

OECD. 2016b. *Skills Matter: Further Results from the Survey of Adult Skills*. Paris: OECD Publishing.

Ostrom, Vincent. 1972, September. "Polycentricity." *Paper Delivered at the Annual Meeting of the American Political Science Association*, Washington, D.C.

Pawell, Walter W., and Kaisa Snellman. 2004. "The Knowledge Economy." *Annual Review of Sociology* 30: 199–220.

Piketty, Thomas. 2013. *Capital in the Twenty-First Century*. Translated by Arthur Goldhammer. Cambridge, MA: Harvard University Press 2014. *Le Capital au XXie Siecie*, Edition du Seuil. Paris: Belnap Press.

Rhodes, Terrell. 2012, September. "Getting Serious About Assessing Authentic Student Learning." *Occasional Paper 15,* National Institute of Learning Outcomes: 19–23. www.NILOA.org.

Ruttan, Vernon W., and Hayami, Yuijiro. 1987. *Agricultural Development: An International Perspective* (2nd ed.). Baltimore, MD: Johns Hopkins University Press.

Simon, Herbert. 1996. *The Sciences of the Artificial*. Boston: M.I.T. Press.

Steedle, Jeffrey. 2012. "Selecting Value-added Models for Postsecondary Institutional Assessment." *Assessment & Evaluation in Higher Education* 37 (6): 637–52.

Zahner, Doris, and Jessalynn James. *Predictive Validity of a Critical Thinking Assessment for Post-College Outcomes*. New York: CAE.org 2015.

Part III

The Rationale for Standardized Assessments in Higher Education

8 The Case for Comparative Institutional Assessment of Higher-Order Thinking Skills

Introduction

Times of threshold change—such as the transformation from the industrial era to the Knowledge Economy of today—and produce pressures to redesign the institutions we live with to respond to or shape this change. In America's Knowledge Economy, there is broad agreement that the only way to preserve the nation's economic edge will be through constant innovation, the creation of ideas that produce new economic value, for which a highly educated workforce is necessary. Since education is the principal venue for human-capital development, it is not surprising that the public gaze has turned to schools and colleges. Specifically, the public and its representatives want to know about the nature and quality of educational outcomes that those institutions generate.

In this context, one of the most contentious questions currently being debated is whether it is possible or desirable to assess and publicly communicate about learning outcomes in a way that permits comparisons between institutions. I contend that comparative assessments are essential and practical. Although we cannot measure all dimensions of learning, it is perfectly possible to comparatively assess the higher-order thinking skills that are etched in most collegiate mission statements, thought to be particularly important in the Knowledge Economy, and shared by most educators as key aims of instruction: critical thinking, analytical reasoning, problem solving, and writing. I also argue that such assessments are a critical part of larger efforts to develop better approaches to teaching and learning—goals all educators share. Finally, I make the case for assessing learning in a way that reveals the "value added" by the institution to students' intellectual development.

The Argument

Why Comparison Is Essential?

Higher education adheres to a transparent system for the evaluation of research proposals and reports based on peer review. Reviewers selected by independent funding agencies such as the National Science Foundation and the National Institutes of Health make decisions about research funding, and peer editors select manuscripts for publication on a competitive basis.

The consequences include rankings of the standing of colleges and universities based on the amount of federal money, publications, citations, and awards that faculty obtain. While these systems to rank institutions' research preeminence are far from ideal, few would argue that the quality of the American research enterprise does not benefit from this system of judgment based on the ability to compare.

Contrast the situation in research to that in undergraduate education. Until the recent development of the Voluntary System of Accountability by the National Association of State Universities and Land Grant Colleges (NASULGC) and the American Association of State Colleges and Universities (AASCU), higher education leaders resisted the idea that comparative information about student learning should be collected for public consumption.

John Lombardi, for example, argued in *Inside Higher Education* (August 2, 2006) that we should not benchmark because we already have a higher education market in which students are free to apply to the schools of their choice. In Lombardi's view, the fact that students of high ability apply to institutions that charge the highest tuition provides us with enough information about the quality of the education they will receive there.

But the effectiveness of market measures to ensure quality requires that the consumer be provided with useful information about the product compared to other choices he or she might make. As Peter McPherson and David Shulenburger, president and vice president of NASULGC respectively, argue (2006), comparative public information about not only student-learning outcomes but class size, student services, per-student endowment, and graduation rates will give consumers (or at least the less than 20% of prospective students who have a choice in the college they attend) the means to make better decisions.

Between-institution comparison is particularly critical now because of the formative stage we are experiencing with respect to the development of useful theories of pedagogy and learning. The university is an organization engaged in continuous improvement in research, a byproduct of the scientific method and rules of scholarly inquiry. It is difficult, however, to find colleges and universities that are engaged in the continuous improvement of teaching and learning. We do not have agreed-upon methods of teaching, strategies for assessment, or standards of learning for which students should be held accountable. Under these conditions, comparative researchers such as Charles Ragin (1989) and others argue it is critical to expand the universe of cases that might be compared with each other. From this larger universe of cases, the researcher can identify outliers that warrant greater examination as possible best practices.

One argument against comparing institutions rests on Ernest Pascarella Patrick Terenzini, and George Kuh's (2006) research, which suggests that *within*-institution variation with respect to student learning and engagement is greater than *between*-institution variation. As Pascarella and Terenzini (2005) write:

> The weight of evidence from the 1990s casts considerable doubt on the premise that the substantial structural, resource, and qualitative differences among postsecondary institutions produce correspondingly large differences in net educational effects on students. Rather, the great majority of postsecondary institutions appear to have surprisingly similar net impacts on student growth. . . . Similarities in between-college effects substantially outweigh the differences.
>
> (p. 590)

If colleges and universities differ less than does student experience within any one of them, the argument goes, one should focus only on internal comparisons.

But Pascarella and Terenzini's review of the learning literature ends at the conclusion of the 1990s. They did not have the available evidence from the comparative measurement instrument with which I am most familiar, the Collegiate Learning Assessment (CLA). The CLA shows not only substantial growth within institutions but differential growth among them. While there is over 1.0 standard deviation value-added growth in CLA scores within institutions (estimated by cross-sectional research design), there are up to 2 standard deviation differences in the results between institutions with similar SAT scores—a large effect, and much greater than within-institution growth (Council for Aid to Education, 2007) (It would also be useful to see how other comparative measures of student learning such as the Measure of Academic Proficiency and Progress (MAPP) and the College Assessment of Academic Progress (CAPP) distinguish among institutions.).

This shows that it does matter where one goes to college. There are significant differences among colleges, at least with respect to their ability to improve higher-order skills. Again, the variance suggests that there are interesting best practices to be studied in those colleges that are doing better than expected, practices that can be adapted by all colleges focused on the improvement of teaching and learning.

One attribute usually and correctly cited in assertions about the superiority of American higher education is its diversity, which is also used to make the case that colleges and universities should not be compared (in contrast to the argument based on the assertion that they are not different enough). Certainly, collegiate missions range widely: some are public and others private; some are nonprofit and others for-profit; some have a liberal arts orientation, while others focus on science and technology, business, music and the other performing arts, art and architecture, and so on. These distinct missions clearly result in different emphases—configurations of majors and minors, types of core curricula, student populations served, and expectations of student performance, among others. The implication of this description of American higher education suggests to some that any effort to compare such a variable group of institutions would be fatally reductionist, but to me it suggests that if one argues for comparative assessment, a clear corollary is that the focus needs to be on a learning goal that virtually all institutions share—i.e., the development of higher-order skills.

Why Higher-Order Skills Should Be a Principal Focus and the Institution the Initial Unit of Analysis?

Academic disciplines were clearly the most important venues for learning during the industrial era, when the transfer of knowledge (content) was thought to be the primary function of undergraduate education, and they have long been the basic building block of the curriculum (although majors account for less than one-third of the courses students take in a typical four-year program). But while students still need to acquire a body of knowledge, it is equally if not more important for them to master the higher-order skills they will need to access, structure, and use information (James Pellegrino et al., 2001).

According to John Immerwahr (2000), employers are not as concerned about what students major in as they are about how well and flexibly they think. Under our present organizational model, faculty have no way of knowing whether their courses—delivered within departments and isolated from one another—in fact develop these greatly valued skills in their students.

Comparative Measures of Higher-Order Skills

There are now at least three standardized instruments—the College Assessment of Academic Progress (CAPP), the Collegiate Learning Assessment (CLA), and the Measure of Academic Proficiency and Progress (MAPP)—that assess various dimensions of higher-order thinking skills. The portfolio of student work, a popular alternative, suffers from serious reliability and validity problems that appear to prevent its use for comparative assessment (Dan Koretz et al., 1993).

The institution as a whole is the appropriate level at which to evaluate success in improving higher-order skills in its students because it is at the level of the institutional mission statement that virtually all institutions commit to improving these higher-order skills. This does not mean the majors are not important in contributing to students' intellectual development; they are crucial to students' mastery of both intellectual skills and disciplinary content. Moreover, it is important to drill down to the individual classroom to understand what changes in pedagogical practice should be affected in order to improve student learning. We will need to identify the systematic steps that link the institutional level results to the faculty in their classroom to complete a continuous system of improvement of teaching and learning. Students develop in a cumulative fashion as they progress through their courses and other experiences at their institutions, so the first goal is to determine the degree of improvement of those skills in the course of students' entire baccalaureate education. This is how we can ascertain the value added by a particular college or university.

Why Comparative Tests Should Supplement, Not Supplant, Local Assessments?

Unique assessments tailored to the individual needs of individual programs are often defended as the only way to make improvements in educational practice. Indeed, faculty generally respond to accreditation requirements to track student learning and other indicators of program effectiveness using a mix of locally developed indicators. Undoubtedly, the information generated by these instruments is of great value in improving programs. The question is whether they provide adequate assistance to faculty and administrators in their effort to improve teaching and learning or whether a measure that enabled them to compare their students' performance to that of similar students at other institutions would give them valuable additional information about their campus's effectiveness. And if comparative measures are to be successful, faculty must see them as important ingredients in their classroom work. In other words, the comparative measures need to be constructed to be direct contributions to teaching and learning; otherwise, the faculty, the ultimate "customer" for assessment instruments, will ignore them.

Comparative measures can produce important signals to the faculty and administration of institutions about where they stand in comparison to other similar institution, but they should not substitute for locally developed instruments. They should be only one of many measures an institution uses to assess its students' learning gains, since no one test can measure everything that is important or provide, by itself, enough information to guide program improvement.

The results of comparative assessments should not be used to rank or rate colleges and universities. Single-dimension rankings mask the great diversity of inputs and outcomes in higher education. Moreover, the field of assessment in higher education is far from reaching maturity, and an overreliance on single measures that are in the process of being tested and improved provides a false sense of certitude where it is not warranted.

Why the Value-Added Approach Is Important?

An important question that every institution needs to ask itself is how much its teaching improves students' intellectual capacities. This is the value-added question that surfaces in today's assessment and accountability debate. It can do this by assessing the performance of freshmen and seniors at the same time (cross-sectional assessment) or by assessing the performance of students when they enter the institution and those same students again when they are about to graduate (longitudinal assessment). Then, to know whether the degree of improvement it makes in those capacities is satisfactory given what is possible with the students it accepts, it needs to know the extent to which that improvement is comparable to the progress of equally able students at other institutions.

There are at least three arguments against using the value-added approach as a way to judge the contribution of the college or university to student learning that must be considered. One is that intellectual mastery at the end of college is overwhelmingly determined by students' preparation when they enter. However, as Klein et al. (2007) have demonstrated in looking at the results of the CLA, some institutions clearly improve the higher-order intellectual skills of their students more than other institutions serving similar students.

A second argument is that there are ceiling effects on student-learning growth in elite institutions: there cannot be as much growth in institutions that admit students with high ability as measured, for example, by the SAT or ACT. If true, this would mean that the value-added approach penalizes those institutions when compared to ones that admit students of lower ability. (Parenthetically, the reverse is the case now. Because colleges and universities neither use the value-added approach nor measure student-learning outcomes in a comparative manner, only those that admit students with high SAT/ACT scores are considered to be of high quality.) In fact, students at the highest SAT/ACT levels only score fifty percent of what is possible on standardized tests currently using the value-added approach. In addition to measuring value added, elite institutions are free to compare the absolute level of student attainment they achieve to that of their peers, since this is the scale on which they excel.

This, however, raises the third argument: that institutions, selective and less-selective alike, may want to assert their contribution to students' intellectual growth not by measuring value added but by setting performance standards. But institutions, even while doing value-added assessment, are free to set standards for minimum proficiency and low to high ranges in performance. Indeed, the producers of testing instruments could provide them with sample answers for well-below, below-average, average, above-average, and well-above-average performance.

Why the Trend Toward Greater Transparency Is Irreversible?

The assessment and accountability debates are not new, but there appears to be a new coalescence of actors pushing for more assessment of student learning; transparency with regard to university operations; and accountability from local government, state legislators and governors, state boards of higher education, Congress, the U.S. Department of Education, journalists, parents, and foundations. They are responding to rising college costs, the nation's need for human-capital development, and the imperative that we do better in ensuring successful educational attainment by minority students, among other motivators.

As the demand for greater transparency and accountability becomes imperative for all institutions, one of the most important issues to address is whether and how information about higher education institutions should be reported publicly. We may be entering a period when we have comparative measurement instruments of sufficient quality to use for assessment and accountability purposes, but we are only in the beginning stages of serious discussion of their public policy implications. For instance, as institutions, associations, systems of higher education, and states devise templates for reporting, they will publicize them. However, raw scores on assessment measures may vary from one year to the next, low graduation rates may signal that an institution is doing a good job of recruiting at-risk students, and so on. The rules of engagement must be worked out through trial-and-error efforts led by national associations, systems of higher education, states, and individual institutions over the next several years.

We should apply to any proposed strategies for assessment and accountability the same logic by which Vannevar Bush (1945) developed the peer review research policy that respects the diversity of institutions and American higher education's institutional design, with its decentralized governance structure and respect for faculty autonomy. But we need to engage in the kind of layered comparison strategy described here to improve the quality of teaching and learning in higher education. If we did not have the ability to do the kind of comparative assessment described here, the status quo might be acceptable. But we now can do sophisticated, meaningful, appropriate comparisons—since we can, there is no legitimate argument against doing so.

References

Bush, Vanevar. 1945. *Science: The Endless Frontier*. Washington, DC: United States Government Printing Office.

CAE (Council for Aid to Education). 2007. *Institutional Report*. New York: CAE.

Immerwahr, John. 2000, August. *Great Expectations: How the Public and Parents of White, African-American and Hispanic Students View Higher Education.* San José, CA: National Center for Higher Education Public Policy.

Klein, Stephen, Richard Shavelson, Roger Benjamin, and Roger Bolus. "The Collegiate Learning Assessment: Facts and Fantasies." *Evaluation Review*, October 2007.

Koretz, Dan., Brian Stecher, Stephen Klein, Dan McCaffrey, and Edward Deibert. 1993. "Can Portfolios Assess Student Performance and Influence Instruction? The 1991–92 Vermont Experience." *CSE Technical Report 371*, RAND Institute on Education and Training and UCLA, National Center for Research on Evaluation, Standards, and Student Testing. Los Angeles, CA: CRESST/UCLA.

Kuh, George. 2007. "Risky Business," *Change*, September/October: 30–5.

Lombardi, John. 2006. *Inside Higher Education*, August 6.

McPherson, Peter and David Shulenberger. 2006, August. *Toward A Public Universities and Colleges Voluntary System of Accountability for Undergraduate Education.* A National Association of State Universities and Land Grant Colleges and Association of American State Colleges and Universities Discussion. www.NASULGC.org.

Pascarella, Ernest and Patrick Terenzini. 2005. *How College Affects Students: A Third Decade of Research, Vol.* 2. San Francisco, CA: Jossey-Bass.

Pellegrino, James W., Norm Chudowsky, and Robert Glaser, eds. 2001. *Knowing What Students Know: The Science and Design of Educational Assessment.* Washington, DC: The National Academy Press.

Ragin, Charles. 1989. *The Comparative Method: Moving Beyond Qualitative and Quantitative Strategies.* Berkeley, CA: University of California Press.

9 The Case for Performance-Based Assessments and Critical-Thinking Tests[1]

The Context

The first version of this chapter was written in 2012 before the current version of the CLA, CLA+, was implemented. This version was written in 2016. The CLA protocol focused exclusively on the improvement of student learning at the institutional level. How much improvement in student learning of its students do institutions produce over the four years of college attendance? A matrix sampling approach was used to sample a minimum of 100 freshmen and 100 seniors. Students who were tested were given 90 minutes to write a constructed essay in response to a performance task or write three shorter essays in response to make-an-argument or critique-an-argument open-ended questions, again in 90 minutes. The degree of representativeness of the sample was corroborated by reviewing the registrar data on the demographic characteristics of all the students at the institution to see whether the demographic characteristics of the sample mirrored the overall demography of the institution's student body. The SAT or ACT scores of freshmen and graduation seniors who were tested were also collected. This measure of the entering competencies of students permits one to estimate the value-added growth in student learning. No stakes were involved for the students taking the CLA.

In 2012, CAE decided to undertake the research and development for a new version of the CLA that would be reliable and valid for judgments about individual students, which is now known as CLA+. CLA+ is in its fifth year of test administration, long enough for significant research on the reliability and validity of the protocol, largely by CAE researchers, to be completed. This new version makes it possible to expand the range of CLA+ applications. Today, the CLA+ is used for the measurement of proficiency levels achieved in critical-thinking skills as well as the value-added growth in these skills. The new protocol, 90 minutes in length of time, features a performance task to be answered within 60 minutes and 26 multiple-choice items aligned with the performance task, which provide additional questions about quantitative and qualitative reasoning and writing skills (see cae.org for more details about the CLA+ protocol).

In this chapter, the case for measuring critical-thinking skills with a performance assessment-anchored protocol has not changed. However, most of the third-party studies in the literature review section, cited below, pages 222–31, are focused on the CLA because the CLA+ has only been operational for four years.

Introduction

Educational institutions across the world are being challenged to improve instruction so that tomorrow's workforce will have the knowledge and skills necessary to meet the demands of modern careers and contribute to the global economy. Indeed, a college education has never been more necessary for productive participation in society. Employers now seek individuals able to think critically and communicate effectively in order to meet the requirements of the new Knowledge Economy (Hart Research Associates, 2006; Levy and Murname, 2004). Therefore, the skills taught in higher education are changing; less emphasis is placed on content-specific knowledge and more is placed on general higher-order skills such as analytic reasoning and evaluation, problem solving, and written communication.

Any rigorous improvement project requires continual evaluation to measure progress toward goals. Consequently, there is a need for standardized assessments such as the Collegiate Learning Assessment (CLA) that measure general higher-order skills. Performance assessments like the CLA evaluate not only whether students are learning higher-order skills required of today's workforce; they also spur educational advances in pedagogy. The CLA presents students with scenarios that are representative of the types of problems they will encounter in the real world and asks them to generate solutions to these problems. Unlike multiple-choice questions where students need only to identify the correct answer—limiting the capacity of those questions to measure students' critical-thinking skills—an open-ended assessment such as the CLA is able to measure how well students formulate hypotheses, recognize fallacious reasoning, and identify implicit and possibly incorrect assumptions. Only open-ended tasks can authentically capture this type of critical thinking as well as the ability to organize and present ideas in a coherent argument.

Because higher-order skills are so critical to national productivity, CAE (the Council for Aid to Education) supports the concept of critical-thinking skills (called generic skills in Europe and Asia). Moreover, from a methodological perspective, CAE believes that critical-thinking skills are the *only* solid basis for cross-institution and cross-national benchmarks that are inclusive of all academic disciplines. Of course, knowledge and skills specific to academic disciplines are important, but there is a multitude of disciplines, each potentially differing across national contexts and evolving over time. This makes it impractical to establish broad, comparative benchmarks based on achievement in academic disciplines. The development of students' critical-thinking skills is central to the missions of modern postsecondary institutions because of growing recognition that these skills fuel innovation and economic growth (Levy and Murname, 2004).

The first section of this chapter provides a rationale for a focus on critical-thinking skills and describes how these skills are operationalized in the development of Performance Tasks for the CLA. The next section describes the CLA, summarizes a decade's worth of validity research pertaining to the use of the CLA in postsecondary institutional assessment programs, and addresses common concerns and critiques related to the CLA. The following section summarizes the validity and reliability research CAE has undertaken. The final section concludes with a summary of the case for measuring critical-thinking skills.

Rationale for Focus on Critical-Thinking Skills

Political and economic leaders everywhere understand that workforce skill level is what determines economic performance. This understanding has led policy analysts to view education policy as being equally as important as other critical policy fields such as healthcare, national security, international trade, and the environment. In other words, education policy is now viewed as one of the top priorities in any society and of any government. The initial credit here goes to Gary Becker and his colleagues in the Economics Department at the University of Chicago, who developed the human-capital school of labor economics. They leveraged the methodological rigor of contemporary economics to formulate the principles of human capital over forty years ago (Becker, 1964; Heckman and Krueger, 2003).Their achievements have been accepted at the highest levels of the Academy, including recognition of several members of the human-capital school by the Nobel Committee.

These scholars defined human capital as the stock of knowledge and skills present in a nation's population. Such capital accrues through education, training, and experience. As the field matured, economists began to mine its implications for education, which is the formal venue for human-capital development. Analysis of the returns on the amount of education achieved has become an important academic pursuit in economics, public policy, and education. This body of research suggests that education must focus on the stock of knowledge and skills required by the economy and society, which today most highly value the ability to access and structure information and apply it to solve new problems.

Recent theories of learning that reflect the change in emphasis from a focus on specific content domains to a focus on higher-order skills are redefining the concept of knowledge. Herbert Simon (1996) argues that the meaning of "knowing" has changed from being able to recall information to being able to find and use information. Bransford et al. (2000) note that the "sheer magnitude of human knowledge renders its coverage by education an impossibility; rather, the goal is conceived as helping students develop the intellectual tools and learning strategies needed to acquire the knowledge to think productively."

The logical extension for some is to say that education should be more explicitly vocational, but this is not the point. As the world economy has evolved from the Industrial Era to the Knowledge Economy, it has become increasingly dependent on a workforce that can generate knowledge that can be a foundation for economic prosperity. Knowledge generation requires strong skills in analytic reasoning, problem solving, and writing—referred to as core "generic skills." Thus, education must prepare students for productive participation in the economy and society, and increasingly this means teaching generic higher-order skills and measuring progress toward desired achievement levels.

Measuring Critical-Thinking Skills

Increasing recognition of the essential role of critical-thinking skills in the Knowledge Economy portends significant changes in teaching and learning as reflected in the educational reform movement now underway and assisted by education technology. Although this reform is present in elementary and secondary education, most advances have occurred in postsecondary or tertiary education in Europe and the United States. The reform movement can be characterized along three dimensions:

- Shift from the longstanding lecture format to a student-centered approach emphasizing students' active class participation and development of analytic writing skills;
- Change in the balance of curricular and textbook focus from its current emphasis on content to case and problem-based materials requiring students to apply what they know to novel situations; and
- Change in assessment instruments from multiple-choice tests that are best used for benchmarking the level of content absorbed by students to open-ended assessments that are aligned with numerous goals of the reform initiative.

Although significant advances have been made on the first two dimensions of this education reform movement, assessment has lagged. As schools and colleges focus increasingly on developing critical-thinking skills in their students, assessment tools need to evolve to measure how well students are learning—and institutions are teaching—such skills.

Multiple-choice and short-answer tests remain the dominant testing regime, not only for facts but also for generic skills. In the United States, they are the principal testing paradigm used by the Educational Testing Service (ETS), ACT, and the College Board. As a result, in postsecondary education and elsewhere, the testing regime is not assessing the most critical skills required of students in the workplace and—just as importantly—is not supporting the other two dimensions of reform. We believe the promise of educational reform developing in today's Knowledge Economy cannot be achieved without employing open-ended, performance-based assessments, not only in postsecondary education but in primary and secondary education as well as other points along the education-to-work continuum.

As an illustration of this point, consider two tests of critical thinking: one multiple choice and the other a performance assessment. To measure students' understanding of correlations and causality, the multiple-choice test requires students to select an answer from a list of four or five provided options. In the performance assessment, students are presented with a research report in which the author incorrectly concludes that there is a causal relationship between the two variables due to a strong correlation between them. The student must evaluate this information and determine how that information does or does not support possible solutions to a real-world problem. The cognitive processes involved in responding to these two assessments are fundamentally different. Recognizing the correct answer from a finite list of possibilities is very different from asking students to generate a critique and explain it clearly. In the latter approach, the student must not only recognize the fallacious reasoning but must also understand how the concepts are confused and explain why the argument fails. This level of fidelity to real-world experience is often viewed as a major advantage of performance assessments over multiple-choice tests. Additionally, performance assessments measure students' written communication skills and their ability to craft an argument and refute counterarguments with relevant and reliable information. Multiple-choice items that assess writing generally measure a student's ability to correctly identify proper use of vocabulary and grammar.

Another important advantage of performance assessments is that they are seen as tests worth teaching to. The practice of "teaching to the test" is generally frowned upon when referring to traditional multiple-choice and short-answer assessments, and there is ample evidence that this practice occurs, especially when educators are held accountable for their students' test performance. However, "teaching to the test" for performance assessments should be encouraged. That is, class time spent preparing students to apply knowledge and skills to complex, real-world problems is time well spent. In line with importance of the instructor in the classroom (see Table 11.2), it has been recognized that a combination of a performance assessment and multiple-choice items would be useful to encourage coherence between instruction, assessments, and the daily complex decisions faced in life (Frederickson, 1984; Steedle et al., 2013). Because of their fidelity to real-world tasks, performance assessments can elicit evidence of students' critical-thinking and written communication skills in addition to knowledge of content such as the English language, the arts and, mathematics. Thus, an assessment containing a mix of performance assessments and multiple-choice items provides similar predictive validity to multiple-choice tests (Zahner et al., 2012) but provides illustrations of the potential for coherence between teaching, instruction, and assessment.

In addition to negative effects on pedagogy, a critical shortcoming of today's principal educational assessment regime is that it pays little attention to how much a school or college contributes to developing the competencies students will need after graduation. For instance, the outcomes that are typically looked at by higher education accreditation teams, such as a college's retention and graduation rates and the percentage of its faculty in tenured positions, say nothing about how well the school fosters the development of its students' analytic reasoning, problem solving, and communication skills. This situation is unfortunate because the ways in which institutions are evaluated significantly affects institutional priorities. If institutions were held accountable for student achievement, they would likely direct greater institutional resources and effort toward improving teaching and learning.

Compounding the challenges of implementing performance assessments is the fact that the development and measurement of performance assessments are rarely taught in schools of education or the social sciences. Consequently, textbooks on assessment devote very little attention to this topic. The main focus of educational assessment courses and textbooks is on item construction and analysis for multiple-choice tests. When performance assessment is taught in these programs, the focus is often on the development of performance tasks for professional licensure or certification purposes. For example, airline pilots are assessed on how competently they handle simulations of a range of realistic problems they may face. Similarly, mocked-up cases that require diagnosis by those studying to become medical doctors, veterinarians, or lawyers also widely use performance assessments (Heinrichs et al., 2007; Klein, 1996).

All these conditions point to the need to support advances in performance assessment, particularly in the field of education. If the human-capital school demonstrates the importance of education, the implications of the Knowledge Economy and recent theories of learning place the focus on improving the higher-order skills of the next generation of students. These developments create an urgent need to generate and implement a testing paradigm that measures and simulates these skills.

The CLA+ Framework

Critical Thinking

While there are many desirable outcomes of college education, there is widespread agreement that *critical-thinking* skills are among the most important. As Derek Bok (2005), former president of Harvard University, states, "With all the controversy over the college curriculum, it is impressive to find faculty members agreeing almost unanimously that teaching students to think critically is the principle aim of undergraduate education" (p. 109). Critical-thinking skills are longstanding desired outcomes of education (Dewey, 1910; Educational Policies Commission, 1961), and, in modern day, they are seen as essential for accessing and analyzing the information needed to address the complex, nonroutine challenges facing workers in the 21st century (The New Commission on the Skills of the American Workforce, 2006; The Secretary's Commission On Achieving Necessary Skills, 1991). In recognition of the central role that critical thinking plays in "The Information Age," leaders in higher education, business, and government stress that such higher-order skills must be assessed at the college level (Business-Higher Education Forum, 2004; Silva, 2008; State Higher Education Executive Officers, 2005; U.S. Department of Education, 2006).

Despite variation in definitions of critical thinking, there is significant agreement on its core components. The American Philosophical Association's (1990) definition, which reflects the consensus of 200 policymakers, employers, and professors, describes critical thinking as "Purposeful, self-regulatory judgment which results in interpretation, analysis, evaluation, and inference as well as explanation of the evidential, conceptual and methodological considerations on which a judgment is based" (p. 2). Along these lines, Pascarella and Terenzini (2005) offer an operational definition of critical thinking largely based on the work of Erwin (2000):

> [. . .] most attempts to define and measure critical thinking operationally focus on an individual's capability to do some or all of the following: identify central issues and assumptions in an argument, recognize important relationships, make correct references from the data, deduce conclusions from information or data provided, interpret whether conclusions are warranted based on given data, evaluate evidence of authority, make self-corrections, and solve problems.
>
> (p. 156)

Bok's (2006) definition of critical thinking captures similar qualities:

> The ability to think critically—ask pertinent questions, recognize and define problems, identify arguments on all sides of an issue, search for and use relevant data and arrive in the end at carefully reasoned judgments—is the indispensable means of making effective use of information and knowledge.
>
> (p. 109)

The aspects of critical thinking measured by the CLA are well-aligned with the definitions of critical thinking provided above. Note that critical thinking may be defined very broadly, so we include *analytic reasoning* and *problem solving* in this construct definition (and in other CLA documentation) to expand upon the critical-thinking skills measured by the CLA and to denote the range of those skills. Students are judged on critical-thinking skills such as analytic reasoning and problem solving during the scoring process, which captures qualities exhibited in student work such as evaluating the reliability and relevance of evidence, identifying logical flaws and holes in the arguments of others, analyzing and synthesizing data from a variety of sources, drawing valid conclusions and supporting them with evidence and examples, and addressing opposing viewpoints. Students obtain higher CLA scores by attending to specific items in a task (e.g., accurately interpreting a graph or identifying a statement as untenable given other information the examinee receives) and by applying the skills described above generally (e.g., overall strength of support for arguments).

Writing

In addition to critical-thinking skills, colleges are expected to teach "top notch writing and speaking skills" (Immerwahr, 2000, p. 10). This derives from recognition that, in many professions, the ability to communicate ideas effectively and articulate problem-solving processes is an important and highly valued skill. In response to CLA prompts, students generate text that describes an analysis of a problem, provides evidence and examples to support a position, explains weaknesses in the arguments of others, and proposes a course of action. CLA scoring rubrics capture whether students write in a style that is well-organized, persuasive, and free from grammatical errors.

The CLA+ Performance-Based Assessment

Traditional learning assessments divide tasks into components, create measures in the form of assessment items for each component (most often using multiple-choice questions), collect scores on each measure, and assume that the aggregated scores are representative of the total construct (or domain) for which the student is being assessed. In contrast, the sampling approach employed by CLA+ assumes that the whole is greater than the sum of its parts and that complex tasks require an integration of abilities than cannot assumed to be measured by summing individual items that are assumed to add up to the whole. CLA+ assessments are based on holistic, real-world tasks that require constructed responses that elicit critical-thinking and communication skills, which are critical for success in the workplace. CLA+ performance tasks are presented in a variety of contexts, including the social sciences, humanities, sciences, engineering, and business. No prior subject knowledge is required.

Students use their analytical reasoning, problem solving, and writing skills to answer open-ended questions that are not framed to elicit "right" or "wrong" answers. Rather, students are asked to compose written responses requiring them to integrate and synthesize information from the different documents provided to them on an online testing platform. Additionally, they are required to support their decisions with relevant facts and ideas from these documents. Twenty-five selective responses are included with the performance task to boost the individual-student reliability of the test results. The selective responses are also document-based and aligned to the same construct as the performance task.

The Conceptual Framework

The framework sets the range of potential outcomes as a continuum ranging from domain-specific knowledge to general ability, or G (Spearman, 1904). At the top of the hierarchy are theories of intelligence, with Spearman (1904) at one extreme and Guilford (1967) and Gardner (2006)at the other end of the spectrum postulating multiple abilities and different independent intelligence. A further premise of the CLA+ conceptual framework is the belief, supported by research, that learning is highly situated and context bound. However, through practice within a particular subject area, the critical-thinking skills derived from learned knowledge (i.e., content) becomes sufficiently generalized to enable the problem solving, qualitative and quantitative reasoning, and written communication skills to be **transferred** to the analysis of other domains (Gick and Holyoak, 1987). In other words, the critical-thinking skills are independent from specific academic fields (see also Chapter 10).

The core critical-thinking skills noted above do not capture all critical-thinking skills. Rather, the CLA+ measures critical thinking as defined specifically on the rubric. We do not claim to measure all critical thinking as that domain is very large. The rubric for the performance tasks and the constructs that it measures were developed by expert measurement scientist to holistically assess analytic reasoning and problem solving and written communication skills. In addition, the rubric does not individually tally every single point that is covered in the performance task and calculate a proportion of missed points.

As an example of a generic skill that is transferrable across domains, consider the task of writing an email to a colleague summarizing the results of a project. Does it matter what field you are in to successfully accomplish this task? Would you use similar skills to report on the results of analyses of different after-school programs as you would on the results of the first quarter returns for a financial institution? We use this example as an illustration of what is meant by transferrable generic skills, which are applicable across multiple domains (Clanchy and Ballard, 1995). Although the content of what is being reported is different, the skills one would use to write these reports are very similar—analysis and written communication.

The Evolution of the CLA Framework

Steve Klein, director of research, CAE, from 2000 to 2014, introduced performance assessment to assess student-learning outcomes in higher education in 2002–03. His approach is an example of what philosophers and scientists call rational empiricism. Rational empiricists believe the best way to arrive at certain knowledge is to use the mind's rational abilities in combination with observations of the empirical world. In Klein's case, he opted for direct performance-based measures of problems or cases from examples across the humanities, social sciences, sciences, engineering, and business (Klein, 2002). He did not believe an overarching conceptual framework was appropriate. His basic assumption was that each student demonstrated their critical thinking as a function of writing the constructed essay response to the problem. He further assumed that each performance task created was itself objectively a part of the empirical world with which all citizens cope. He further assumed that the skills demonstrated in taking a test based on a problem in the humanities could be transferred to analysis of a problem in science or engineering.

Klein's colleague, Richard Shavelson, describes the approach using different but aligned language. For Shavelson, the criterion-sampling approach employed by the CLA assumes that the whole is greater than the sum of its parts and that complex tasks require an integration of abilities that cannot be measured when deconstructed into individual components. The criterion-sampling approach is based on a simple principle: if you want to know what a person knows and can do, sample tasks from the domain in which that person is to act, observe his or her performance, and infer competence and learn (Shavelson, 2008).[2] In short, the CLA samples tasks from "real-world" domains; the samples are holistic, real-world tasks drawn from life experiences. The samples require constructed responses (not selected) and elicit complex critical thinking, analytic reasoning, and problem-solving skills.

One Key Issue: Context Matters

An underlying question is whether a performance-based assessment developed in one national context can be translated and adapted into another language in a way that preserves its reliability and validity. The answer is yes—with a caveat. Measurement scientists, like all social scientists, should not retreat to the position that reliable and valid performance-based assessments of critical-thinking skills are impossible, including applications of such assessments internationally. Equally unwarranted is the position that ignores the fact that individuals, groups, institutions and societies exist within changing contexts. In other words, we should develop and apply new methods and new types of items to measure core cognitive critical-thinking skills as rigorously as possible. However, while core cognitive skills may be invariant, the way they are expressed changes across time and national cultural contexts. Unlike physics or biology, social science is not an ahistorical subject (Goodenough, 1970; Benjamin, 1982). History matters.[3]

The CLA+ Program

The CLA represents a paradigm shift in testing and is a good example of how performance assessment can be used effectively. Unlike multiple-choice or short-answer tests, the CLA combines performance tasks and multiple-choice items. Performance tasks are concrete exercises that require students to apply a wide range of higher-order thinking and communication skills to solve a complex problem. In these tasks, students are allotted 60 minutes to examine a set of documents related to a real-world problem, write responses to explain their analysis of the documents, and propose a solution to the problem at hand. The documents, which contain a mix of dependable and questionable information, appear as newspaper articles, research abstracts, emails, web pages, transcripts, graphics, maps, and other forms of written and visual media. CLA Performance Tasks are presented in a variety of contexts, including the arts, social science, natural sciences, business, education, political science, and other fields. However, no prior subject knowledge is required. Students use their analytical reasoning, problem solving, and writing skills to answer open-ended questions that are not framed to elicit "right" or "wrong" answers. Rather, students are asked to compose written responses, requiring them to integrate information from the different provided documents and support their decisions with relevant facts and ideas.

There are a number of applications of CLA+.

The Value-Added Approach (the principal protocol from 2004–05 to 2012):

- *Unit of analysis*. CAE considers the institution, rather than the individual student, as the initial unit of analysis. Additionally, while higher-order skills measured by the CLA are not a function of any one particular course or even a specific academic major, some institutions are using the CLA to assess differences between programs. Nonetheless, the primary goal of the CLA is to be sensitive to an important portion of the summative effects of the courses and educational experiences students encounter over the course of an entire undergraduate program. This point is one of the most innovative features of the CLA: it assesses the institution, rather than the individual student.

- *Benchmarking.* The great majority of standardized assessments do not document the level of proficiency of their entering students. Thus, it is impossible to gauge how much improvement an institution itself contributes to the growth in student learning. The CLA controls for the competencies that students bring to the college, and results are reported in terms of "value added" (i.e., how much value an institution adds to students over the period of time they are at the institution) and other indices. Research shows that CLA value-added scores are sufficiently reliable to make inferences about student learning relative to other institutions (Klein, 2007; Klein et al., 2005; Steedle, 2011 online first).
- *Value-added scores.* An institution's CLA value-added score gives faculty and administrators a benchmark of where their institution stands relative to other institutions admitting students with similar entering academic ability. There is significant variation between similarly situated institutions along this value-added continuum. In other words, there are very large differences in CLA value-added scores among institutions that accept students with similar entering academic ability. This means there is a large canvas for studying best practices in the institutions that perform better than the equation predicts as opposed to those that perform worse. There is also ample opportunity for those institutions that perform more poorly than predicted to improve upon their contribution to their students' education.
- *Reporting.* In reports to the institution, an institution's CLA value-added score is presented to provide an indicator of the growth in skills measured by the CLA relative to similarly selective institutions. In addition, absolute score levels are provided to show where an institution falls in the overall distribution before controlling for entering academic ability. The CLA results for each participating institution are sent only to that institution. Each participating student also receives their individual test results. Some institutions also share results publicly with prospective students as part of the Voluntary System of Accountability (McPherson and Shulenburger, 2006), a network of public, four-year colleges and universities that use a common web template for presenting information about institutional characteristics as well as student experiences and outcomes.

New Applications of CLA+ From 2013–14 to Present

The new applications include a focus on the critical thinking of graduating seniors only for which certified mastery-level badges are provided (see Chapter 6), the attainment agenda, and the international agenda (see Chapter 11).

Internet Delivery

An important feature of the CLA is its use of a secure Internet browser for administration and delivery of the assessment. The Internet has provided two important benefits for the CLA. First, the Internet-based delivery platform makes it possible to increase the complexity and richness of the performance assessments created. The performance assessments are comprised of a considerable number of pertinent documents that include tables, figures, and graphs. An Internet browser makes it possible to present and organize the information on the documents without overwhelming the students. Second, delivering the CLA over the Internet significantly reduces cost and frequency of errors related to test administration, scoring, and reporting. The CLA would not exist without the Internet.

Psychometric Properties of the CLA

There are several studies that speak to the reliability of CLA scores and to the validity of CLA score interpretations. Some of the key studies are highlighted below. A more comprehensive list of studies is given in Appendix B and the list of references.

Reliability

In institutional assessment programs, reliability is achieved when test results are consistent across different samples of students drawn from the same population. Here, the focus is on the reliability of aggregate institutional results rather than those of individual test takers. When the institution is the unit of analysis, the CLA's reliability is approximately 0.90 (Klein et al. 2007a). This indicates that the relative standings of institutions would be highly consistent if testing was repeated with different samples of students. Moreover, an institution's CLA value-added scores has a reliability of approximately 0.75 (Steedle, 2011 online first).

Validity

Construct validity refers to the degree to which test scores can be interpreted as indicators of whatever skill (i.e., construct) the test purports to measure. While gathering validity evidence in any testing program is an ongoing activity, a substantial amount of validity research has already been done by both CAE researchers and independent third parties. Some of these studies are summarized below.

Face Validity

An assessment is said to have face validity when it appears to measure what it claims to measure. For the CLA to have face validity, CLA tasks must emulate the critical thinking and writing challenges that students will face outside the classroom. These characteristics of the CLA were vetted by a sample of 41 college professors selected to be representative of faculty from a wide range of institutions (Hardison and Vilamovska, 2008). After an in-depth review of CLA Performance Tasks and reading a range of student responses, these professors completed a survey on their perceptions of the CLA Performance Tasks. As shown in Graph 9.1, results indicate that the professors considered the Performance Tasks to be good assessments of critical thinking, writing, problem solving, and decision-making. For example, using a rating scale of 1–5, professors felt that the CLA measures what it intends to measure (Mean 4.14, SD 0.46); it measures important skills that college graduates should possess (Mean 4.70, SD 0.53); students need good critical-thinking skills to do well on the task (Mean 4.60, SD 0.46); and students who do well on the task would also perform well in a job requiring good written communication (Mean 4.20, SD 0.83) or decision-making (Mean 4.10, SD 0.70). Respondents also agreed, after viewing the tasks, that college seniors should perform better on this task than college freshman (Mean 4.70, SD 0.48).

Concurrent Validity

Concurrent validity is commonly evaluated by examining the pattern of correlations between a test and other tests of similar and different skills (Campbell, 1959). For example, if the CLA measures critical-thinking skills, then it should be highly (positively) correlated with other tasks that measure critical thinking. In the fall semester of 2008, CAE collaborated

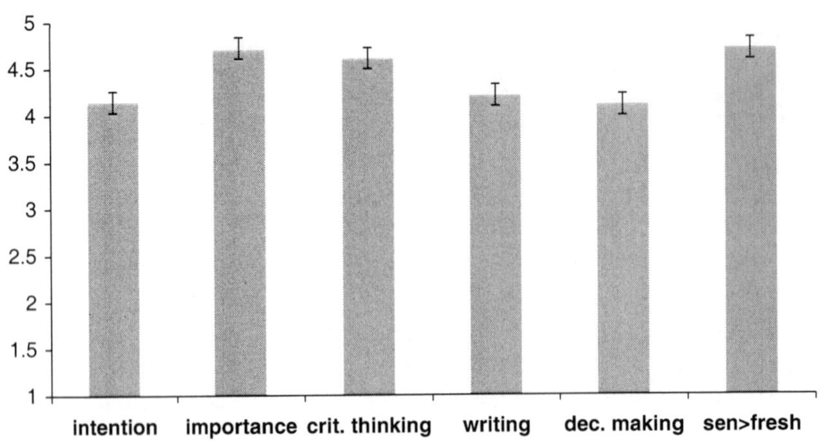

Graph 9.1 Average Face Validity Evaluations of the CLA

in a validity study with ACT and ETS to investigate the validity of the CLA, ACT's Collegiate Assessment of Academic Proficiency (CAAP), and ETS's Measure of Academic Proficiency and Progress (MAPP—currently known as the ETS Proficiency Profile) (Klein et al., 2009a). Results from the study show that for critical thinking, the CLA is indeed strongly positively correlated with other tasks that measure critical thinking. The correlations at the institutional level between CLA scores and the critical-thinking tests for MAPP and CAAP were .83 and .79, respectively. This evidence is consistent with the notion that the CLA measures critical-thinking skills. Additional studies have also corroborated these results by showing that the CLA correlated highly with other measures of critical thinking (Carini et al., 2006; Klein et al., 2005).

In this context, it is important to note that a moderate to high correlation between open-ended and multiple-choice test scores does not mean these measures assess the same construct. First, how one would prepare for a multiple-choice test is different than how one would prepare for an essay test. Second, a high correlation between the scores on a general-skills measure (such as the SAT or ACT) earned in high school and grades earned in a college-level organic chemistry course does not mean that high school seniors with high verbal and quantitative admission test scores know anything about organic chemistry.

Predictive Validity

The predictive validity of an assessment refers to how well a test score predicts some future criterion that is conceptually connected to the skills measured by the test. Traditionally, indicators of college readiness such as high school grade point average (HSGPA) and college entrance exam scores (SAT or ACT) are used to predict academic success in college as measured by college GPA. Results from a study using the CLA as a replacement for or supplement to college entrance exam scores showed that the most accurate prediction of students' senior-year GPA was achieved using the combination of SAT's and the CLA scores (Zahner et al., 2012). These results indicate that the CLA scores may capture knowledge and abilities that are different from content-based college entrance exams such as the SAT and ACT and underscore the apparent value of open-ended performance assessments as indicators of college readiness and therefore as predictors of college success. Recent findings from a large, multicollege, longitudinal study found that students who perform well on the CLA as college seniors tended to have better postgraduate outcomes such as securing employment and having less credit card debt (Arum et al., 2012). Another study by Zahner and James (2015) finds that students who score higher on the CLA+ earn higher salaries several years after graduating from college than students who score lower.

Common CLA Concerns and Critiques

Any new testing program that challenges the status quo and is used widely is bound to receive public and professional scrutiny as well as generate criticism. This is especially so if it has or may have consequences for students, faculty members, and their schools. The CLA is not an exception. This section addresses the most common concerns that have been raised about the CLA (Appendix A summarizes the critiques of the CLA and CAE's responses to each critique).

Critique: if multiple-choice test scores are correlated with performance assessment scores, they provide the same information about student abilities

A high correlation between two tests—for example, a multiple-choice critical-thinking test and a CLA Performance Task—indicates that the relative standings of examinees on the two tests are similar. A high correlation does not necessarily mean that the two tests are providing the same information about student abilities. Indeed, it is common to find high correlations between obviously different constructs. For example, in the aforementioned validity study, the school average ETS Proficiency Profile Math and Writing test scores correlated .92. Put simply, a high correlation between two tests is consistent with the idea that they measure the same construct, but it does not prove that they measure the same construct (Steedle et al., 2010). Multiple-choice questions cannot adequately assess students' ability to use their analytic and problem-solving skills to identify important strengths and weaknesses of arguments made by others (such as critical but unstated assumptions); present a coherent, succinct, and well-organized discussion of the issues; and independently generate a solution to a real-world problem.

Critique: performance assessments are too costly to administer and score

Performance assessment is increasingly being implemented in large-scale testing programs because it is recognized as being more valid than multiple-choice testing. Importantly, for instance, the new K–12 assessment programs being widely adopted in the United States are all focusing on the use of performance assessments. As a result, all the U.S. testing companies, including CAE, have made major commitments to building their capacity to develop and deliver performance assessments.

With this increase in demand, innovative approaches are being employed to address cost issues. Internet test delivery and reporting have been central to making performance assessment affordable. Computer-assisted scoring is also serving to reduce costs. Training human scorers, actual scoring, and maintaining scorer calibration account for a significant portion of the cost of performance assessments. Initially, human scorers need to be trained on how to score the student responses for Performance Tasks. However, once a sufficient number of responses have been collected, computer-assisted, automated scoring in all languages is available. This lowers the cost of scoring Performance Tasks substantially, and the inter-rater consistency between two humans and between the computer and a human is comparable (Steedle and Elliot, 2012).

Critique: results do not generalize

Critics of the CLA make claims that sampling only 100 students will lead to a nonrepresentative sample of the entire student body, thereby questioning the generalizability of CLA results. However, analyses of sample representativeness show that CLA participants are demographically similar to nonparticipants (e.g., in average SAT scores, percentage of minority students, and percentage of women) and that controlling for student characteristics has negligible effects on the relative standings of institutions (Klein et al., 2008), suggesting that CLA results are indeed generalizable to an institution.

Critique: students are not motivated

Low motivation is a persistent threat to the validity of score interpretations, especially for low-stakes tests like the National Assessment of Educational Progress (NAEP), Trends in International Mathematics and Science Study (TIMSS), and the CLA. That is, if examinees are not motivated, their scores will not be accurate reflections of their maximum level of proficiency. To address this concern, studies have been carried out to evaluate the relationship between motivation and performance assessment scores, identify the reasons students are motivated (or not) on performance assessments, and measure differences in motivation on performance assessments observed in low- and high-stakes environments (Steedle, 2010a). Results from these studies show that aggregate student motivation is not a significant predictor of aggregate CLA performance. Therefore, the relative standings of institutions are not affected by student motivation. Moreover, that the types of incentives that students prefer (e.g., money, public recognition) are not related to motivation and performance (Steedle, 2010a).

Finally, as noted in Chapter 11, CLA+, the current version of the CLA, reliable and valid at the individual-student level, provides moderate stakes that give students greater motivation to take the test and do well on it.

Critique: as a test of generic skills, CLA results cannot be usefully applied to improve educational programs

The CLA is a standardized test (i.e., a test administered in the same conditions for all examinees), and it is often the belief that such assessments are not useful for improving classroom instruction. However, there is increasing evidence that performance tasks like those included in the CLA can play an important role in classroom learning and assessment (Chun, 2010).This is important because, in order for faculty to take assessment seriously, they must view measures as authentic and useful to them in the classroom. Dr. Chun has given over 100 faculty academies, including eight in countries besides the United States. Appendix B provides examples of how the CLA has contributed to the improvement of teaching and learning in higher education.

Critique: critical-thinking skills are not independent of discipline-specific knowledge

Critics question whether generic skills like analytic reasoning and problem solving can be measured independently from discipline-specific contexts. Recent research on this found no significant interaction between CLA Performance Task content and students' fields of study (Steedle and Bradley, 2012). For example, students in the "hard" sciences do no better or worse on a performance task set in the context of a scientific inquiry than they do on a task set in a social science or business context. His finding suggests that generic skills can be measured using complex, authentic assessments without great concern for the potential confounding effect of content knowledge on test performance (see Chapter 8 for additional points on this issue).

Observations

Critical-thinking skills can be identified and measured. For nearly a decade, the CLA has been measuring higher-order thinking skills that are important to all students regardless of their academic background (see Chapters 8 and 10). There is considerable research support for the CLA, but more research is needed on a variety of issues. As is the case with other testing organizations, CAE researchers carry out much of the research on reliability and validity issues. However, CAE-based research continues to be published in peer-reviewed journals. Moreover, CAE's policy is to provide extensive data sets, when requested, to independent researchers to carry out their own studies (cf. Arum et al., 2012; Arum and Roksa, 2011). Finally, CAE welcomes the independent studies and reports on the use of CLA results noted in Appendices A and B.

Appendix A

Summary of the Critiques of the CLA and Responses to the Critiques

Topic	*Critique*	*Response*
General/ Background	The CLA is a one-size-fits-all measure designed for accountability only (Douglass et al. (2012). The CLA crowds out more nuanced assessments such as portfolios and surveys (Douglass et al., 2012). The CLA is designed to create a ranking system (Douglass et al., 2012).	■ Seven Red Herrings on Assessment in Higher Education (Benjamin, 2012). The CLA program rejects one-size-fits-all measures. The CLA program is opposed to ranking systems of colleges and universities. Appropriate standardized tests that permit interinstitution comparison are necessary but not sufficient. Comparison is needed to frame within-institution formative assessments. Formative assessments are supported, indeed undertaken by the CLA education program as well. ■ CLA background and context (Klein, 2002; Shavelson, 2007a, 2007b, 2010; Steedle, 2010b). ■ CLA constructs (Shavelson and Huang, 2003).
Value-Added Scores	■ CLA value-added scores are not reliable (Banta, 2008; Banta and Pike, 2007). ■ Value-added scores should account for more than just the SAT (e.g., age, race, sex). ■ Different value-added models can produce very different results (Liu, 2011c). ■ Value-added approach weakens correlations (Kuh, 2006).	■ Average CLA scores are highly reliable, especially when the unit of analysis is the institution (Freshman = .94; Seniors = .86) (Klein et al., 2007a; Klein et al., 2005). ■ Adding age, race, and sex to the model does not affect value-added results. Since the variables are correlated with each other, the estimates are less precise due to multicollinearity (Klein et al., 2008). ■ It is not true that different value-added models produce different results, as long as you are controlling for EAA* (Steedle, 2011 online first).*Entering Academic Ability

(*Continued*)

Appendix A (Continued)

Topic	*Critique*	*Response*
Reliability	■ Tests measure the same thing if they are highly correlated (numerous sources).	■ CLA and multiple-choice tests like CAAP are highly correlated, but many tests of obviously different constructs are also highly correlated (e.g., science and reading). Just because the tests are correlated does not necessarily mean they are measuring the same thing (Klein et al., 2009a; Steedle et al., 2010).
Motivation	■ Student motivation affects CLA scores (Banta, 2008; Liu, 2011c, Douglass et al., 2012).	■ Aggregate student motivation is not a significant predictor of aggregate CLA performance. It does not invalidate the comparison of schools based upon CLA scores. The types of incentives that students prefer (e.g., money, public recognition) are not related to motivation and performance (Steedle, 2010a). Moreover, CLA+ adds moderate stakes to encourage students to do well on CLA+ and use their certified Badge results as additional information to send to potential employers.
Validity	■ Tests like the CLA do not measure every important outcome of higher education. "... standardized measures currently address only a small part of what matters in college" (Association of American Colleges and Universities & Council for Higher Education Accreditation, 2008, p. 5). ■ The CLA tests primarily entering ability (e.g., when the institution is the unit of analysis, the correlation between scores on these tests and entering ACT/SAT scores is quite high, ranging from .7 to .9), therefore differences in test scores reflect individual differences among students taking the test more accurately than they illustrate differences in the quality of education offered at different institutions (Banta, 2007).	■ Critical thinking may only be a small part of what students are expected to learn in college. However, it is still a very important skill. In fact, many colleges have a set of general learning outcomes for all students regardless of their concentration, and critical thinking and writing frequently occur at the top of the list (Hart Research Associates, 2009). ■ Although the CLA is correlated with entering academic ability, it does not test the same constructs as college entrance exams like the SAT and ACT (Klein et al., 2007a; Zahner et al., 2012). ■ There is no interaction between CLA task content and field of study (Klein et al., 2007a; Steedle and Bradley, 2012). ■ Isn't it excellent that an assessment measures 30% of the knowledge and skills that faculty want? What assessment out there measures more than this (Klein et al., 2007b)? ■ The CLA has face validity (Hardison and Vilamovska, 2008, pp. 107–9). ■ The CLA is sensitive to differences between freshmen and seniors (Klein et al., 2007a).

	■ CLA tasks are not content neutral, thus they disadvantage students specializing in some disciplines (Banta, 2007, 2008; Banta and Pike, 2007) (Douglass, et al., 2012). ■ Contain questions and problems that do not match the learning experiences of all students at any given institution (Banta, 2007; Douglass et al., 2012). ■ Measures at best 30% of the knowledge and skills that faculty want students to develop in the course of their general education experiences (Banta, 2007). ■ CLA is not a valid assessment. ■ The CLA is highly intercorrelated with the SAT (Douglass et al., 2012) and therefore not credible.	■ The most accurate prediction of college senior GPA was achieved using high school GPA plus CLA scores (predictive validity) (Zahner et al., 2012). ■ Evidence of CLA reliability, convergent validity, and differences between freshmen and seniors (Klein et al., 2009b). ■ Correlations between CLA and the National Survey of Student Engagement (Carini et al., 2006). ■ Correlations among Performance Tasks and the GRE (convergent validity) (Klein et al., 2005).
Test Administration	■ Test administration procedures need to be standardized because they appear to influence student motivation and test performance (Hosch, 2010).	■ This is a legitimate concern, but we do not have any research published on this issue.
Sampling	■ Cannot be given to samples of volunteers if scores are to be generalized to all students and used in making important decisions such as the ranking of institutions on the basis of presumed quality (Banta, 2007). ■ Longitudinal and cross-sectional data are not comparable (Garcia, 2007). ■ Freshmen and seniors in a cross-sectional sample are not similar. ■ No way to determine whether sample is representative (Douglass et al., 2012). ■ Small sample required only valid for small liberal arts colleges.	■ CLA participants are like nonparticipants (in terms of SAT scores, ethnicity, and sex) (Klein et al., 2008). The degree of representativeness is checked with that of the overall student body. ■ Provides some arguments against longitudinal approach (e.g., expensive, large attrition, and students not progressing in their studies at the same rate within and across schools). May be providing biased results. We can never really know which approach is better or worse. The approaches have different pros and cons, and neither is likely to produce an unbiased result (Klein et al., 2008). ■ Freshmen and seniors do not differ much from each other except for their CLA scores (Klein et al., 2008). ■ Cross-sectional provides comparable results to longitudinal (Klein et al., 2009b). ■ Small sample is adequate for large universities who, however, may test more students to drill down to departments and programs.

(*Continued*)

Appendix A (Continued)

Topic	*Critique*	*Response*
Pedagogy	■ Faculty may narrow the curriculum to focus on test content (Banta, 2007) (Douglass et al., 2012).	■ How the CLA relates to what occurs in the classroom and if the CLA results can be used to improve pedagogy (Chun, 2010). ■ CLA focuses on broad competencies that are mentioned that cut across academic disciplines. Faculty cannot "teach to the test" (Klein et al., 2007a).
Miscellaneous Articles	■ Study focused on ETS's Tasks in Critical Thinking and its relation to General Education coursework (Erwin and Sebrell, 2003). ■ Cross-sectional assessments are difficult to interpret because they inevitably reflect characteristics of the same students when they first entered college; variation is attributable to entering freshman characteristics not institutional policies or practices (Astin and Lee, 2003). ■ Cannot make America smarter, so there is no need for measures such as the CLA (Hacker, 2009).	■ Measuring learning outcomes in higher education (Liu, 2008, 2011a, 2011b). ■ Limitations of portfolios (Shavelson et al., 2009, October 16). ■ Klein (2002).. ■ Machine-scoring of assessments (Klein, 2008). ■ Performance testing on the bar exam (Klein, 1996). ■ Recommends cooperation by critical-thinking faculty and administrators if there is less comparability and deeper transparency of tests (Ennis, 2008). ■ Nontechnical guide to popular methods and tests for assessing how well students acquire critical-thinking skills in school and college (Possin, 2008). ■ Comparison of the methodology and potential uses of three tools ■ For measuring learning outcomes: the CLA, the National Survey of Student Engagement (NSSE), and the University of California's Undergraduate Experience Survey (UCUES) (Thomson and Douglas, 2009). ■ Examination of the strengths and limitations of some common approaches to measuring student learning outcomes (Erisman, 2009). ■ The Hacker Critique is not based on appropriate statistical evidence. ■ Recommendation of the CLA for formative assessment use (Hutchings, 2010). ■ Comparison of the CLA, CAAP, and Academic Profiles (*Report of the cuny task force on system-wide assessment of undergraduate learning gains*, 2011). ■ Use of the CLA as a dependent variable (Arum and Roksa, 2011).

Appendix B

Examples of How the CLA Can Contribute to the Improvement of Teaching and Learning in Higher Education

The CLA is a testing program. Equally, however, it can be viewed as an instrument for reform of teaching and learning in higher education. It is important to give examples of what this means because the word "assessment" places the CLA in a box occupied by many other assessments, including multiple-choice tests. When examined for its contributions to teaching and learning, the CLA is in a league of its own. Here is a template that indicates how an institution might respond to the initial institutional-level CLA scores followed by illustrations of how administrators and faculty are benefiting from using the CLA along with other measures related to student learning. These illustrations are offered as early examples of productive uses of the CLA.

From the Institution to the Classroom: The CLA Comparison Strategy

1. The CLA's single, global, institutional score is based on the average performance of the sample of freshmen and senior students taking the CLA. In reports to the institution, its score is presented in comparison to other similarly selective participating institutions. To account for variation in competencies the students bring to college, the CLA institution scores are adjusted for the SAT scores of the participating students. The CLA score, then, reflect the amount of value-added improvement in performance between the freshman and the senior-year graduating students. When the scores of all institutions taking the CLA are placed in a regression equation, the institutions cluster along a straight line. More specifically, a college can be compared against the performance of colleges with similar average SAT scores.

   The first time the institution tests, CLA results provide faculty and administrators a benchmark, a signal about where their institution stands. There is up to a 2.0 standard deviation in estimated CLA gains between similarly situated institutions. In other words, there are very large differences in CLA scores between institutions that accept students with similar incoming cognitive ability. This means there is a large canvas for studying best practices in the institutions that perform better than the equation predicts as opposed to those that perform worse. The question then is what should the faculty and administrators of institutions do to improve the degree of their value added? That leads to the following subsequent steps.

2. Correlate inputs, processes, and outputs. A logical next step is for the college's institutional research office to correlate the inputs and processes (or their proxies such as class size, expenditures per pupil, incoming SAT scores of the freshmen, per-student endowment expenditures, etc.) with outputs of undergraduate education such as retention and graduation rates and, of course, CLA outcomes and other measures of learning. The goal here is to develop an efficient description of the factors that correlate with CLA results.
3. Conduct in-depth analysis. While the institutional score signals the place of the college compared to other colleges administering the CLA, college administrators and faculty members will want to know more about the relative contributions to that score by colleges (if the institution is a university) or by certain departments or programs (if the institution is a college). Which departments or programs, for example, are particularly strong or weak contributors to their CLA results?
4. Conduct audits of existing assessments. There is a saying in the assessment world that a curriculum is determined by what faculty assess. Thus, it will be useful to understand the extent to which faculty are using multiple-choice or essay tests in their classrooms. Are the tests given measuring what is important, such as critical thinking, problem solving, or analytical reasoning? How well are the students doing on current tests?
5. Examine best practices found to produce good CLA results. Many colleges participating in the CLA are working together in consortia of similar institutions. They are highlighting and sharing best practices that are correlated with noteworthy CLA scores. For example, it appears that schools that require more analytic-based writing do better on the CLA than those that do not.
6. The most important step: get published CLA Performance Tasks into the hands of the faculty so that they can:

   a. Use them in their classroom, where they have greater knowledge of the strengths and weaknesses of their students;
   b. Develop Performance Tasks that are based on the scoring guide of the published tasks;
   c. Choose case studies and problems for text material that is congruent with the documents in the CLA Performance Tasks rather than the content-dominated textbooks extant; and

d. Adopt a student-centered approach to teaching that calls for much more analytic-based writing on the part of the students and diagnostic feedback to the student about how they can improve their performance.

In sum, the above steps comprise an early version of what we hope will become a reinforcing system of continuous improvement of teaching and learning.[4] The institution's global score provides a critical signal that triggers an internal focus on what correlates with the score. It does not really matter where the institution is on the initial test administrations. The important questions become related to (a) understanding what led to those results and (b) deciding what improvement goals might make sense for the future.

See a few links (Point No. 2 CLA+ Education in the CLA+ Analytics section of Coda) illustrating how students can improve their CLA scores.

Notes

1. Klein, S., Steedle, J., Zahner, D., Elliot, S., and Patterson, J. co-authored this chapter. D. Zahner contributed significantly to the conceptual framework, pp. 11–14.
2. See also Klein et al. (2009), authored by Klein, Benjamin, Shavelson, and Bolus, which incorporates Shavelson's and Klein's approaches to the conceptual framework.
3. A number of measurement scientists and cognitive scientists take this position including Singley and Anderson (1989), Pellegrino et al. (2001); Miller (2003), Lakatos (1970). "Falsification and the Methodology of Scientific Research Programmes"; Bransford et al. (2000); Haskell (2002).
4. This is precisely what higher education has in the research realm. Through peer review, research has a public face that encourages and requires researchers to respond to criticism and evaluate the claims of other researchers: in short, engage in a never-ending process of continuous improvement. If we followed the above steps for undergraduate assessment, we could hope to eventually also create a continuous system of improvement of teaching and learning.

References

American Philosophical Association. 1990. *Critical Thinking: A Statement of Expert Consensus for Purposes of Educational Assessment and Instruction "the delphi report"*. Committee on Pre-College Philosophy. Millbrae, CA: The California Academic Press.

Arum, R., E. Cho, J. Kim, and J. Roksa. 2012. *Documenting Uncertain Times: Post-graduate Transitions of the Academically Adrift Cohort*. Brooklyn, NY: Social Science Research Council.

Arum, Richard, and Josepi Roksa. 2011. *Academically Adrift: Limited Learning on College Campuses*. Chicago, IL: University of Chicago Press.

Association of American Colleges and Universities, & Council for Higher Education Accreditation. 2008. *New Leadership for Student Learning and*

Accountability: A Statement of Principles, Commitments to Action. Washington, DC: Association of American Colleges and Universities and the Council for Higher Education Accreditation.

Astin, A., and J. Lee 2003. "How Risky Are One-shot Cross-sectional Assessments of Undergraduate Students?" *Research in Higher Education* 44: 657–72.

Banta, Trudi. W. 2007. "A Warning on Measuring Learning Outcomes." *Inside Higher Ed*. January 26.

Banta, Trudi. W. 2008. "Editor's Notes: Trying to Clothe the Emperor." *Assessment Update* 20 (2): 3–4, 15–16.

Banta, Trudi. W., and Gary. R. Pike. 2007. "Revisiting the Blind Alley of Value Added." *Assessment Update* 19 (1): 1–2, 14–15.

Becker, Gary. 1964. *Human Capital*. Chicago: University of Chicago Press.

Benjamin, Roger. 1982. "The Historical Nature of Social Scientific Knowledge: The Case of Comparative Political Inquiry." In *Strategies of Political Inquiry*, edited by Elinor Ostrom, 69–82. Beverly Hills, CA: SAGE Publications.

Benjamin, Roger. 2012. *The New Limits of Education Policy*. London: Edward Elgar.

Bok, Derek. 2005. *Our Underachieving Colleges: A Candid Look at How Much Students Learn and Why they Should Be Learning More*. Princeton, NJ: Princeton University Press.

———. 2006. *Our Underachieving Colleges: A Candid Look at How Much Students Learn and Why they Should Be Learning More*. Princeton, NJ: Princeton University Press.

Bransford, Jonathan, A. Brown, and R. Cocking, eds. 2000. *How People Learn*. Washington, DC: The National Academy Press.

Business-Higher Education Forum. 2004. *Public Accountability for Student Learning in Higher Education: Issues and Options*. Washington, DC: American Council on Education.

Campbell, Donald. T. 1959. Convergent and Discriminant Validation by the Multitrait-Multimethod Matrix." *Psychological Bulletin* 56 (2): 81–105.

Carini, R. M., G. D. Kuh, and S. P. Klein. 2006. "Student Engagement and Student Learning: Testing the Linkages." *Research in Higher Education* 47 (1): 1–32.

Chun, Marc. 2010. "Taking Teaching to (performance) Task: Linking Pedagogical and Assessment Practice." *Change* 42 (2): 22–9.

Clanchy, John, and Brigid Ballard. 1995. "Generic Skills in the Context of Higher Education." *Higher Education Research and Development* 14 (2): 155–66.

Dewey, John. 1910. *How We Think*. Boston, MA: D.C. Heath.

Douglass, John A., Gregg Thomson, and Chun Mei Zhao. 2012. "Searching for the Holy Grail of Learning Outcomes." *Research & Occasional Paper Series*. CSHE3,12, Berkeley, CA: Center for Studies in Higher Education.

Educational Policies Commission. 1961. *The Central Purpose of American Education*. Washington, DC: National Education Association.

Elliot, Scott. 2011. *Computer-Assisted Scoring for Performance Tasks for the CLA and CWRA*. New York: Council for Aid to Education.

Ennis, Robert H. 2008. "Nationwide Testing of Critical Thinking for Higher Education: Vigilance Required." *Teaching Philosophy* 31 (1): 1–26.

Erisman, Wendy. 2009. *Measuring Student Learning as an Indicator of Institutional Effectiveness: Practices, Challenges, and Possibilities*. Austin, TX: Higher Education Policy Institute.

Erwin, T. Dary. 2000. *The NPEC Sourcebook on Assessment, Volume 1: Definitions and Assessment Methods for Critical Thinking, Problem Solving, and Writing*. Harrisonburg, VA: Center for Assessment and Research Studies, James Madison University.

Erwin, T. Dary, and Kimberly. W. Sebrell. 2003. "Assessmnet of Critical Thinking: Ets's Tasks in Critical Thinking." *The Journal of General Education* 52 (1): 50–70.

Fredericksen, Norman. 1984. "The Real Test Bias: Influence of Testing on Teaching and Learning." *American Psychologist* 39 (3): 193–202.

Garcia, Phillip. 2007. "How to Assess Expected Value Sdded: The CLA Method." *Paper Presented at the California Association of Institutional Research Conference*, Monterey, CA.

Gardner, Howard. 2006. *Multiple Intelligences: New Horizons*. New York: Basic Books.

Gick, Mary L., and Keith J. Holyoak. 1987. "The Cognitive Basis of Knowledge Transfer." In *Transfer of Learning: Contemporary Research and Applications*, edited by S. M. Cormier and J. D. Hagman, 9–46. The Education Technology Serioes. San Diego, CA: Academic Press.

Goodenough, Ward H. 1970. *Description and Comparison in Cultural Anthropology*. Chicago: Aldine Publishing Co.

Guilford, Joy. Paul. 1967. *The Nature of Human Intelligence*. New York: McGraw Hill.

Hacker, Andrew. 2009. Can We Make America Smarter? *New York Review of Books*, February 24.

Hardison, Chaitra. M., and Anna-Marie Vilamovska. 2008. *The Collegiate Learning Assessment: Setting Standards for Performance at a College or University* (No. PM-2487-1-CAE). Santa Monica, CA: RAND.

Hart Research Associates. 2006. *How Should Colleges Prepare Students to Succeed in Today's Global Economy?—Based on Surveys among Employers and Recent College Graduates*. Washington, DC: Hart Research Associates.

———. 2009. *Learning and Assessment: Trends in Undergraduate Education—A Survey among Members of the Association of American Colleges and Universities*. Washington, DC: Hart Research Associates.

Haskell, Robert E. 2002. *Transfer of Learning* (1st ed.). Cambridge, MA: Academic Press.

Heckman, James., and Alan. B. Krueger. 2003. *Inequality in America: What Role for Human Capital Policies?* Boston: MIT Press.

Heinrichs, W. Leroy, Brian Lukoff, Patricia Youngblood, Parvati Dev, Richard Shavelson, and H. M. Hasson. 2007. "Criterion-based Training with Surgical Simulators: Proficienty of Experiences Surgeons." *Journal of the Society of Laparoendoscopic Surgeons* 11 (3): 273–302.

Hosch, Braden. J. 2010. "Time on Test, Student Motivation, and Performance on the Collegiate Learning Assessment: Implications for institutional accountability." *Paper Presented at the Association for Institutional Research Annual Forum*, Chicago, IL.

Hutchings, Patricia. 2010. *Opening Doors to Faculty Involvement in Assessment*. University of Illinois at Urbana-Champaign: National Institute for Learning Outcomes Assessment.

Immerwahr, John. 2000. *Great Expectations: How the Public and Parents—White, African American, and Hispanic—View Higher Education.* San Jose, CA: The National Center for Public Policy and Higher Education.

Klein, Steve. 1996. "The Costs and Benefits of Performance Testing on the Bar Examination." *The Bar Examiner* 65 (3): 13–20.

———. 2002. "Direct Assessment of Cumulative Student Learning." *Peer Review* 4 (2/3): 26–8.

———. 2008. "Characteristics of Hand and Machine-assigned Scores to College Students' Answers to Open-ended Tasks." In *Probability and Statistics: Essays in Honor of David a. Freedman*, edited D. Nolan and T. Speed, Vol. 2, 76–89. Beachwood, OH: Institute of Mathematical Statistics.

Klein, Steve, Roger Benjamin, Richard Shavelson, and Roger Bolus. 2007a. "The Collegiate Learning Assessment: Facts and Fantasies." *Evaluation Review* 31 (5): 415–39.

Klein, Steve, David Freedman, Richard Shavelson, and Roger Bolus. 2008. "Assessing School Effectiveness." *Evaluation Review* 32 (6): 511–25.

Klein, Steve, George D. Kuh, Marc Chun, Laura Hamilton, and Richard Shavelson. 2005. "An Approach to Measuring Cognitive Outcomes across Higher Education Institutions." *Research in Higher Education* 46 (3): 251–76.

Klein, S., Ou L. Liu, James Sconing, R. Bolus, Brent Bridgeman, and Heather Kugelmass. 2009a. *Test Validity Study (TVS) Report.* Supported by the fund for the improvement of postsecondary education. from www.voluntarysystem.org/docs/reports/TVSReport_Final.pdf.

Klein, Steve, Richard Shavelson, and Roger Benjamin. 2007b. "Setting the Record Straight." *Inside Higher Ed*, February 8.

Klein, Steve, Jeffrey Steedle, and Heather Kugelmass. 2009b. *CLA Lumina Longitudinal Study Summary Findings.* New York: Council for Aid to Education.

Kuh, George D. 2006. *Director's Message—Engaged Learning: Fostering Success For All Students.* Bloomington, IN: National Survey of Student Engagement.

Lakatos, Imre. 1970. "Falsification and the Methodology of Scientific Research Programmes." In *Criticism and the Growth of Knowledge*, edited by Imre Lakatos, and Alan Musgrave, 91–196. Cambridge: Cambridge University Press.

Levy, Frank, and Richard J. Murname. 2004. "Education and the Changing Job Market: An Education Centered on Complex Thinking and Communicating Is a Graduate's Passport to Prosperity." *Educational Leadership* 62 (2): 80–3.

Liu, Ou. L. 2008. *Measuring Learning Outcomes in Higher Education using the Measure of Academic Proficiency and Progress (mapp).* (ETS RR-08-47). Princeton, NJ: ETS.

Liu, Ou L. 2011a. "Measuring Value-added in Higher Education: Conditions and Caveats. Results From using the Measure of academic Proficiency and Progress (mapp)." *Assessment and Evaluation in Higher Education* 36 (1): 81–94.

Liu, Ou L. 2011b. "Outcomes Assessment in Higher Education: Challenges and Future Research in the Context of Voluntary System of Accountability." *Educational Measurement: Issues and Practice* 30 (3): 2–9.

Liu, Ou L. 2011c. "Value-added Assessment in Higher Education: A Comparison of Two Methods." *Higher Education* 61 (4): 445–61.

McPherson, Michael, and David Shulenburger. 2006. *Toward a Voluntary System of Accountability (vsa) for Public Universities and Colleges.* Washington, DC: National Association of State Universities and Land-Grant Colleges.

Miller, George. 2003. "The Cognitive Revolution: A Historical Perspective." *Trends in Cognitive Sciences* 7: 141–4.

The New Commission on the Skills of the American Workforce. 2006. *Tough Choices or Tough Times*. Washington, DC: National Center on Education and the Economy.

Pascarella, Ernest. T., and Patrick T. Terenzini. 2005. *How College Affects Students: A Third Decade of Research*. San Francisco, CA: Jossey-Bass.

Pellegrino, James. W., Norm Chudowsky, and Robert Glaser, eds. 2001. *Knowing What Students Know: The Science and Design of Educational Assessment*. Washington DC: The National Academy Press.

Possin, Kevin. 2008. "A Field Guide to Critical-thinking Assessment." *Teaching Philosophy* 31 (3): 201–28.

Report of the Cuny Task Force on System-wide Assessment of Undergraduate Learning Gains. 2011.

The Secretary's Commission On Achieving Necessary Skills. 1991. *What Work Requires of Schools: A Scans Report for America 2000*. Washington, DC: U.S. Department of Labor.

Shavelson, Richard J. 2007a. "Assessing Student Learning Responsibly: From History to An Audacious Proposal." *Change* 39 (1): 26–33.

———. 2007b. *A Brief History of Student Learning Assessment: How We Got Where We Are and a Proposal For Where to Go Next*. Washington, DC: Association of American Colleges and Universities.

———. 2008. "The Collegiate Learning Assessment." *Paper Presented at the Forom for the Future of Higher Education*, Cambridge, MA.

Shavelson, Richard J., Steve Klein, and Roger Benjamin. 2009, October 16. *The Limitations of Portfolios*. Washington, DC: Inside Higher Ed.

Shavelson, R. J., and Leta Huang. 2003. "Responding Responsibly to the Frenzy to Assess Learning in Higher Education." *Change* 35 (1): 10–19.

Silva, Elena. 2008. *Measuring Skills for the 21st Century*. Washington, DC: Education Sector.

Simon, Herbert. 1996. *The Sciences of the Artificial*. Boston, MA: MIT Press.

Singley, Mark K., and Anderson, John R. 1989. *The Transfer of Cognitive Skills*. Cambridge, MA: Harvard University Press.

Spearman, Charles. 1904. "General Intelligence Objectively Determined and Measured." *American Journal of Psychology* 15: 201–93.

State Higher Education Executive Officers. 2005. *Accountability For Better Results: A National Imperative for Higher Education*. Boulder, CO: State Higher Education Executive Officers.

Steedle, Jeffrey T. 2010a. "Incentives, Motivation, and Performance on a Low-stakes Test of College Pearning." *Paper Presented at the Annual Meeting of the American Educational Research Association*, Denver, CO.

———. 2010b. "On the Foundations of Standardized Assessment of College Outcomes and Estimating Value Added." In *Accountability in American Higher Education*, edited by Carey Kevin, and Schneider, Mark. New York, NY: Palgrave Macmillan.

Steedle, Jeffrey T., Heather Kugelmass, and Alex Nemeth. 2010c. "What Do they Measure? Comparing Three Learning Outcomes Assessments." *Change* 42 (4): 33–7.

———. 2011 online first. "Selecting Value-added Models for Postsecondary Institutional Assessment." *Assessment & Evaluation in Higher Education* 1–16.

Steedle, Jeffrey T., and Michael Bradley. 2012. "Majors Matter: Differential Performance on a Test of General College Outcomes." Paper *Presented at the Annual Meeting of the American Educational Research Association,* Vancouver, Canada.

Steedle, Jeffrey, and Scott Elliot. 2012. *The Efficacy of Automated Essay Scoring for Evaluating Student Responses to Complex Critical Thinking Performance Tasks.* New York: CAE.

Steedle, Jeffrey T., Doris Zahner, and Julie A. Patterson. 2013, May 13. *Common Core State Standards Validation through Assessment (CCSSVA) Report.* New York: Council for Aid to Education.

Thomson, Gregg, and John A. Douglas. 2009. *Decoding Learning Gains: Measuring Outcomes and the Pivotal Role of the Major and Student Backgrounds.* Berkeley, CA: Center for Studies in Higher Education.

U.S. Department of Education. 2006. *A Test of Leadership: Charting the Future of U.S. Higher Education.* Washington, DC.

Zahner, D., Lisa M. Ramsaran, Jeffrey T. Steedle. 2012. "Comparing Alternatives in the Prediction of College Success." *Paper Presented at the Annual Meeting of the American Educational Research Association*, Vancouver, Canada.

Zahner, Doris, and Jessalynn James. 2015. *Predictive Validity of a Critical Thinking Assessment for Post-College Outcomes.* New York, NY: www.CAE.org.

10 Two Questions About Critical-Thinking Tests

Critical-Thinking Skills and the Discipline

Referring to the CLA, some critics (e.g., Douglass et al., 2012; Banta and Pike, 2012; Ewell, 2012) question whether critical-thinking skills exist independent of the academic disciplines. They argue that, even if the answer is yes, interaction effects between test contents and disciplinary knowledge create confounding effects that make the use of such tests problematic.

They claim that, for example, majors in business and engineering will be more comfortable than those in the humanities and the arts in addressing a scenario in which the test taker must decide whether or not to recommend purchase of a particular plane (Banta and Pike, 2012, p. 25). If they are right, comparisons between institutions based on student learning would be problematic because some institutions would be advantaged over others if they have a preponderance of students who major in academic disciplines better aligned with the content of the scenario presented in the test. These critics are correct that no test is devoid of content. However, that does not mean that such tests are inevitably confounded by interaction effects with academic majors. To understand why this is the case, it is important to first place critical-thinking skills in the context of notions of intelligence.

Theories of intelligence have at one extreme Spearman (1904), who postulated a single, undifferentiated general intelligence, which he called *g*. At the other end are Guilford (1967) and Gardner (2006), who hypothesized differing and independent kinds of intelligence. The concept of critical thinking for which I argue is between the two; it is based on the understanding that learning is highly situated and context bound and that it can be defined as applying what one knows to new situations (Bransford et al., 2000; Simon, 1996).

In this view, critical-thinking skills are seen as broad abilities that are applicable over an array of academic disciplines or domains. Through practice within a subject area, critical thinking becomes sufficiently generalized to be used across content domains. This view is reflected in the shift now underway in both K–12 and postsecondary education from learning defined as mastery of content to learning defined as mastery of analytic reasoning, problem solving, and written communication.

Over 40 states are beginning to implement a new set of Common Core Standards for middle schools and high schools, designed to foster "the knowledge and skills that our young people need for success in college and careers." Sample standards include:

- Writing—students can make logical arguments based on claims, solid reasoning, and relevant evidence.
- Mathematics—students can make sense of problems, reason abstractly and quantitatively, construct viable arguments and critique others, model with mathematics, and use appropriate tools strategically (www.corestandards.org).

This notion of "deeper" learning has a parallel in postsecondary education, where graduating seniors are increasingly expected to be able to perform tasks that demonstrate agreed-upon levels of skill in analytic and quantitative reasoning, problem solving, and writing. Here is a typical passage from a college mission statement:

Each candidate for the bachelor's degree must complete a series of broad and rigorous learning experiences crossing disciplinary content areas and skill development, especially critical thinking, analysis, writing and speaking (Pepperdine University).

Seventy-eight percent of the Association of American Colleges and Universities' (AAC&U) member institutions report they have a common set of critical-thinking and writing goals for their undergraduate students (Hart Research Associates, 2009, p. 1).

Students can be assessed for such learning. Consider a teacher who instructs students in her chemistry course on how to determine the characteristics of different substances, such as how each responds to fire (the so-called *flame test*). The instructor then gives each student a different unknown and asks him or her to determine its chemical composition. Students are evaluated on their ability to figure out what the unknown substance is but also on the appropriateness of the tests they ran, the sequence of those tests, and the rationale for their conclusions.

This unknown-substance test certainly requires substantive and procedural knowledge about chemistry (such as how to run a flame test), but it also assesses generic problem-solving and reasoning skills. A task that provides students with the knowledge they need (in the figures, graphs, technical reports, and newspaper articles in the Document Library) can also focus on assessing critical thinking (see www.cae.org/sampletask). That is what the CLA does.

Interaction Effects

Even if critical-thinking skills go above and beyond disciplinary skills, critics argue that there are there are interaction effects between the performance tasks and academic majors. Three articles attempt to refute this position.

In the first paper, Stephen Klein and his colleagues describe a study by Richard Shavelson of college seniors who performed a CLA Performance Task during spring 2007 (Klein et al., 2009). Each task had content from one of three areas: science, the social sciences, or the humanities. Students identified the area of their major as science and engineering, social science, humanities, or other. Ultimately, five individual, student-level regression equations were constructed to predict CLA scores, using measures of the students' high school records, their SAT scores, and indicator variables for the task area and academic major area. When adjusted for entering academic ability (the students' high-school GPAs and SAT or ACT scores), other variables such as academic major had almost no effect on the accuracy of the prediction regarding how well each student would do. Shavelson expanded upon this study in 2010 and came to the same conclusion. The most recent study using data from 12,632 graduating seniors from 236 four-year institutions in the United States corroborates the two previous ones.

The analysis of Jeffrey Steedle and Michael Bradley (2012) revealed significant differences in performance between seniors at four-year colleges in different fields of study, which seems to support the conclusions of Banta and Pike (2012). For example, students studying the natural sciences, social sciences, humanities, and languages scored the highest, and students studying business and education scored the lowest on a variety of performance tasks. These differences persisted after controlling for entering academic ability, sex, race, and language spoken at home.

However, "there was no significant interaction between the students' field of study and the content of the CLA task." This suggests that we may move forward "without great concern for the confounding influence of content knowledge on performance tasks" (Steedle and Bradley, 2012, p. 2).

Why might arts and science students do better on performance tasks overall? One hypothesis is that there is more writing and analysis required of students in those fields.

In short, we conclude that there is no empirical interaction between the content of a performance-task prompt and an examinee's academic major. The performance-task format, structure, and approach do a good job of isolating the skills and abilities we want to measure (Klein, personal communication).

Assessing Critical-Thinking Skills

Portfolios Versus Tests

Many faculty and administrators join Rhodes (2012) in claiming that portfolios are a better means of assessing students' general intellectual skills than standardized tests (see AAC&U's Valid Assessment of Learning in Undergraduate Education or VALUE project at www.aacu.org/

value). States such as Massachusetts, which is spearheading the Multi-State Collaborative to Advance Learning Outcomes Assessment, plan to use the VALUE rubrics to assess student artifacts that demonstrate their skills in written communication, quantitative thinking, and critical thinking.

Faculty understandably give portfolios high face validity because they directly present the work of students. However, most measurement scientists remain skeptical of claims that portfolios are equal or superior to standardized assessments because they have doubts about the reliability of assessments based on portfolios.

These scientists have developed criteria to evaluate assessment protocols. They are particularly concerned with validity and reliability. Validity is about the extent to which the test measures the knowledge, skills, and abilities it was designed to measure. Reliability refers to the degree of consistency of students' (or schools') scores across a test's questions, the consistency of scores across different assessors, and whether the tests are given to students under the same conditions and over the same time period (Klein, 2002).

Its critics also argue that the CLA's value-added scores are not reliable (Banta and Pike, 2012). Indeed, they are not—at the individual-student level. But these scores are highly reliable when the unit of analysis is the institution (freshmen .94, seniors .86; Klein et al., 2007; cf. Steedle, 2012).

Lydia Liu's 2011 critique of the CLA's reliability is based on the fact that that different value-added models produce different results. However, Liu did not aggregate the student test results to the institutional level, either. When the mean SAT for the institution (which serves as an estimate of entering academic ability for CAE's value-added model) is introduced, different value-added models do not produce different results (Steedle, 2012).

Until adherents of the portfolio approach make their evaluation criteria for judging the reliability and validity of portfolios explicit and those criteria pass muster with measurement scientists and until the critics of matrix-sample tests such as the CLA work at the institutional rather than at the individual-student level, it is unlikely there will be productive dialogue between researchers in these two camps.

Value Added

Their proponents argue that one advantage of portfolios as assessment platforms is that in them, we see students' development over time—that is, we see the value added to students' skills by the college or university. We constructed the CLA to be a value-added measure as well, but some critics have questioned the claim that it is one.

Value-added models are used to estimate growth in learning between freshmen and graduating seniors. Cross-sectional value-added measures (designed to simulate longitudinal studies for four years of college) compare the freshmen tested in a given year with the senior cohort tested in that same year. The term *effect size* is a quantification of the difference between the two groups (Cole, 2002).

Students' entering academic ability (EAA) scores are made up of their SAT math and critical reading scores or their ACT scores converted to the SAT measures. Critics argue that if the EAA scores of graduating seniors are significantly higher than the scores of the entering freshmen cohort, one may assume effect sizes to be overstated. Such a difference might be expected because of the presumably higher drop out rate of less-successful students; therefore, the effect size may be seen as an artifact of attrition rather than a result of college itself.

When we look at the results of several CLA administrations over a range of colleges and universities, though, we find that that difference between the freshman and senior cohorts is not large. Exiting seniors, on average, have only 20 points higher EAA scores than entering freshmen. This means that the freshmen and senior samples are within 2% of each other, certainly not large enough a spread to significantly affect the CLA scores across institutions.

A number of critics also argue that the strong correlation between the SAT and the CLA for individual students does not leave much for the CLA to explain. However, when the institution is the unit of analysis, the SAT accounts for about 70% of the variance in CLA scores. Self-reported effort accounts for another 3–7%, depending upon the sample (e g., freshmen versus seniors).

That means the CLA itself accounts for about 25% of the variance of CLA test scores. This is a substantial effect. To place this in context, in predicting freshman GPAs, the SAT adds only 7.2–30% of variance explained by high school GPA (Kobrin et al., 2008).

In addition, the differences between the average performance of freshmen and seniors on the tests are significant. The average effect size reflecting differences in CLA performance between entering freshmen and graduating seniors was .73 over several annual test administrations. This equates to a 19% variance.

The distribution of effect sizes shown in Figure 10.1 suggests two things: that CLA scores increase significantly over the course of college and some colleges contribute substantially more than others to students' learning. The distribution of value-added scores shown in Figure 10.2 corroborates the latter point, with the overall variance explained rising to 96%, a highly significant result (see Sample Institutional Report at www.cae.org for more statistical information).

The symmetric bell-shaped curves of Figures 6 and 7 present a picture of student-learning growth. Institutions with very low effect sizes or value-added scores are in precarious territory, but there are also sizable numbers of institutions with growth of 1.0 and above.

The results suggest that it is time to implement a research program aimed at understanding the pedagogical practices of the institutions at the high end of the curves. Regardless of whether institutions are above or below the average effect size or value-added score, why not commit to shift the entire distribution upward by 10% over 5 years, then another 10% over the next 5 years, and so on?

Comparing Institutions

The proponents of portfolios tend to eschew institutional comparisons. Those who administer standardized tests believe that their measures are reliable enough to make comparisons between colleges, whether or not they believe that such comparisons *should* be made (see Chapter 8).

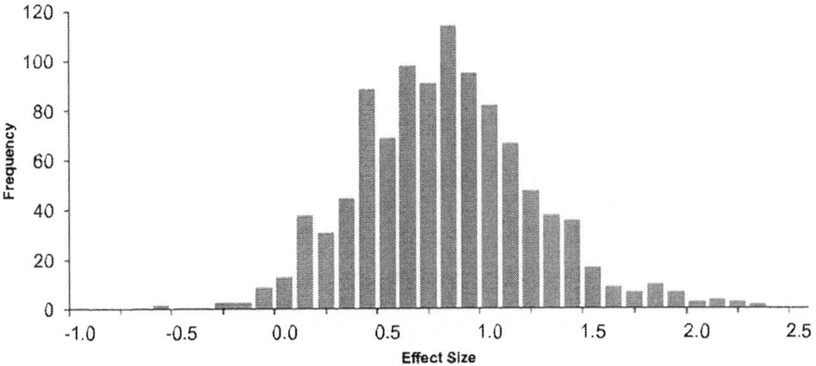

Figure 10.1 Distribution of Effect Sizes Across Schools, 2005–12 (N=1,038)

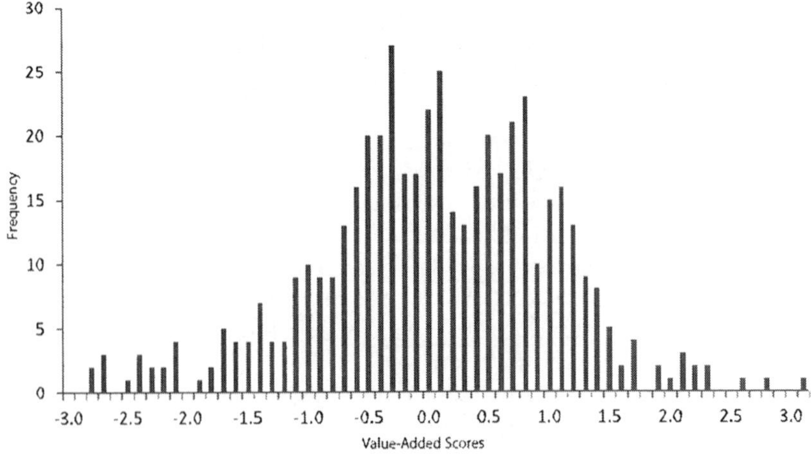

Figure 10.2 Distribution of Value-Added Scores Across Institutions, 2009–12 (N=431)

The Massachusetts initiative currently plans to publicly present only results aggregated at the state level (which enables comparisons among states but not institutions).

Meanwhile, the Voluntary System of Accountability (VSA) has presented the results of the CLA and other tests of critical thinking in a way that makes such comparisons possible.

In the VSA presentation of learning results, a school's value-added score is described as meeting, exceeding, or being below expectations established by (1) the average EAA of the senior cohort and (2) the mean critical-thinking performance of freshmen at that school. Value-added scores indicate senior performance relative to those expectations. This approach allows schools to compare their learning results to the results of similarly selective institutions.

Motivation

Another argument for portfolios is that students are motivated to include in them the best work of which they are capable, produced in high-stakes environments (i.e., class rooms and for grades). Tests of critical thinking such as the CLA are typically low stakes (see Chapter 6 for a high-stakes use of CLA+).

Liu (2011a) and John Douglass et al. (2012) argue that motivation issues overwhelm the results of the three critical-thinking tests since the test taker is not given compelling incentives to do well on the test. Similar arguments have been made about international tests such as the National Assessment of Educational Progress (NAEP), the Trends in International Mathematics and Science Study (TIMSS), and the Assessment of Higher Education Learning Outcomes (AHELO) feasibility study.

There is widespread agreement that motivation is a significant issue for no-stakes approaches at the individual-student level, as documented by Liu et al. (2012). Steedle and Bradley (2012 agree, stating that "students with low motivation and low performance may not receive scores that can be validly interpreted."

But Klein et al. (2009) and Steedle and Bradley (2012) find that student motivation aggregated at the institution level is not a statistically significant predictor of CLA value-added scores.

Steedle and Bradley (2012) also find that the relative standings of institutions on value-added scores are not affected by student motivation, again at the institutional level. Presumably, this is also the case at the country level (one of the units of analysis in the AHELO feasibility study), but no study has yet been done to answer this question.

Because there is such a widespread concern about low-stakes testing in general, the testing organizations are experimenting with moderate-stakes testing (Fain, 2013). We may expect increased value-added growth in student learning between freshmen and graduating seniors if stakes are added to the tests (Liu, 2011b), but the relative positions of institutions should remain unchanged.

Liu et al. (2012) carried out an experimental design in which she gave the ETS Proficiency Profile (its critical-thinking test) to several groups of students. For the first group, there were no stakes attached to the test. The second was told that the test results would be given to their professors and administrators, who would use the information to award scholarships or to allow students to test out of some general education courses. The final group of students was told that their test results would be on their transcripts when they graduated. The second group had twice as much learning growth as the first, and group three did even better. But the relative ranking of students did not change in any of the three groups.

Teaching to the Test

One critique of standardized testing in general is that the results cannot be used in the classroom and that teachers are then reduced to "teaching to the test." But the CLA is a test worth teaching to. To illustrate the utility of performance assessments for classroom use, consider whether students can be taught to improve their performance on the CLA. What would such teaching look like? The students would be given a series of CLA-like tasks and work through the tasks in small groups. Then they would explain their answers to their peers, who would give them constructive feedback. The discussion generated would serve as a basis for developing the competencies underlying the CLA. In a nutshell, if we taught students to do well on CLA tasks, which mimic the real-world tasks we expect them to perform, we would be teaching the competencies we want to develop in students (see Carpenter et al., 1990; Richard Shavelson, private communication).

Conclusion

Entrants to today's workforce can expect to change jobs several times over the course of their careers. The skills required for specific jobs are likely to change quickly as well. In contrast, the importance of critical-thinking skills is enduring. There are additional core cognitive skills—such as leadership, teamwork, moral decision-making—that are worthy of measuring as soon as this can be done reliably. But critical-thinking skills, at the heart of most definitions of core cognitive skills, can be measured in a way that is independent from academic disciplines.

The results show that college matters substantially and that some colleges and universities have much more impact on the growth of critical-thinking skills than others. This means all colleges can improve their teaching and learning. The stakes are too high for them not to do so.

References

Banta, Trudi W., and Gary R. Pike. 2012. "Making the Case Against—One More Time." *Occasional Paper 15*, National Institute of Learning Outcomes, September 24–30. www.NILOA.org

Bransford, John D., Ann L. Brown, and Rodney R. Cocking. 2000. *How People Learn: Brain, Mind, Experience, School.* Washington, DC: National Academy Press.

Carpenter, Patricia A., Adam J. Marcel, and Peter Shell. 1990, July. "What One Intelligence Measures: A Theoretical Account of the Processing in the Raven Progressive Matrices Test." *Psychological Review* 97 (3): 404–31.

Cole, Gerald A. 2002. *Personnel and Human Resource Management.* London: Continuum Publisher.

Douglass, John A., G. Thomson, and C. Zhao. 2012. "Searching for the Holy Grail of Learning Outcomes." *Research & Occasional Paper Series*, Center for Studies in Higher Education CSHE3,12, Berkeley, CA.

Ewell, P. 2012. "Preface." "Making the Case Against—One More Time." *Occasional Paper 15*, National Institute of Learning Outcomes: 24–30. www.NILOA.org

Fain, Paul. 2013. "Beyond Grades." *Inside Higher Ed.* August 2.

Gardner, Howard. 2006. *Multiple Intelligences: New Horizons.* New York: Basic Books.

Guilford, Joy Paul. 1967. "Creativity: Yesterday, Today, Tomorrow." *Journal of Creative Behavior* 1 (1): 3–14.

Hart Research Associates. 2009. *Learning and Assessment: Trends in Undergraduate Education---A Survey Among Members of the Association of American Colleges and Universities.* Washington, D. C.: Hart Research Associates.

Klein, Steve. 2002. "Direct Assessment of Cumulative Student Learning." *Peer Review* 4 (2/3): 26–8.

Klein, Steve, Roger Benjamin, Richard Shavelson, and Roger Bolus. 2007. "The Collegiate Learning Assessment: Facts and Fantasies." *Evaluation Review*, 31 (5): 415–39.

Klein, Steve, Jeffrey Steedle, and Heather Kugelmass. 2009. *CLA Lumina Longitudinal Study Summary Findings.* New York: Council for Aid to Education.

Kobrin, Jennifer L., Brian F. Patterson, Emily J. Shaw, Krista D. Mattern, and Sandra M. Barbuti. 2008. *Validity of the SAT for Predicting First Year College Grade Point Average* (College Board Research Report No. 2008–5). Accessed the College Board website: https://professionals.collfegeboard.com/profdownload/Validity_of_the_SAT_for_Predicting_First_Year_College_Grade_ Point_Average.pdf.

Ou, Liu. 2011a. "Value-added Assessment in Higher Education: A Comparison of Two Methods." *Higher Education* 61 (4): 445–61.

———. 2011b. "Measuring Value-added in Higher Education: Conditions and Caveats. Results from Using the Measure of Academic Proficiency and Progress (mapp)." *Assessment and Evaluation in Higher Education* 36 (1): 81–94.

Ou, Liu, Brent Bridgeman, and Rachel Adler. 2012. "Measuring Learning Outcomes in Higher Education: Motivation Matters." *Education Researcher* 41 (9): 3 352–62.

Rhodes, Terrell. 2012. "Getting Serious about Assessing Authentic Student Learning." *Occasional Paper 15*, National Institute of Learning Outcomes, September 19–23. www.NILOA.org.

Spearman, Charles. 1904. "General Intelligence Objectively Determined and Measured." *American Journal of Psychology* 15: 201–93.

Steedle, J., and M. Bradley. 2012. "Selecting Value-added Models for Postsecondary Institutional Assessment." *Assessment & Evaluation in Higher Education* 37 (6): 637–52.

11 Conclusion

The Implications of Pasteur's Quadrant for Research on Higher Education

In a recent review, Foroohar (2016) points to a negative cycle between post secondary education and economic growth that accelerated after the 1980s. Crediting Goldin and Katz (2008) for uncovering the positive link between education and productivity, she noted the importance of the correlation between the decline in the United States' postsecondary education attainment and faltering economic productivity growth. The United States now ranks third from the bottom of the 35-member OECD top-ranked economies in gains in education attainment in education beyond high school (Bowen and McPherson, 2016). Whether the decline in growth of postsecondary graduates causes the declining economic growth, the fact is the slower economic growth of the past two decades has led to "less tax money, and less public financial support for public post- secondary education" (Foroohar, 2016, p. 28). In turn, this leads to the poor postsecondary education outcomes cited by the authors Foroohar reviewed.

Business and society have reoriented their orbit around the financial sector. This negative change has led to the financialization of postsecondary education. Johanson states "consumers seek out personalized education and training that will make them marketable" (Foroohar, 2016, p. 29). In Faoorhar's view, this transformation disconnects postsecondary education from its value as a public good. The net result, in Foroohar's view, is a growing bifurcation between students in the lower quintiles and higher quintiles of family income that increases inequality in postsecondary education. Evidence for this is shown in the cost issues revealed in Figure 10.1, p. 13, and the high student-loan debt problem noted on p. 14.

Foroohar believes the concept of free college would overly benefit middle- and upper-class students. She also does not think the debate over whether STEM (Science, Technology, Engineering, Mathematics) fields should be focused on while non-STEM liberal arts, the humanities and social science fields is worthwhile. As she puts it:

> We need both, not only because it's impossible to predict exactly what the jobs of the future will be, but also because critical thinking

> in any field is the measure of economic and civic success. We need a deeper shift in the American system—we must once again start to think about public education as an investment in our future as a nation, the way our leaders did forty years ago. It is, after all, an asset, rather than a cost, on our national balance sheet.
>
> (Foroohar, 2016, p. 300)
>
> Foroohar concludes by stating that students and parents should be asked to pay part of their higher education costs based on a percent of their income that is progressive—the higher the family income, the higher the percentage of tuition they should be asked to pay.

Her view appears to be balanced, but, in any case, what does not appear to be debatable is that we need more objective tools to improve the ability of higher education decision makers to make better decisions about how we can reduce costs and improve the quality of undergraduate education. Let us turn, then, to the implications of the UIR approach in higher education.

Standardized assessment of student-learning outcomes is an important part of the UIR approach because such assessments are needed to tie the other science-based fields of inquiry together. Practically, this may be accomplished by bringing researchers from cognitive science, economics, data analytics, education technology, measurement science, and teaching and learning fields together physically or virtually. In this model, the interdisciplinary research team is tasked with creating objective tools of analysis that can assist the practitioners to better carry out their mission.

In postsecondary education, the practitioners, the faculty, are the leaders that translate theoretical knowledge about content and approaches to learning into practice. Table 11.1 illustrates the distinction between the research and practice-focused groups in the use-inspired research programs generated in the three historical examples listed above and the proposed functions of the research and practice groups in postsecondary education.

What is common in the three established UIR major policy domains of agriculture, health, and national security and suggested in the proposed higher education case is that the practitioners take the lead in establishing the goals on which to focus, receive the results of the interdisciplinary research teams, revise their goals, and suggest new research ideas to the interdisciplinary research teams who also suggest new research and implementation ideas. Whether or how quickly the professor in the classroom, teaching and learning specialists, and colleges of education can become as effective as the lead practitioners in agriculture and health is an important question. For example, the agricultural extension agent has become a model for several technology transfers. Without their presence,

Table 11.1 The Model and Examples of Use-Inspired Research Programs in Agriculture, Health, and National Security and the Proposed Design for Higher Education

EXAMPLES OF RESEARCH FOCUS			
Agriculture	*Health*	*National Security*	*Education*
Key Fields	**Key Fields**	**Key Fields**	**Key Fields**
Food Science, Plant Genetics	Biochemistry, Molecular Biology	Cost-Benefit Analysis, Game Theory, Systems Theory	To Be Determined Candidate Fields
Agronomy	Biomedical Engineering		Cognitive Science, Neuroscience Education Economics • Returns to Education • Incentive Theory • Microeconomics • Public Goods Theory • Behavioral Economics
Animal Science, Soil Chemistry, Natural Resources	Biostatistics	Defense Data Analytics	Education Technology • Online Education • Gamification • Data Miner Applications
Agricultural Economics, Agricultural Engineering	Health Economics	Information Theory	Education Statistics, Data Analytics
	Medical Data Analytics Medical Imaging Technology	New Defense Technologies	Education Assessment of Learning Outcomes

(*Continued*)

Table 11.1 (Continued)

FACILITATORS			
Agriculture	*Health*	*National Security*	*Education*
U.S. Department of Agriculture	National Institute of Health	Defense Contractors, Federally Funded Research Centers	U.S. Department of Education
Agriculture Banks	Healthcare Insurance	Congress	Pell Grants
Kellogg, Rockefeller, Gates, National Institute of Food and Agriculture	Hughes Medical Research Center		Fund for the Improvement of Post-Secondary Education (FIPS), National Science Foundation
	Johnson Wood, Kresge, Gates	Alfred Sloan, Ford,	Gates, Hewlett, Lumina, Carnegie, and Packard Foundations
THE PRACTITIONERS			
Farmers	Primary Care Doctors	General Officers/Joint Chiefs of Staff	Professors, Instructors, Teaching Assistants
Agriculture Extension Agents	Specialist Doctors	Secretary of Defense	Teaching and Learning Specialists
		National Security Council, Office of the President	College of Education?
		Secretary of State	
		Defense Advanced Research Projects Agency (DARPA)	

it is not clear that the scientific progress in Colleges of Agriculture would have been as quickly and effectively transferred to the farm.

Designing Assessments of Learning Outcomes for the Postsecondary Sector

The institution of postsecondary education appears to be under stress in most countries because public and private leaders understand the critical role formal education plays in preserving and enhancing their national human capital. They want to improve the quality of undergraduate education. Policymakers increasingly place the spotlight on the outcomes: the return on investment they perceive from their colleges and universities. However, increased costs and the challenges associated with educating many new college students not as college ready as in previous generations are creating the disruptive forces noted in Chapter 2.

The governance model for colleges and universities devolves substantial authority to faculty in academic disciplines, particularly for the decisions about what subfields of inquiry to emphasize, what the curriculum should be for the subjects taught, and how students should be assessed. For their part, then, faculty naturally privilege subject matter assessments focused on the subjects they teach. It seems only logical that faculty in academic disciplines should be in the lead for any requests for more systematic assessments that could be used to evaluate the progress their students are making. Moreover, a voluntary approach in which faculty are encouraged to work collaboratively to develop assessments seems best aligned with the traditions of the Academy. Indeed, the voluntary approach has been adopted by the founders of the European Union's Colohee project and another recently proposed promising project, PAL (Performance Assessment Learning at KokoHs). While the voluntary approach has virtues, it presents a problem. Without an overarching agreement or mandate to actually produce a credible assessment, who will make sure conceptual and assessment frameworks are turned into solid assessments?

While faculty prefer subject matter assessments, thought leaders, policymakers, and employers place critical-thinking skills at the top of their agenda. Problem solving, qualitative and quantitative reasoning, and writing ability are viewed by these stakeholders as essential for success in work. Fortunately, faculty also view these skills as essential for success in college. The growth of these skills in students is a joint function of their entire academic and nonacademic experience at an institution. How might we more concretely differentiate the contribution of academic disciplines to the holistic outcome of critical-thinking skills? One possibility is to group disciplines into professional versus arts and sciences categories. Here, evidence so far suggests that arts and sciences students do better on critical-thinking tests than in professional fields. Another strategy might be to group academic disciplines into STEM, the humanities, and the social sciences.

Thus, one would create large enough samples of students from each of these groupings. This would give researchers significant information they could use for better understanding the contribution of these three distinctive approaches to learning. Finally, the development of standardized assessments for academic disciplines, as well as generic skills, should be encouraged.

[1] It is not a question of either focus on academic disciplines or generic skills. We need both.

The Preferred Strategy: Continuous Improvement of Undergraduate Education

Remember that postsecondary education produces two principal public goods: research and undergraduate education. We have a continuous system of improvement in research through widespread adherence to transparency, peer review, and the need to demonstrate the ability to replicate research results. Is it impossible to set the goal of designing such a system of continuous improvement for undergraduate education, a system that would seek always to better align teaching, learning, and assessment?

Reliable and valid standardized assessments are important for any comparisons because without the ability to compare, the student, department, institution, and national policymakers will remain isolated from each other. They do not have appropriate information that lets them know where they stand in terms of student-learning outcomes in comparison to others that may be similar and different.

However, all these approaches should adhere to three principles in order to make sure we start going down the road of creating a continuous system of improvement in teaching and learning:

1. The assessment must be seen to be reliable and valid within and across national boundaries if the test also has any stakes attached to it that motivate students to agree to take the assessment and try their best to do well on it.
2. The test results must be actionable and:

    - Provide tangible benefits for students who take the test, institutions, national consortia of institutions, and ministry of education and other ministries in the government and
    - Be aligned with and leading to improvements in teaching and learning

Third, standardized assessments are not typically adopted or aligned with important practical issues faculty and administrators, students, and employers face. That needs to change if these critical actors are able to use standardized assessments as one of the objective tools of analysis they require in order to make improvements. Here is a list of examples at ascending units and levels of analysis of important practical issues faculty, administrators, students, and employers face plus examples of major education-based policy issues.[2]

The problem of declining economic growth over the past 40 years has increasingly puzzled economists. Estimates from the Bureau of Labor Statistics, Department of Labor, William Nordhaus (2016), and Robert Gordon (2016), among many others, leave no doubt that the per-year annual productivity growth rate of 2.5% from 1947 to 1970 now stands at 1.5% per year. One year of lower growth in productivity is trivial. However, a permanent decline in the annual rate of productivity growth is a very large problem. There are numerous theories about the decline

Table 11.2 CLA+—Examples of Use-Inspired Research at Different Levels of Analysis

Student Level	Diagnostic assessment of strengths and weaknesses in reading, writing, qualitative and quantitative reasoning, and ability to critique and make arguments at freshmen entry level.
	Certified mastery-level badges indicating the proficiency level of critical-thinking skills students have reached at graduation as seniors (see Chapter 6).
	Progress level in development of critical-thinking skills at the rising junior level.[3]
Curriculum Level	Evaluation of general education curriculum improvement designed to improve the critical-thinking skills of students.[4]
Institution Level	Increasing two-year and four-year graduation rates.[5]
	Meeting attainment goals for students from underrepresented groups—increased access, retention, graduation rates, and assistance in attainment of success in the workplace.[6]
	Value-added improvement in critical-thinking skills from freshmen to graduating senior level (see Chapter 10).
Evidence-Based Policy Issues	The impact of increased instruction by adjuncts on student-learning proficiency levels achieved and value-added growth of student learning (see Chapter 2).
	The impact of resources on student-learning growth and proficiency levels of students achieved (see Chapter 2).
	The relationship of critical-thinking skills attainment to declining economic productivity growth (see Chapter 7).
	The predictive validity of CLA+ of success level attained in the workplace (see Zahner and James, 2015).
	Leveling the playing field from college to career—increasing the employment opportunities for high-ability students in less-selective colleges (see Chapter 6).

in productivity growth.[7] However, one issue that may be examined with metrics of critical-thinking skills is the declining utility of use of the B.A. degree and college grade point average as the metrics to benchmark the relationship between educational attainment and productivity growth. If the mean national graduating college senior's GPA is 3.3 on a 4.0 scale, students have little to differentiate themselves, and it is difficult for employers to evaluate college transcripts. In other words, it may be interesting to explore whether it is useful to construct a measure of critical thinking that can be used, in addition to the B.A. degree and grades, to predict success in the workplace (see also Chapter 7).

There must also be agreement on basic principles of governance:

- Participating institutions, national consortia of universities, and participating countries must own their data.
- Students decide, at their choice, whether and how to use their test data, including the badges recording the mastery levels for which they are eligible.

At every level of analysis—the academic department, institution, system of institutions, consortia, or countries—the goal should be a testing protocol that is seen to be reliable and valid and produces actionable test results that benefit the participants. After the initial test administration is completed, the representatives of the participants evaluate the test results with the support of researchers from the testing organization that carried out the test administration. Errors are corrected and new proposed solutions for technical issues and substantive improvements are piloted and, if successful, implemented in the subsequent test administration. The process of adjustments to the conceptual framework, the assessment model, the testing protocol, and the related research on causes and policy issues to which the test results may be relevant is continuous.

The rationale for assessment of student learning, then, recognizes that colleges and universities are too important and too fragile not to provide the best objective tools of analysis to assist their leaders in developing their institutions to become more effective and efficient. It is also recognized that we already have a system of continuous improvement for research based on peer review to measure the quantity and quality of research that researchers, their research facilities, and universities create. We also need a system of continuous improvement for teaching and learning.

Overall, national leaders want to know how well their universities are preparing their students for today's Knowledge Economy. Faculty and administrators want to know how to improve their teaching and learning. Students want credible, third-party certificates attesting to what they know and are able to perform when they graduate from college. And employers want credible evidence beyond the grade point average of graduating students of the skill levels job candidates have reached. More specifically, assessments of postsecondary education are proposed for:

- The improvement of teaching and learning
- Diagnosis of the strengths and weaknesses of students entering college
- Evaluation of new or proposed improvements in curriculum and teaching methods
- Additional credentials for students to show employers and for employers to use in evaluating students
- Assisting administrators and policymakers in deciding where to invest resources for improvement of their institution

Benefits of Focus on Academic Disciplines

Giving faculty the lead in developing assessments in disciplines increases the validity of the assessments and increases the probability that the assessments will be accepted by the faculty. Development of discipline-based assessments throughout the arts and sciences, engineering, and business can capture critical-thinking skills in the discipline contexts. Therefore, development of assessments for disciplines will assist in legitimizing the role of assessment throughout postsecondary education. The process should follow the three principles of the use-inspired assessment initiative.

The Limits of Focusing on Disciplines Only

Overall, there are too many disciplines, and universities differ significantly in the mix of disciplines they offer. Thus, it is difficult to make apples-to-apples comparisons across universities. Second, unlike core cognitive skills, the agreed-upon essential concepts and competencies attributed to many disciplines change over time and/or are defined differently from one institution to another. This problem is greatly magnified if the focus is on international comparisons. However, there are additional substantive reasons why comparison at the discipline level only is problematic.

Critical-thinking skills, including problem solving, qualitative and quantitative reasoning, and writing skills, are judged by employers, professors, and thought leaders to be very important skills in today's Knowledge Economy (Hart Associates, 2014). When one can Google for facts, it becomes more important to be able to access, structure, and use information rather than merely memorizing content. Critical-thinking skills are aligned with a historical shift in the definition of knowledge and education itself. From the focus on content primarily, the new definition defines knowledge as the ability to apply what one knows to new situations.

The benefit of focusing on critical-thinking skills is that these skills are appropriate to measure at the graduating-college stage because of 1) the interest of employers in them and 2) the relevance of these skills at the institutional level. The critical-thinking skills that graduating seniors have attained in college are a joint product of all the courses they have taken and the sum of all the experiences they have had over the course of their stay at the college. Therefore, critical-thinking skills are holistic in nature, not simply the sum of the parts accounted for by academic disciplines alone.

Finally, there is the question of what testing format to use: multiple-choice or performance-based assessments. In line with importance of the instructor in the classroom (see Table 11.2), it has been recognized that a combination of a performance assessment and multiple-choice items would be useful to encourage coherence between instruction, assessments, and the daily complex decisions faced in life (Fredericksen, 1984; Steedle et al., 2013). Because of their fidelity to real-world tasks, performance assessments can elicit evidence of students' critical thinking and written communication skills in addition to knowledge of content such as the English language, the arts, and mathematics. Thus, an assessment containing a mix of performance assessments and multiple-choice items provides similar predictive validity to multiple-choice tests (Zahner, 2013) but provides illustrations of the potential for coherence between teaching, instruction, and assessment.

The Rationale for an International Focus

College graduates and employers do not only stay within the country in which they started; they move from the country in which they are born. Moreover, there are approximately 100 million college students worldwide today. By 2030, estimates of the number of college students worldwide range from 350 to 500 million. Grade point average and the brand of the university will not be enough points of information for employers to find graduating students qualified to fill their positions. New metrics that benchmark the skills of graduates from college will be necessary. Second, no matter how big or small countries are, international comparisons widen our landscape; all countries can benefit from enlarging the pool of students and institutions they use for comparisons beyond their national borders. Third, placing an international focus on postsecondary learning outcomes is likely to better engage the interest and support of policymakers everywhere.

Conclusion

The most urgent problem to solve in postsecondary education is the absence of a level playing field for too many students from underrepresented groups with demonstrated high ability, as defined by CLA+ scores. Social mobility and social class are now determined by mericratic principles rather than race or ethnicity in the United States. That is a good thing. However, if the selective or "branded" colleges are positional goods that determine the economic fates of all graduating college students, we need to find ways to widen the opportunity structure for students who graduate from less-selective colleges. We should agree upon additional metrics that can be used by all students to attest to the skill levels they have achieved upon graduation. This is a serious problem that we need to remedy as soon as possible and not just in the United States.

Notes

1. This is what Richard Arum and his colleagues have proposed, initially for six academic fields—economics, sociology, communications, biology, history, and business—in the measuring learning project. Supported by funding from the Gates and other foundations, notable faculty in these disciplines have reached a consensus about the core concepts that define their disciplines. Currently, an implementation effort is underway that brings subject matter experts from these disciplines together with measurement scientists aimed at developing reliable and valid discipline-based assessments. The strategy privileges the faculty by placing them in the lead but using the technical expertise of measurement scientists from the start of this phase of the project. See Arum et al. (2016).
2. This list is based on interviews with faculty and administrators and policy experts in a number of fields.
3. Here the individual student can monitor their progress in developing critical-thinking skills.
4. The institution can evaluate the efficacy of the general education program in place at the freshmen and sophomore levels to improve their students' critical-thinking skills.
5. The current six-year graduation rate is between 50 and 55%, depending on the demographics of the students at the university. Use of data analytics to examine the importance of resource allocation on academic and nonacademic variables that affect this percentage is an important evidence-based objective.
6. Improving the attainment results for students from underrepresented groups has become a major goal for many universities. The City University of New York's ASAP program (Accelerated Study in Associate Programs) shows significant results. See Scrivner et al. (2015).
7. Here are three examples. Gordon (2016) argues that the major technological innovations are behind us in the "special century" from 1770 to 1870. Solomon (2016) believes the causes of the decline in productivity is twofold. The patent system has been degraded. and the competitive configuration of the technology industry has become highly concentrated. Both changes have resulted in a technological stagnation. Olson (1982) argues that the decline of productivity is caused by the growth of special interests who engage in collective action to protect their economic gains. This leads to the overall decline in economic growth in a nation. Finally, many view the concept of the Gross Domestic Product as biased toward measurement of physical goods. Today, in the Knowledge Economy where service goods prevail, it is more difficult to measure them (Hirsch, 1976).

References

Arum, Richard, Josipa Roksa, Amanda Cook. 2016. *Improving Quality in American Higher Education*. San Francisco, CA: Jossey-Bass.

Bowen, William G., and Michael S. McPherson. 2016. *Lesson Plan an Agenda for Change in American Higher Education*. Princeton, NJ: Princeton University Press.

Foroohar, Rana. 2016. "How the Financing of Colleges May Lead to Disaster!" *The New York Review of Books*, October 13.

Fredericksen, Norman. 1984. "The Real Test Bias: Influence of Testing on Teaching and Learning." *American Psychologist* 39 (3): 193–202.

Goldin, Claudia, and Lawrence F. Katz. 2008. *The Race between Education and Technology*. Cambridge, MA: Harvard University Press.

Gordon, Robert. 2016. *The Rise and Fall of American Growth: The US Standard of Living Since the Civil War*. Princeton, NJ: Princeton University Press.

Hart Research Associates. 2014. *It Takes More than a Major: Employer Priorities for College Learning and Student Success*. www.aacu.org/leap/documents/2013_EmployerSurvey.pdf

Hirsch, Fred. 1976. *Social Limits to Growth*. Cambridge, MA: Harvard University Press.

Nordhaus, William D. 2016, August 18. "Why Growth Will Fall." *New York Review of Books*, Issue: 1–9.

Olson, Mancur. 1982. *The Rise and Fall of Nations*. New Haven, CT: Yale University Press.

Scrivner, Susan, Colleen Sommo, Michael Weiss, Timothy Rudd, Michelle Ware, Michelle S. Manno, Alysea Ratledge, and Himani Gupta. 2015, February. *Doubling Graduation Rates: Three-Year Effects of CUNY's Accelerated Study in Associate Programs (ASAP) for Developmental Education Students*. New York: MDRC.

Solomon, Neal. 2016. *Policy Solutions to the Productivity Growth Crisis*. Accessed SSRN: https: ssrn.com.

Steedle, Jeffrey T., Doris Zahner, Julie A. Patterson. 2013, May 13. *Common Core State Standards Validation Through Assessment (CCSSVA)*. Report to the Gates Foundation.

Zahner, Doris. 2013. *Reliability and Validity of CLA+*. New York, NY. CAE.org.

Zahner, Doris, and Jessalynn James. 2015. *Predictive Validity of a Critical Thinking Assessment for Post-College Outcomes*. New York, NY: www.CAE.org

Coda

CLA+ Analytics: Making Data Relevant Through Data Mining in Real Time

The premise for CLA+ (Collegiate Learning Assessment) Analytics is based on the judgment that it makes immediate sense to introduce the UIR model to the higher education sector through data mining and other Internet-based tools. This is a different UIR strategy than the one followed in agriculture, healthcare, and national security policy domains. The ways UIR was implemented in agriculture, healthcare, and national security policy differed in each case because of the nature and context for these three major policy domains. Congress established the land-grant university in 1862 for the purpose of improving agriculture, a vital part of the economy. Since World War II, the resources devoted to UIR in healthcare have been exceeded only by resources provided to national defense. For example, 6,000 scientists work at the Bethesda, MD, health research facility alone. In addition, significant research grants are awarded by the National Institute of Health to researchers in medical schools and the biological-related sciences throughout the country. Because of the nature of national security policy, it made sense to create and fund Federally Funded Research Development Centers such as the RAND Corporation to assemble a critical mass of researchers from across the sciences and social sciences in a single-purpose facility to conduct UIR. This supplemented the strategies that introduced UIR to the three major policy domains noted above.

For UIR in the higher education sector, the most immediate problem is how to overcome the absence of tight channels of communication across and among academic departments, administrators, and faculty committees (see Chapter 5). Universities, after all, are aptly characterized as loosely coupled organizations featuring colleges within universities in silos, isolated one from the other and governance responsibilities delegated to departments. This is in sharp contrast to the command and control system of the military or the hierarchical, centralized organization of healthcare institutions. The need, therefore, is to create a virtual network that permits and encourages researchers from many academic disciplines, along with administrators and faculty leaders, to share information in a timely fashion and to use that information on demand when they need it. As a first step, my colleagues and I have created a prototype tool called CLA+ Analytics that is designed to provide the virtual infrastructure that allows for collaboration between faculty, who are engaged in formative efforts to improve teaching and learning, and researchers from several scientific, empirical-based research fields.

CLA+ Analytics allows leaders and researchers to network horizontally within the institution and across to other institutions to access and share data. In turn, this offers leaders of institutions the ability to access information and carry out analyses in real time that assist them in making better-informed decisions.[1] The intent is that, instead of operating in individual silos, economists of education, cognitive scientists, teaching and learning specialists, education measurement specialists, and experts in data analytics can operate in a more integrated way to tackle the daily issues higher education leaders face, as well as mount longer-term research programs designed to assist the higher education sector in dealing with its problems.

In today's information-saturated environment, unless research findings can be provided to the intended users in real time, the information may not be useful. Administrators and faculty at colleges and universities need data to assist them in making better decisions when they are in the process of making decisions, not months after the fact. Students need to be able to access their test results along with their transcripts and other supporting documents in real time as well. We have created CAE (Council for Aid to Education) Data Miner, a software tool that can be used to introduce on-demand, use-inspired access to information relevant to higher education decision makers. This coda describes the CLA+ Analytics tool and how we visualize its use.

Attacking Pasteur's Quadrant in Higher Education Through CLA+ Analytics

CAE's Data Miner affords the opportunity to link CLA+ test results to the several disciplines noted above, among others, through new analytical tools that can be used for colleges, students, and employers. The CLA+ test reports will provide information to students and colleges along with opportunities for colleges, systems of colleges, states, and countries to create their own analyses. CLA+ Analytics are to be used in a dynamic, interactive manner by the user.

Three analytic tools will be available for the initial set of deliverables to students and college leaders when they participate in CLA+ testing. The goal is for the first beta test delivery of the tools to be ready for a selected number of schools and student testing in the spring of 2018. Here is a description of what is embedded in each analytic tool so far.

1. **CLA+ CareerConnect**—provides certified badges to CLA+ students scoring Proficient or better to indicate critical-thinking skills to potential employers

   Students who take CLA+ will be offered certificates featuring badges that certify their critical-thinking skills mastery level. Using the results from the standard setting study (Zahner, 2013), students who score at the Proficient, Accomplished, or Advanced mastery levels will be eligible to receive badges certifying their aptitude in critical thinking. To date, about 60% of CLA+ students have been found to be eligible for a badge. These badges allow students to demonstrate their critical-thinking attainment levels to potential employers and graduate school admission officers. Students will also be able to share their CLA+ scores and certificates directly on the CLA+ Analytics jobs board, as well as through social media and their résumés. (See Chapter 11 for a further rationale and description of CLA+ CareerConnect.)

2. **CLA+ Education**—used to promote growth in teaching and learning aligned with the skills measured by CLA+

   a. For institutions:

      - A compendium of resources detailing established instructional practices, which promote the skills assessed by CLA+; these resources will focus on feasible practices that can be implemented at the classroom level
      - A variety of practices for institutions from which to choose to improve their students' scores

   b. For students:

      - Videos that help students understand their performance level and improve their critical-thinking skills
      - Additional online resources that allow students to understand and improve their test scores
      - Student reports that provide diagnostic information to students, which can be used to improve their writing, analytic, problem solving, and quantitative reasoning

3. **CLA+ Data Analytics**—using the new opportunities provided by the CAE Data Miner:

   Provides data to be used across university offices to compare cross-university performance based on key indicators such as

Figure 1 CareerConnect-Certified Badges

Figure 2 Examples of Possible Data Analyses. APS, Analysis and Problem Solving; WE, Writing Effectiveness; WM, Writing Mechanics.

size, total costs and fees, selectivity, and per-student expenditures organized in a variety of data analyses, including advanced data analysis. See examples of possible data analyses in Figure 2.

How CLA+ Analytics Works?

When CLA+ data are placed on the CAE Data Miner, the information needed to complete CLA+ CareerConnect, CLA+ Education, and CLA+ Data Analytics are also computed. Previously, CLA+ reports for each test administration were sent to the Office of Institutional Research, and CLA+ student reports were sent to each student. Now, CLA+ Analytics will be sent to eight to 10 offices at the institution with the information relevant to each office highlighted.

Figure 3 illustrates how the specific applications could be accessed by colleagues in offices throughout the institution in real time.

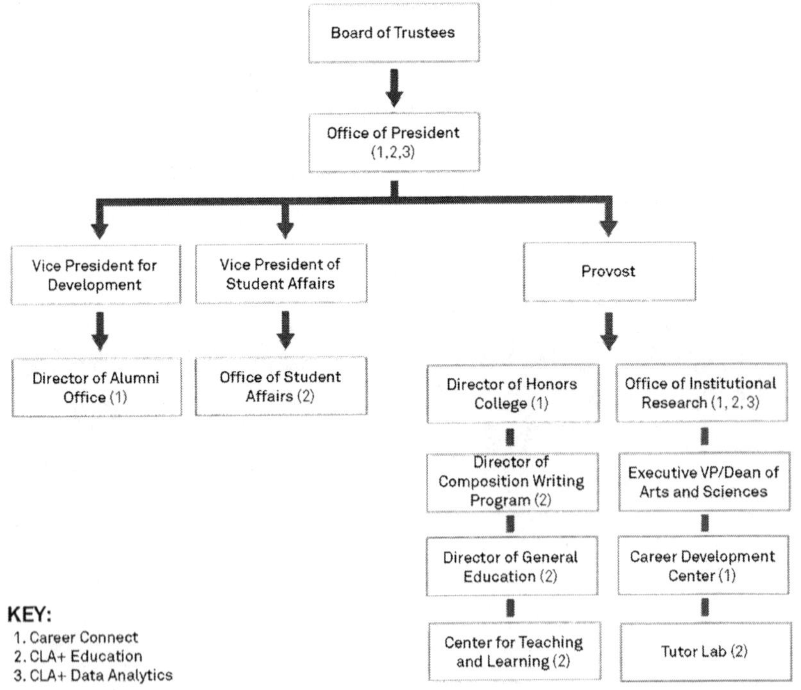

Figure 3 Possible Destinations of CLA+ Analytics Applications in the University Organization Flow Chart

An Example of Advanced Data Analytics

A research study assisted in creating a plan for dealing with Nevada's rapid population increase, which placed pressure on the postsecondary education system from 2000 to 2003. As a result, in part by R. Lempert's analysis in Benjamin et al. (2002, pp. 20–32, a report for the Regents of the Nevada postsecondary system), a new four-year college was established to absorb the increased demand for postsecondary education. (See the Nevada system of postsecondary education's website for more information about the related decisions made following the Regents' deliberations were informed by the analysis.) Here is a synopsis of Lempert's analysis

RAND was asked to explore the possible ramifications of various levels of increased undergraduate enrollment. For this purpose, we employed computer models that project enrollment and other attributes of Nevada's higher education system into the future, based on Nevada's projected demography and data on the current flows of students through Nevada higher education. Because the future is often highly unpredictable, we consider a wide range of scenarios and report conclusions across these scenarios. Such an "exploratory modeling" process can be useful for strategic planning because it reveals the key driving forces and tradeoffs any strategy must address. It can also allow decision makers to "test drive" choices across key scenarios before committing to action.

The findings of our exploratory modeling exercise strongly suggest that Nevada must make significant changes in its higher education system to meet its goals in the face of rapid population growth. Accommodating this population growth within the current structure could require heroic increases in the rates at which students enter and progress through existing institutions. Changing the structure of the Nevada higher education system, in this case by establishing new four-year campuses, could meet goals with other, less aggressive changes.

The exploratory modeling-based findings confirm the qualitative assessment discussed in the first part of this draft report that the Regents need a strategic plan, a road map giving them stronger decision-making tools and a logic for the management of growth.

References

Benjamin, Roger, Arthur Hauptman, Richard Hersh, and Robert Lempert. 2002, March. *The Road Less Traveled: Redesigning the Higher Education System of Nevada*. Santa Monica, CA: RAND, DRU-2508-CAE.

Lempert, Robert, David G. Groves, Steve Popper, and Steve Bankes. 2006, March. "A General, Analytic Method for Generating Robust Strategies and Narrative Scenarios." *Management Science* 52 (4): 514–28.

Zahner, Doris. 2013. *CLA+ Standard Setting Report*. New York: CAE.

Note

1. Until the late 1960s, social science researchers needed to learn FORTRAN to carry out standard statistical tests such as regression and causal modeling analysis on data sets. Because of the complexity of this process, the time and effort involved in statistical corroboration of hypotheses often took as long as, or longer than, other steps in the research process itself. The invention of the Statistical Package for the Social Sciences (SPSS) made the statistical tests much quicker and easier. The researcher could now choose the appropriate statistical package and carry out the tests quickly, in real time. The technological breakthrough of the SPSS (2015) made social research a more robust, more vigorous enterprise. Researchers could spend more time on the actual research itself. New tools such as CAE's Data Miner give promise of assisting decision makers in higher education and related stakeholders, such as employers and policymakers, to make better decisions.

Index

Page numbers in *italics* indicate figures and graphs and those in **bold** indicate tables. Notes are indicated by the page number followed by n.